# Bioinformatics for
# Everyone

# Bioinformatics for Everyone

## Mohammad Yaseen Sofi

*Transcriptomics Laboratory (K-Lab),*
*Division of Plant Biotechnology,*
*Sher-e-Kashmir University of Agricultural Sciences*
*and Technology of Kashmir, J&K, India*

## Afshana Shafi

*Transcriptomics Laboratory (K-Lab),*
*Division of Plant Biotechnology,*
*Sher-e-Kashmir University of Agricultural Sciences*
*and Technology of Kashmir, J&K, India*

## Khalid Z. Masoodi

*Transcriptomics Laboratory (K-Lab),*
*Division of Plant Biotechnology,*
*Sher-e-Kashmir University of Agricultural Sciences*
*and Technology of Kashmir, J&K, India*

ELSEVIER

**ACADEMIC PRESS**

An imprint of Elsevier

Academic Press is an imprint of Elsevier
125 London Wall, London EC2Y 5AS, United Kingdom
525 B Street, Suite 1650, San Diego, CA 92101, United States
50 Hampshire Street, 5th Floor, Cambridge, MA 02139, United States
The Boulevard, Langford Lane, Kidlington, Oxford OX5 1GB, United Kingdom

**Notices**

Knowledge and best practice in this field are constantly changing. As new research and experience broaden our understanding, changes in research methods, professional practices, or medical treatment may become necessary.

Practitioners and researchers must always rely on their own experience and knowledge in evaluating and using any information, methods, compounds, or experiments described herein. In using such information or methods they should be mindful of their own safety and the safety of others, including parties for whom they have a professional responsibility.

To the fullest extent of the law, neither the Publisher nor the authors, contributors, or editors, assume any liability for any injury and/or damage to persons or property as a matter of products liability, negligence or otherwise, or from any use or operation of any methods, products, instructions, or ideas contained in the material herein.

**Library of Congress Cataloging-in-Publication Data**
A catalog record for this book is available from the Library of Congress

**British Library Cataloguing-in-Publication Data**
A catalogue record for this book is available from the British Library

ISBN: 978-0-323-91128-3

For information on all Academic Press publications visit our website at
https://www.elsevier.com/books-and-journals

*Publisher:* Stacy Masucci
*Acquisitions Editor:* Rafael Teixeira
*Editorial Project Manager:* Tracy Tufaga
*Production Project Manager:* Sreejith Viswanathan
*Cover designer:* Alan Studholme

Typeset by TNQ Technologies

*We dedicate this book to Professor J. P. Sharma, Hon'ble Vice Chancellor, SKUAST-K, for his vibrant leadership*

*and*

*Professor Nazir. A. Ganai, Director Planning and Monitoring, for his constant encouragement and unending support.*

# Contents

# Foreword

To write the foreword for *Bioinformatics for Everyone* by my bright colleagues gives me great joy. It is an incredible achievement for the authors following the successful publication of *Advanced Methods in Molecular Biology and Biotechnology: A Practical Lab Manual*, a succinct reference on common procedures and procedures for advanced molecular biology and biotechnology testing.

Bioinformatics, often referred to as life science informatics, is a modern discipline of biotechnology that provides biologists with a critical tool for expediting biotechnology and Molecular Biology research. Bioinformatics refers to how biotechnology and information technology have converged.

Bioinformatics has long been recognised as a critical tool for mining, analysing, searching, integrating and modeling molecular biological data in life science. I found this book a compact yet comprehensive bioinformatics textbook that provides an overview of the entire discipline along with thorough techniques. Written primarily for a life science audience, this book covers the fundamentals of bioinformatics before delving into the state-of-the-art computational methods available for solving biological research challenges. This book covers all critical areas of bioinformatics, including biological databases, sequence alignment and a variety of fundamental bioinformatics software and tools. This book provides a concise review of each bio-informatic software which includes a variety of online and offline bioinformatics tools and applications along with their step-by-step protocols that might act as a consolation for undergraduate and postgraduate students who are in desperate need of assistance at this point. The material provided by this book is suitable for both academic and research use. Additionally, the concept underlying this book transcends the frequently encountered restricted understanding of bioinformatic software and tools, which may be limited to specific tasks such as attempting to identify genes in a DNA sequence.

Moreover, I congratulate Dr Khalid Z. Masoodi and his PhD students Mr Mohd Yaseen Sofi and Ms Afshana Shaft on this outstanding publication, and I am convinced that this book will provide many opportunity for students and researchers to rapidly instill concepts and ideas in *Bioinformatics for Everyone*.

**Professor J.P. Sharma**
*Vice-Chancellor*
*Sher-e-Kashmir University of Agricultural Sciences*
*and Technology of Kashmir,*
*Srinagar, J&K, India*

*Place: SKUAST-K, Shalimar*
*Date June 7, 2021*

# Preface

Bioinformatics is a rapidly developing new field of research in which computational tools are used to gather, store and analyse biological data. This book focusses on applied bioinformatics with a certain applicability for crops and model plants. In recent years, considerable progress has led to an explosive expansion of biological data provided through a range of biological databases in the area of molecular biology and biotechnology which has led to further developments in genome technologies. The National Center of Biological Information website (http://www.ncbi.nlm.nih.gov/Genomes/index.html) now contains a collection of genomes from different species. The number of items listed on this list is expanding at an unprecedented rate. The biggest issue academics have today is in learning how to synthesise and understand this immense amount of data in order to identify and develop new global biological insights for the benefit of mankind. To overcome these impediments, we have designed this book that is easy to comprehend and is easily applicable to day-to-day research that students and researchers of universities across the globe come through. Which in turn include applying computational approaches to aid in understanding various biological processes. Equally important, bioinformaticians have to have a rudimentary understanding of biological issues to efficiently implement their computer talents in the bioinformatics industry. This book is designed to provide the most up-to-date bioinformatics techniques for scientists, researchers and students.

*Bioinformatics for Everyone* is a concise yet comprehensive bioinformatics textbook that provides a thorough overview of the entire topic. Written primarily for a life science audience, the fundamentals of bioinformatics are introduced, followed by explanations of the most cutting-edge computer methods for solving biological research challenges. Biological databases, data visualisation, sequence alignment, restriction analysis, primer designing, gene and promoter prediction, molecular phylogenetics, structural bioinformatics, genomics and proteomics are all covered under one umbrella, *Bioinformatics for Everyone*. This book focusses on how computational methods function and examines the advantages and disadvantages of various methods. This well-balanced but easily accessible text will be beneficial to students who do not have advanced computational backgrounds. Technical intricacies of computational algorithms are described using graphical illustrations rather than mathematical formulas to enhance comprehension. This book is ideal for all bioinformatics courses taken by life science students, as well as for researchers wishing to develop their knowledge of bioinformatics to aid their research, due to its user-friendly structure and in-depth and up-to-date coverage of all key topics in bioinformatics.

# Acknowledgement

We acknowledge the Science and Engineering Research Board (SERB), Department of Science and Technology, Government of India for providing Research Grant under SERB project No.: SERB/EMR/2016/005598 to Dr. Khalid Z. Masoodi, Assistant Professor, Division of Plant Biotechnology, Sher-e-Kashmir University of Agricultural Sciences and Technology of Kashmir, J&K, India.

# Prologue to bioinformatics

1

## 1.1 Definition

The computer-assisted study of biology and genetics is known as bioinformatics. In other words, it refers to the analysis of genetics and other biological data using a computer. Bioinformatics is now gaining prominence in life science, especially in the fields of molecular biology and plant genetic resources. Bioinformatics is a field that combines biology and computer sciences. Bioinformatics is a relatively new science that uses data to better understand biological phenomena. It covers a wide range of statistical tools and methods for managing, analysing and manipulating large amounts of biological data. Some computer biologists refer to bioinformatics as subset of computational biology. The above is devoted to biological systems modelling and problem solving in the context of quantitative analysis. Bioinformatics is a study of molecular processes that demands a complex combination of science, math and statistics (Fig. 1.1).

## 1.2 Concept of bioinformatics

Bioinformatics, also known as life science informatics, is a modern branch of biotechnology that gives biologists a vital tool for commercialising biotechnology faster. Bioinformatics is a classic example of the merging of biotechnology and information technology. Bioinformatics has long been one of the most important methods in life science for mining, analysing, searching, integrating and simulating molecular biological data.

However, data storage and genome sequence research have been implicated as its top priorities. Bioinformatics is a cutting-edge technology that arose from the exponential growth of information technology and the exceptional growth of molecular biology and recombinant DNA technologies, as well as their interrelated studies. Bioinformatics may also be referred to as biocomputing or computational biology. In recent years, genomics has become increasingly important in bioinformatics, or the study of basic life processes.

Bioinformatics for Everyone. https://doi.org/10.1016/B978 0 323 91128-3.00018-5

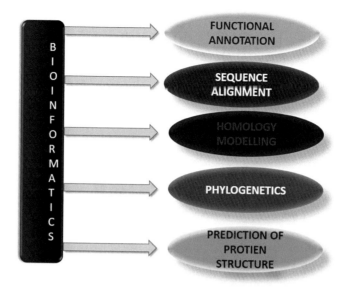

**FIGURE 1.1**

Bioinformatics— A crosstalk between different Sciences.

## 1.3 Advancements in bioinformatics

The first bioinformatic scientific literature was published in 1991 under the title "Bioinformatics a New Age." Prophet, a unix-based software package that enabled scientists to store, analyse and perform mathematical modelling, was one of the first attempts to construct a database and develop analysis algorithms. Indeed, a free database named Gen Bank was established in 1982 to store DNA sequence data.

This database currently contains approximately 17 billion bases from over a million genes. Intell-Genetics developed PC/GENE, a bioinformatics programme that converts gene sequences to proteins, in the 1980s. This software was created to predict the secondary structure of proteins. Amos Bairoca introduced a database in 1991 namely Swiss-PROT, which is actually a protein sequence database where different details of proteins and their sub-structures are stored.

Swiss-PROT is currently a curated protein database under EXPASY (Export Protein Analysis System) proteomics, and the release of the draught sequence of the human genome to the public was a watershed moment in the history of modern biology and research. This has resulted in a powerful tool that can create entire gene catalogues for a variety of microbes as well as the plant *Arabidopsis*.

## 1.4 Objectives of bioinformatics

The authoritative goal of bioinformatics is to almost certainly comprehend a living cell and how it works at the sub-atomic level. By analysing rough sub-atomic gathering and vital data, bioinformatics research will generate new pieces of information and provide an "around the world" perspective of the cell. The explanation that the components of a cell can be best understood by separating progression details is finally because the flow of inherited knowledge is organised by science's "central dogma," in which DNA is unwrapped to RNA, which translates into proteins. Normally, cell boundaries are imposed by proteins, whose capacities are largely dictated by their progressions. As a result, dealing with viable problems using advanced and, to a large degree, critical methods has proven to be a fruitful endeavour. The three significant targets of bioinformatics are

1. Deconstruct the massive amount of Biological Data,
2. Develop more genius devices to deal with the increasing complexities,
3. Interpret the outcomes from both the wet-lab and *in silico* tests.

A portion of the major bioinformatics applications are

1. Mapping of different biomolecules data,
2. Comparing DNA/RNA/Protein Sequences,
3. Predicting 3-D structures of Gene-Products/Proteins,
4. Predicting functions of Gene-Products/Proteins,
5. Designing of Primers.

## 1.5 Components of bioinformatics

There are three components which are used in bioinformatics:

1. **Establishment of a database:** This entails arranging, storing and managing biological data sets. Researchers may use existing information databases to make separate entries, such as the molecular structure protein sequence data bank. Databases are useless before they are analysed.
2. **Creation of algorithms and statistics:** This emphasises the application of tools and resources to predict the association between members of large sets of data, for example, by comparing data on protein sequence with protein sequences already reported.
3. **Data and perception evaluation:** The proper usage components 1 and 2 (listed above) for biologically relevant analysis and interpretation of data. All examples of which include DNA, RNA, sequence of proteins, protein structure, profiling of gene expression and metabolic changes.

## 1.6 Biological terminology

The most abundant data which are used in bioinformatics are the DNA and protein (amino acid) sequences. The four bases that constitute DNA are Adenine, Guanine, Cytosine and Thymine. If genetic material can be used to produce protein, it can also perform non-coding functions. There can be thousands of bases for a gene, and millions of bases for a normal bacterial genome. There are almost 3.2 billion bases in the entire genes. The nucleotide series contains 20 different types of amino acids, which codes for different proteins. There are about 300 different amino acids in a standard-length protein. Proteins sequences include an extremely large numbers of codons. You only have traits as a result of having a certain mix of genotypes, or DNA and protein sequences. The main purpose of a protein is accomplished when it has a definite structure. Although one of the greatest challenges in physics and bioinformatics in modern science is finding out how proteins fold from their amino acid sequences, or structures, the issue of protein prediction is exceedingly difficult. There are different knowledge-based techniques such as homology modelling and threading, as well as ab-initio techniques based on energy minimisation. The method of synthesising messenger RNA (mRNA) from DNA information is known as gene expression (transcription). The mRNA that has been transcribed is then translated to generate the corresponding protein. This whole process in molecular biology is known as the central dogma. Identifying which genes are expressed and which are not in a specific tissue or disease is a difficulty in molecular biology. This issue is addressed by the field of transcriptomics, and recent advances in biotechnology have allowed researchers to assay gene expression on a large scale in a high-throughput manner. Microarrays (also known as gene expression arrays or gene chips) gather a vast amount of data about genetic alterations in a specific circumstance or biological sample. Interaction assays also show which proteins interact with one another, enabling researchers to examine the cell as a whole. Data on experiences have been collected in a variety of databases, including MINT, Intact and DIP, which are constantly expanding. Many issues arise when analysing molecular biology data, including redundancy and multiplicity, noise and incompleteness. There are thousands of sources for molecular biology information. The Nucleic Acids Research online database set lists 1380 carefully curated databases covering various aspects of molecular and cell biology as of January 2012. NCBI Entrez, EBI Ensemble, UCSC Genome Browser and KEGG are the most commonly used database. While data standardisation initiatives, such as the Gene Ontology consortium, are under way, most databases have their own format and the specifics of a database have to be understood in order to make effective use of the data.

## 1.7 The evolution of bioinformatics

In the 1990s, the term "bioinformatics" was introduced. Its initial goal was to treat and analyse the data related to sequences of DNA, RNA and proteins. Bioinformatics is needed to handle and interpret biological data because it is being produced at an unparallelled rate. As a result, bioinformatics now encompasses a wide range of biological data.

The following are a few of the most important:

1. Profiles of gene expression
2. Structure of proteins
3. Interactions of different proteins

**4.** Microarrays/DNA chips
**5.** Functional analysis of biomolecules
**6.** Designing of drugs.

Bioinformatics is primarily (but not entirely) a computer-based field. Huge quantities of biological data, as well as their storage and retrieval, necessitate the use of computers. We must agree that no machine on the planet (no matter how advanced) can store information and perform the functions of a living cell. As a result, an organism's cells contain a highly sophisticated information technology. This specifically refers to the organism's genes and the instructions they provide for biological processes and behaviour.

## 1.8 Applications

The introduction of bioinformatics has revolutionised biological research. Bioinformatics is also beneficial to biotechnology. The most notable example is the rapid sequencing of the human genome, which would have been impossible without the use of bioinformatics. The expandable list of bioinformatics applications is presented below:

**1.** Underlined graphs/sequential mapping of biomolecules such as DNA, RNA or proteins.
**2.** Nucleotide sequence identification of activated genes.
**3.** Identifying sites in the sequence where different restriction enzymes can sever.
**4.** Designing of primer sequence for use in amplification of gene in PCR.
**5.** Prediction of functional genetically engineered products.
**6.** To rebuild evolutionary genetic trees.
**7.** For forecasting the three-dimensional structure of proteins.
**8.** Computational molecular modelling of molecules.
**9.** The ability to find new treatments for new medical needs.
**10.** Handling vast quantities of biological data that would be difficult to handle otherwise.
**11.** Create models for the functioning of various cells, tissues and organs.

The above list of applications, however, should be considered incomplete, as bioinformatics is now used in every area of biological science.

## 1.9 Limitations

Computer-based projects have helped in better comprehension of different cycles of life science. In any case, there are a few restrictions of bioinformatics which are recorded beneath:

**1.** Bioinformatics requires modern research centre of molecular science for top-to-bottom investigation of biomolecules. Foundation of such research facilities requires parcel of assets.

2. Computer-based investigation of life science requires some preparation about different computer programmes pertinent for the investigation of various cycles of life science. Thus, special training is required for handling of computer-based biological data.

3. There ought to be continuous (power) supply for PC-supported natural examinations. Interference of force may now and again prompt loss of enormous information from the computer memory.

4. There ought to be ordinary checking of computer viruses in light of the fact that viruses may represent a few issues like erasure of information and defilement of the projects.

5. The upkeep and upkeeping of molecular labs includes parcel of consumption which now and then turns into a restricting variable for computer-based molecular studies.

## 1.10 Branches of bioinformatics

The science of bioinformatics can be divided into several branches based on the experimental material used for the study. Bioinformatics is broadly divided into two groups, viz., animal bioinformatics and plant bioinformatics. Various branches of bioinformatics are defined below:

1. Animal Bioinformatics

   It focusses on computer-assisted genomics, proteomics and metabolomics research in a variety of animal species. It entails research into gene mapping, gene sequencing, animal breeds and animal genetic capital, among other things. Bioinformatics of mammals, reptiles, insects, birds and fishes, for example, can be subdivided.

2. Plant Bioinformatics

   It deals with computer-aided study of plant species. It includes gene mapping, gene sequencing, plant genetic resources, database, etc.

   It can be further divided into following branches:

1. Agricultural Bioinformatics

   It deals with computer-based study of various agricultural crop species. It is also referred to as crop bioinformatics.

2. Horticultural Bioinformatics

   It refers to computer-aided study of horticultural crops, viz. fruit crops, vegetable crops and flower crops.

3. Medicinal Plants Bioinformatics

   It deals with computer-based study of various medicinal plant species.

4. Forest Plant Bioinformatics

   It deals with computer-based study of forest plant species.

## Further reading

Chatr-aryamontri, A., Ceol, A., Palazzi, L.M., 2007. MINT: the molecular interaction database. Nucleic Acids Res. 35, 572–D574.

Flicek, P., Amode, M.R., Barrell, D., 2012. Ensemble. Nucleic Acids Res. 40, 84–D90.

Kanehisa, M., Goto, S., Sato, Y., 2012. KEGG for integration and interpretation of large-scale molecular datasets. Nucleic Acids Res. 40, 109–114.

Kent, W.J., Sugnet, C.W., Furey, T.S., 2002. The human genome browser at UCSC. Genome Res. 12 (6), 996–1006.

Kerrien, S., Aranda, B., Breuza, L., 2012. The IntAct molecular interaction database in 2012. Nucleic Acids Res. 40, 841–846.

Maglott, D., Ostell, J., Pruitt, K.D., Tatusova, T., 2010. Entrez Gene: gene-centered information at NCBI. Nucleic Acids Res. 33, 54–58.

The Gene Ontology Consortium, 2000. Gene ontology: tool for the unification of biology. Nat. Genet. 25 (1), 25, 32.

Xenarios, I., Rice, D.W., Salwinski, L., 2000. DIP: the database of interacting proteins. Nucleic Acids Res. 28, 289–291.

Zvelebil, M., Baum, J., 2007. Understanding Bioinformatics. Garland Science, New York, NY. ISBN 978-0815340249.

# Advances in DNA sequencing

2

## 2.1 Introduction

**Genome:** "Complete set of genetic information present in a haploid cell of an organism including its protoplasm" — *Hans Winkler 1920*

Prior to the mid-1970s, there was no system for specifically sequencing DNA. Centred on Rosalind Franklin's fundamental DNA crystallography and X-ray diffraction experiments, Watson and Crick were the two scientists who developed the DNA structure. The Phi-X174 bacteriophage was the very first organism to have the whole genome sequenced in 1977. Various research groups began sequencing DNA, with Fredrick Sanger and colleagues introducing the chain-termination process in 1977, resulting in a breakthrough. The first automatic DNA sequencing system was developed in 1986. This was the beginning of a golden age for sequencing platform creation and refining, including the pivotal DNA capillary sequencer.

## 2.2 DNA sequencing process

DNA sequencing is a lengthy procedure. It includes the following tasks in order to produce a sequenced DNA fragment. There are several DNA sequencing bioinformatics companies that use these measures (Fig. 2.1).

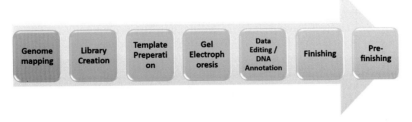

**FIGURE 2.1**

DNA sequencing process.

Bioinformatics for Everyone. https://doi.org/10.1016/B978-0-323-91128-3.00006-9

**Extraction of Genomic DNA:** To sequence the organism's DNA, the first step is to remove high-quality DNA from it. To extract clean and efficient genomic DNA from the respective organism, various kits and protocols are available.

**Genome Mapping:** The genome map is a must-have for any DNA sequencing project. The period area of the genome to be sequenced is identified first using the genome map. This region's identity group of clones is chosen; these are the mapped clones. The amplification for this gene region is then completed.

**Library Creation:** Cloning is used to create collections of smaller clones from the chosen mapped clones. This collection of clones serves as a clone archive for future sequencing projects.

**Template Perpetration:** DNA is purified from smaller clones at this point. The wet-lab setup for sequencing chemistries (using some of the methods described above) is complete.

**Gel Electrophoresis:** In assessing the sequence of smaller clones, gel electrophoresis will be used.

**Pre-finishing:** To generate high-quality sequences, certain unique sequencing techniques are employed. This is a critical move since it is here that the DNA sequence is cleaned up.

**Finishing:** This is the point at which the sequenced DNA becomes a finished product. This sequenced DNA is now able to be processed and used as DNA sequence results.

**Data Editing/DNA Annotation:** It is essential to store sequenced DNA in a library or genome bank in order to make it accessible to future bioinformatics research. Any quality assurance, verification and biological annotation are required prior to submission to public databases (Table 2.1).

**Table 2.1** Web-based resources for completed genome projects.

| Resource | Description | URL |
|---|---|---|
| EBI | European Bioinformatics Institute | http://www.ebi.ac.uk/genomes/ |
| NCBI | Entrez at National Center for Biotechnology Information | http://www.ncbi.nlm.nih.gov/Entrez/ |
| TIGR | The Institute for Genomic Research | http://www.tigr.org.tdb |
| GNN | Genome News Network | http://gnn.tigr.org/sequenced.genomes/genome.guide.p1.shtml |
| GOLD | Genomes Online Database | http://www.ergo.integratedgenomics.com/GOLD/ |
| Cyanobase | Kazusa Research Institute | http://bacteria.kazusa.or.jp/cyano/ (google − cyanobase) |
| Infobiogen | Complete Microbial Genomes | http://www.infobiogen.fr/doc/data/complete.genome.html |

## 2.3 DNA sequencing in real time

Think, what if you had a doctor and your doctor asked you to do some diagnostic blood tests along with an additional test to find the DNA sequence in a particular genome area. For that region of the genome, the doctor will need sequence details to conclude that there is or is no DNA pattern in this area. One day it will be almost a regular job in nursing practices for a fragment of DNA. The primary requirements are super-fast DNA sequencing mechanisms for enabling that kind of scenario. Many institutes, researchers and companies in bioinformatics science are focussing on this approach. These prospective DNA sequencing approaches need to differ materially from existing and likely next-generation sequencing approaches with very high throughput. The nanopore sequencing method is such a technique for sequencing which can open the future door.

In this phase, a nanopore prompts nucleic acids (a biological protein membrane such as alpha-haemolysin or a synthetic pore). DNA permeability changes by the pore or observations of individual base interactions with pore will infer the sequence of nucleotides. While there has been improvement on early demonstrations of proof of concept for such approaches, significant technological hurdles remain on the road to a genuinely functional nanopore-based sequence platform.

## 2.4 Maxam—Gilbert chemical cleavage method

Allan Maxam and Walter Gilbert introduced a detailed method of DNA sequencing using a two-stage catalytic mechanism that includes piperidines and two chemicals that pick purines and pyrimidines. The three phases of a chemical attack are base modification, processed base removal from its sugar and a breakup of DNA strand. Dimethyl sulphate with hydrazine can be used by purines and pyrimidines to disrupt the glycoside bond in between the ribose sugar as well as the base. The cleavage of phosphodiester bonds where the bases are displaced is catalysed by piperidine. Even if dimethyl sulphate and piperidine are to be separated from the guanine nucleic acids, dimethyl sulphate or piperidine are to be separated in formic acid, both guanine can then be split into a single stranded DNA substrate, with a radioactive label at 5″ end that splits both guanines and a single stranded DNA substratum with such a radioactive label on the 5′ end. The reactions will be run on polyacrylamide gels with a high polyacrylamide content, and the fragments will be separated by electrophoresis. Acid fragments are resolved with acrylamide or agarose matrix in an opposite length range, which means that smaller fragments are faster than large fragments in the polyacrylamide gel matrix. The autoradiographic bands (dark) on the film represent the 5′3′ DNA chain while reading from bottom up. The banding pattern is part of the basic calling process when it is considered in relation to four chemical reactions. In the world of genome sequencing, the sequencing of the reference human genome was the pinnacle. The method employed approximately 20,000 massive bacterial artificial chromosome or BAC clones, each of which represented a 100 kb fragment of the human genome (Fig. 2.2).

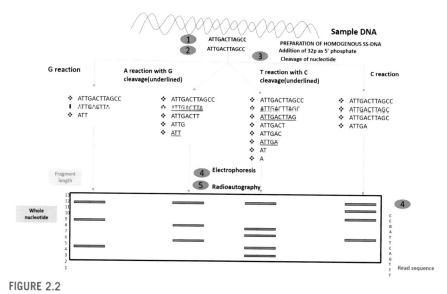

**FIGURE 2.2**

Sequencing by Maxam—Gilbert method.

## 2.5 Sanger chain-termination method

The first DNA sequence method of Sanger and Coulson for rapid DNA sequencing was known as "plus and minus" method. The *Escherichia coli* DNA polymerase I as well as DNA polymerase T4 method was used with separate restriction of nucleoside triphosphates. The acrylamide gel ionophoresis was used to counteract the products of the polymerases. Sanger and his colleagues found 2 years later, because of the inefficiency of the plus and minus process, a new pioneering technique for sequencing oligonucleotides by enzymatic polymerisation. A catalysed enzyme reaction has been developed which polymerises complementary DNA fragments into the DNA target template (unknown DNA). A P32-labelled primer was ran into the same known area of a template DNA, providing the point of departure for the synthesis of DNA, a short oligonucleotide with such a complementary sequence of the template DNA. In presence of DNA polymerases, deoxynucleoside triphosphates (dNTPs) are catalytically polymerised to DNA. The polymerisation was carried on until a modified nucleoside (named as terminator or dideoxynucleoside triphosphate) was inserted in a raised chain (ddNTP). This procedure was performed in four tubes with one of the four terminators having the required volume. The dideoxynucleotide used throughout the reaction determined the residue of the 3-end, while all the fragments produced had the same 5-end. After all four reactions, an electrophoresis of a polyacrylamide denaturation gel in four parallel lanes was performed for the mixture of different sized DNA fragments. The pattern of the bands revealed the distribution of the ends in the synthesised DNA strand, and an autoradiography was used to read the unknown sequence (Fig. 2.3).

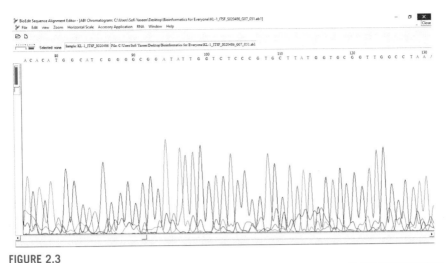

**FIGURE 2.3**

Chromatogram of Sanger sequencing (*Brassica oleraceae variety*).

## 2.6 **Automated fluorescence sequencing**

Automatic sequencing was the major advance in sequencing with fluorescence-labelled dideoxy terminators and pushed DNA sequencing to a high-performance environment. In 1986, Leroy Hood and his colleagues concentrated their efforts on the methods of DNA sequencing, using fluorescent labelling, laser-induced detection and computerised base calls rather than radioactive labelling and autoradiography as well as manual base calls. The primers have been labelled with one of four fluorescent colours, and one of the four dideoxynucleotides with all four deoxynucleotides have been placed in separate sequencing reactions accordingly. The four reactions were grouped into a sequencing gel of polyacrylamide until completion. A fluorescent detector scans the gel while the fragments of reaction are drifting by a four-colour laser. To produce an image, a computer analyses the data and assembles it into a gel, which can be read in the form of a ladder from the bottom to the top. Multiple sequencing reactions on different templates are run in parallel, and each ladder's bands are read as a separate electropherogram or chromatogram. Applied Biosystems launched this approach in 1987. James M. Prober from DuPont and colleagues promoted "a rather more sophisticated chemistry" for the approach of Fluorescent Sequence. They named the terminators themselves instead of using fluorescence-labelled primers. Succinyl fluorescein was used in the first "dye kit." DuPont commercialised the invention for a short time before selling the patent to Applied Biosystems.

Applied Biosystems worked into the 1990s to improve the terminator chemistries as well as the detection/base calling schemes. Two big chemistry changes were the change in the colour marks on the terminators and the enhancement of fragment resolution. In the early 1990s, Harold Swerdlow and associates concentrated on using capillaries to retrieve DNA sequences. Capillary electrophoresis was a very well method in analytical chemistry by the late 1980s. Once the experiment reagents have been pumped out, DNA sequencing reactions could be performed in a single reaction tube and loaded. The capillary system is developed to supply the capillary with new polymer, load the sequencing reaction in the capillary system, use a continuous electric current through the capillary system and allow the solved fragments to pass via an optical window in which a laser exits a colour control, a detector collects the emission fluorescence wavelengths and software interprets the emission wave. In a shorter time, these systems can now produce 500 to1000 bases of high-quality DNA sequence.

## 2.7 Next-generation DNA sequencing

New-generation gequencing or NGS is a high-performance technique which is focussed on parallelising the sequencing process, allowing thousands to millions of sequences to be read at the same time. There are presently eight major huge sequencing networks, each of which differs in terms of how the models are prepared for sequencing, the sequencing reaction itself and the detection systems used. Moreover, the various facilities, production thresholds and number of readings of each of these platforms will result in differing costs for every sequencing reaction (Table 2.2).

Note: Discussions about the next-generation sequencing tools will be thoroughly discussed in Chapter 20.

## 2.8 Sequence platform pros and cons

**Table 2.2** Pros and cons of sequencing platforms.

| Platform | Pros | Cons |
| --- | --- | --- |
| 454 Roche | The reading time is very long. Analysis time is short. For small trials, the cost is low. | Homopolymers have a high error rate. Low performance. Instrumental costs are high. Data have a high cost per gigabyte. |
| SOLiD | Throughput is high. Data at a low cost per gigabyte. High precision. | Reading time is limited. Instrumental costs are high. |
| Illumina | High flow rate. Low cost per gigabyte of information. Excellent precision. | Limited reading time. Costly instrumentation. |
| Ion Torrent | Low-operational, cost-effective instrumentation, short execution time. | Price per gigabyte of data is in the middle. Needs more experience. |
| Pacific Bioscence | Availability of longest period for reading. Short instrument execution time. | High error rate. High cost data per gigabyte. |
| Oxford Nanopore | Small, compact and cost-effective instrumentation. | High error rate. Errors that are biased. Expensive readings. |

## 2.9  Usage of DNA sequencing

- **Preventive Medicine Design:** The sequenced DNA of each human genome can be used as a factor in the development of preventive medicine.
- **Genetic Hypothesis Testing:** Rapid genotype phenotype relationship hypothesis testing.
- **Gene Expression Profiling:** DNA sequencing is needed for in vitro and in situ gene expression profiling at all stages of multicellular organism growth.
- **Cancer Research:** For example, in cancer research, DNA sequencing is used to determine detailed mutation sets for individual clones.
- **Pathogen Identification:** Identifying existing and novel pathogens, as well as developing biowarfare sensors.
- **Precision Genome Annotation:** The secret to a detailed genome annotation is sequenced DNA.
- **Evolutionary Research:** Evolution can be researched in great depth, including the clarification of single nucleotide polymorphisms or SNPs and other forms of mutations and speciation using correctly sequenced DNA.

## 2.10  Challenges of DNA sequencing

The biggest difficulty with DNA sequencing is that there is no computer that can take long DNA as an input and produce the whole sequence. Current approaches can only sequence around 500 letters (base pairs) at a time. It is critical to improve the sensitivity of existing instruments (in terms of sequence length). Additional flour combinations are needed in the chemistry lab to allow reaction multiplexing, which can save time and money. Along with raising throughput, lowering the cost of sequencing is another task ahead of us. Many cost reductions in the past have been gradual rather than massive. According to figures, existing DNA sequencing setups (laboratory standards) (e.g. 3100 Genetic Analyzer) can sequence about 100 samples a day on average. One run contains 16−20 tests, a plate contains 6−10 runs, and two plates are used at the same time. So, on a regular basis, the total capacity for sequencing is about 200 samples. This is insufficient sequencing throughput to meet existing and future demands for sequenced DNA.

## Further reading

Breathnach, R., Benoist, 1978. Ovalbumin gene: evidence for a leader sequence in mRNA and DNA sequences at the exon-intron boundaries. Proc. Natl. Acad. Sci. U.S.A 75, 4853−4857.

Breathnach, R., Mandel, J.L., Chambon, P., 1977. Ovalbumin gene is split in chicken DNA. Nature 270, 314−319.

Dovichi, N.J., Zhang, J., 2000. How capillary electrophoresis sequenced the human genome. Angew. Chem. Int. Ed. 39, 4463−4468.

Franklin, R.E., Gosling, R.G., 1953. Molecular configuration in sodium thymonucleate. Nature 171 (4356), 740–741.

Hood, L.E., Hunkapiller, M.W., Smith, L.M., 1987. Automated DNA sequencing and analysis of the human genome. Genomics 1 (3), 201–212.

Jeffries, A.J., Flavell, R.A., 1977. The rabbit β-globin gene contains a large insert in the coding sequence. Cell 12, 1097–1108.

Maxam, A.M., Gilbert, W., 1977. A new method for sequencing DNA. Proc. Natl. Acad. Sci. U.S.A 74, 560–564.

Mount, D.W., 2001. Bioinformatics: Sequence and Genome Analysis. Cold Spring Harbor. Cold Spring Harbor Laboratory Press, New York.

Prober, J.M., Trainor, G.L., 1987. A system for rapid DNA sequencing with fluorescent chain-terminating dideoxynucleotides. Science 238, 336–341.

Ruiz-Martinez, M.C., Berka, 1993. DNA sequencing by capillary electrophoresis with replaceable linear polyacrylamide and laser-induced fluorescence detection. Anal. Chem. 65, 2851–2858.

Sanger, F., Micklen, S., Coulson, A.R., 1977. DNA sequencing and chain-terminating inhibitors. Proc. Natl. Acad. Sci. U.S.A 74, 5463–5467.

Smith, L.M., Sanders, J.Z., 1986. Fluorescence detection in automated DNA sequence analysis. Nature 321, 674–679.

Swerdlow, H., Wu, S.L., 1990. Capillary gel electrophoresis for DNA sequencing. Laser-induced fluorescence detection with the sheath flow cuvette. J. Chromatogr. 516, 61–67.

Swerdlow, H., Zhang, J.Z., 1991. Three DNA sequencing methods using capillary gel electrophoresis and laser-induced fluorescence. Anal. Chem. 63, 2835–2841.

Watson, J.D., Crick, F.H.C., 1953. Molecular structure of nucleic acids: a structure for deoxyribose nucleic acid. Nature 171 (4356), 737–738.

Zhang, J.Z., Fang, Y., 1995. Use of non-cross-linked polyacrylamide for four-color DNA sequencing by capillary electrophoresis separation of fragments up to 640 bases in length in two hours. Anal. Chem. 67, 4589–4593.

# Bioinformatics databases and tools

Biological databases have evolved extensively in recent years and have become part of the daily toolbox of the biodiversity. Searching databases, for example, has many reasons:

1. If a new DNA sequence is obtained, one has to know if it is already entirely or partly stored in databases or whether it contains a homologous sequences.
2. Each of the indexes has an annotation attached to a particular sequence. The quest will promote its analysis by finding annotations for the sequence search.
3. Search for identical non-coding stretches of DNA on the database, i.e. repeat elements or regulatory sequences.
4. Other applications, such as finding the wrong priming sites for a group of PCR oligonucleotides, for particular purposes.
5. Find homologous proteins — identical in sequence and in their supposed folding or form.

The web offers a large number of online bioinformatics databases.

## 3.1 List of databases

- **NAR databases** — The international journal *Nucleic Acids Research* has held the largest lists of biological databases, publishing in the first issue of each year since 1996, a special edition for molecular biology databases. You can freely read any of these website documents.
- **NCBI databases** — NCBI maintains molecular databases. There are six major classes in the databases: nucleotides, proteins, structure, expression, taxonomy and genome. It also contains links to the description of each database page.
- **EBI databases** — The fundamental passage to EBI databases is isolated into the accompanying classes: literature, microarrays, nucleotides, protein, design, pathway and ontology.

Bioinformatics for Everyone. https://doi.org/10.1016/B978-0-323-91128-3.00009-4

## 3.2 Database query systems

- **NCBI Entrez** — the special NCBI search interface.
- **EBI SRS** — it is the EBI-maintained database query system. In the early 1990s, in the European Molecular Biology Laboratory, SRS stands for sequence recovery method originally designed by Thure Etzold. Initially, it was an open infrastructure implemented in a dozen different database organisations. SRS was made a commercial kit in the late 1990s, but was still open to be used academically. The tech corporation headquartered in Cambridge, UK, Bio-Wisdom purchased SRS in 2006.
- **EMBL SRS** — maintained by EMBL, at Germany.
- **DKFZ SRS** — it is kept up by the German Cancer Research Centre.
- **Columbia SRS** — maintained by Columbia University, USA (Table 3.1).

## 3.3 Genome databases

Hundreds of species have been sequenced on a genome scale because of the rapid evolution of DNA sequencing technology. On the Internet, genome databases and associated research platforms are available.

## 3.4 List of genome databases

- **GOLD:** it is also called as Genomes Online Database. A full and continuing gene sequencing resource with flow charts and predictive data tables.
- **Karyn's genome:** a short overview and reference list for each genome. It is exceptionally valuable for the user community because of direct connections to the EMBL or ENSEMBL annotations.
- **CropNet:** UK Crop Plant Network-based website for the production, executives and scattering of relative planning and genome analysis data in crop plants.

**Table 3.1** Major databases.

| Database | Country or region | Link to website |
|---|---|---|
| European Nucleotide Archive (ENA) | Europe | https://www.ebi.ac.uk/ |
| Data Bank of Japan (DDBJ) | Japan | https://www.ddbj.nig.ac.jp/index-e.html |
| GenBank | United States | www.ncbi.nlm.nih.gov/genbank/ |

## 3.5 Genome browsers and analysis platforms

- **NCBI Genome** — the entry to different NCBI RESOURCES and genomic tools like the Map Viewer, Genome Database and PGC.
- **GoldenPath** — the site for the genomic programme at the University of California, Santa Cruz, which includes a guide series and draught assemblies for a large genomic collection (UCSC).
- **ENSEMBL** — European eukaryotic genome resource web server. It was created in collaboration with the EBI and the Sanger Institute.
- **VISTA** — an exhaustive collection of genomic sequence analysis programmes and databases.
- **Genomics of the TIGR Plant** — TIGR plant genome databases and resources.
- **TIGR gene indices** — it is maintained at Harvard.

## 3.6 Genome database of model organisms

- **Gramene** — Open access data resource for comparison of genomes, e.g. rice, maize, wheat, barley, sorghum, *Arabidopsis*, poplar, grape, etc. It is also noted that genome sequencing products, structure of proteins, functional analysis, gene mapping and physical mapping are used to produce cross-species homology relationships.
- **TAIR** — It consists of the entire *Arabidopsis* genome sequence, genetic markers, physical markers, knowledge of the scientific community, genetics, metabolism, gene expression, DNA and inventories of seeds as well as the genetics structure.
- **AtENSEMBL** — A genome browser for the *Arabidopsis thaliana*.
- **Oryzabase** — It is maintained by Japan's National Institute of Genetics. It includes material on the genetic resources, genetic dictionaries, chromosome maps, photographs of mutants and basic rice science awareness.
- **FlyBase** — An extensive collection of genes and genomes of *Drosophila* maintained by the University of Indiana.
- **CyanoBase** — Developed by the Kazusa Institute, Japan. It is genomic database for cyanobacteria (Table 3.2).

## 3.7 Sequence databases

Several databases developed in various parts of the world at the beginning of the 1980s. Two major groups of databases are available: DNA databases and protein databases. Over the years, the database series has expanded enormously.

**Table 3.2** Genomic databases.

| Resource | Description | URL |
|---|---|---|
| EBI | European Bioinforatics Institute | http://www.ebi.ac.uk/genomes/ |
| NCBI | Entrez at National Center for Biotechnology Information | http://www.ncbi.nlm.nih.gov/Entrez/ |
| TIGR | The Institute for Genomic Research | http://www.tigr.org.tdb |
| GNN | Genome News Network | http://gnn.tigr.org/sequenced. genomes/genome.guide.p1.shtml |
| GOLD c v | Genomes Online Database | http://www.ergo.integratedgenomics. com/GOLD/ |
| Cyanobase | Kazusa Research Institute | http://bacteria.kazusa.or.jp/cyano/ (google – cyanobase) |
| Infobiogen | Complete Microbial Genomes | http://www.infobiogen.fr/doc/data/ complete.genome.html |

## 3.8 DNA sequence databases

- **GenBank** – likewise an online interface of NIH Genetic Sequence Database oversaw by NCBI as a feature of the International Cluster Nucleotide Collaboration Network.
- **EMBL** – an International Nucleotide Database Collaborative, maintained as an EMBL nuclear sequence database.
- **RefSeq** – the NCBI-built reference sequence series for providing an extensive, interconnected, non-redundant range of protein and DNA sequences. It gives a steady reference to the ID and characterisation of genomes, genes, mutation and polymorphism investigation, gene expression research and comparative analysis.
- **UniGene** – it is the NCBI's Organized Transcriptome View. Each UniGene passage contains a bunch of transcript sequences that ordinarily get from a similar locus, just as data about protein likenesses, gene expression, clone cDNA reagents and gene position.
- **dbSNP** – NCBI-preserved SNP site.
- **EMBLCDS** – EMBL coding sequence database of nucleotides (Figs. 3.1 and 3.2).

## 3.9 Protein sequence databases

- **Swiss-Prot** – the site of the SIB Geneva, Switzerland, links to a well-noted protein sequence data archive. A list of sources is provided, as well as a comprehensive user manual and flowcharts statistics.

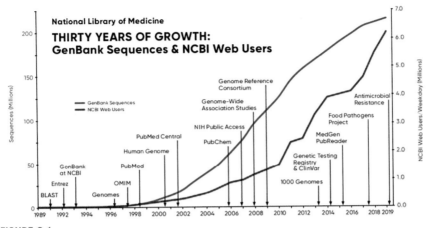

**FIGURE 3.1**

Thirty years of expansion for GenBank sequences and NCBI Web users.

*Source: (Dept. of health and human services national institute of health).*

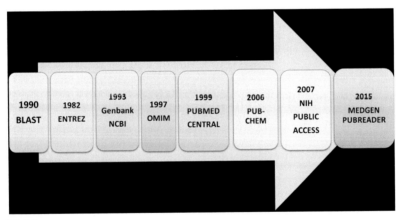

**FIGURE 3.2**

Brief timeline of various NCBI databases.

- **UniProt** — the international database for protein sequences that comprises a UniProtKB (protein knowledge base), UniReF (cluster sequence) and UniParc (sequence archive).
- **HPOI** — the UniProtKB/Swiss-Prot Consistency Requirements for EBI initiative in recording all known human sequences. It gives enormous details to each known protein, including the function definition, domain composition, subcellular position, posttranslational changes, variants and resemblances to other proteins.
- **IPI** — it is the International Protein Index-related website providing a high-level guidance on topical database describing proteomes in higher eukaryotic species.

Protein molecules play an essential function in living organisms. Typically, they are categorised in families according to their various roles. Proteins have sequence and fingerprints, blocks or functional domains in the same family and subfamily which can be conserved. With the large number of sequence data available it was possible to create secondary databases of protein molecules.

## 3.10  Databases of protein domain

- **Prosite** — It is a database maintained and developed by the Swiss Institute for Protein Domain, Family and Functional Sites.
- **PRINTS** — It is a set of preserved motif-based protein fingerprints created and stored by the University of Manchester, UK, within the protein family.
- **BLOCKS** — It is the most well-preserved protein regions in a variety of lined ungapped segments that have been kept archived at the Fred Hutchinson Cancer Research Centre in the United States of America.
- **CDD** — Database of Conserved Protein Domains of the National Biotechnology Centre.
- **ProDom** — A detailed database of protein domain families generated and maintained automatically by the Claude Bernard University in France using the Swiss-Prot and TrEMBL sequence databases.

## 3.11  Databases of protein family

- **Pfam** — It is the database of protein families, made and managed by the Sanger Institute, UK, representing various sequence alignments as well as Markov secret designs.

## 3.12  Databases of protein function

- **IMGT** — It is developed and run by the University of Montpellier, France, an international immunogenetic information system. The integrated high-quality information for human and other vertebrates' immune system.
- **HPA** — Website of the Proteome Resource Centre in Sweden, for a wide spectrum of normal human tissues, cancer cells and cell lines showing the expression and position of proteins by immunohistochemistry.

## 3.13  Structure databases

It is the Protein Data Bank (PDB), developed at the end of 1970s at the United States Brookhaven National Laboratory. It serves as the protein structure database's focal point. In 1999, the RSCB was created to administer the PDB. RSCB is the key entrance to macromolecular structures, protein structures which can also be found via the EBI MSDLite server and the NCBI Entrez system.

## 3.14 Protein structures database portals

- **MSD** — the EBI macromolecular structure client's entry advantage.
- **MSDLite** — an EBI web server that allows you to scan for structures of proteins quickly.
- **PDBSUM** — the web server of an EBI which provides high-level definition, structural interaction and schematic diagrams.
- **BMRB** — the University of Wisconsin-biological Madison's magnetic resonance data bank.
- **ModBase** — a database of similar protein structure models created and kept up at the University of California, San Francisco.

## 3.15 Protein structures — classification

- **Structure Classification of Proteins (SCOP)** — Cambridge University developed and maintains this database.
- **CATH** — it is a database that is created and maintained by University College London. It is named according to the hierarchy used in classification: Class, Architecture, Topography and Homology.

## 3.16 Protein structures — visualisation

**JenaLib** — The Jena Biological Macromolecules Library focussing on macromolecular structure simulation and analysis.

## Further reading

Gaffney, J., Tibebu, R., Bart, R., Beyene, G., Girma, D., Kane, N.A., Mace, E.S., Mockler, T., Nickson, T.E., Taylor, N., Zastrow-Hayes, G., 2020. Open access to genetic sequence data maximizes value to scientists, farmers, and society. Global Food Sec. 26, 100411. ISSN 2211-9124.

Luo, J., 2013. Chapter 9 Applied Bioinformatics Tools. Springer Science and Business Media LLC, p. 2.

# Nucleic acid sequence databases

4

## 4.1 Introduction

Specialised and generalised databases were used to classify biological databases. Protein and nucleic acid sequences are kept in generalised databases, whereas the solved structure of transcripts and proteins are saved in structural/specialised databases (Figs. 4.1–4.8).

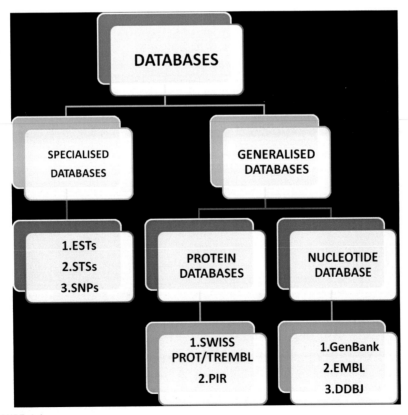

FIGURE 4.1

Classification of databases.

Bioinformatics for Everyone. https://doi.org/10.1016/B978-0-323-91128-3.00016-1

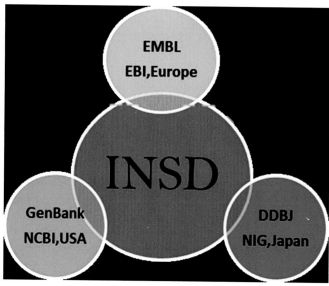

FIGURE 4.2

Data from GenBank, EMBL and DDBJ are exchanged.

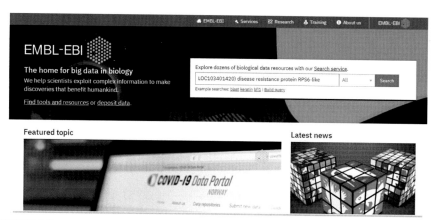

FIGURE 4.3

Homepage of EMBL database.

## 4.2 Nucleic acid sequence databases

Nucleic acid sequences provide an initial basis for understanding genetically diverse organisms' structure, function and growth. The simultaneous efforts to capture, process and disseminate them in various parts of the world have been a testament to their central significance in modern biology. Biological databases started to appear

GenBank ▾

## Oryza sativa 28S rRNA, complete sequence

GenBank: AH001750.2

FASTA   Graphics

Go to: ⊙

```
LOCUS        AH001750                 996 bp    rRNA    linear   PLN 25-AUG-2016
DEFINITION   Oryza sativa 28S rRNA, complete sequence.
ACCESSION    AH001750 M82048 M82049 M82050 M82051 M82052
VERSION      AH001750.2
KEYWORDS     28S ribosomal RNA.
SOURCE       Oryza sativa (rice)
  ORGANISM   Oryza sativa
             Eukaryota; Viridiplantae; Streptophyta; Embryophyta; Tracheophyta;
             Spermatophyta; Magnoliopsida; Liliopsida; Poales; Poaceae; BOP
             clade; Oryzoideae; Oryzeae; Oryzinae; Oryza.
REFERENCE    1 (sites)
  AUTHORS    Doyle,J.A., Donoghue,M.J. and Zimmer,E.A.
  TITLE      Integration of morphological and ribosomal RNA data on the origin
             of angiosperms
  JOURNAL    Ann. Mo. Bot. Gard. 81 (3), 419-450 (1994)
REFERENCE    2 (bases 1 to 996)
  AUTHORS    Hamby,R.K., Suh,Y.B., Bult,C.J., Kallersjo,M. and Zimmer,E.A.
  TITLE      Darwin's abominable mystery revisited: Ribosomal RNA insights into
             flowering plant evolution
  JOURNAL    Unpublished
COMMENT      On or before Aug 25, 2016 this sequence version replaced M82048.1,
             M82049.1, M82050.1, M82051.1, M82052.1, AH001750.1.
FEATURES             Location/Qualifiers
     source          1..996
                     /organism="Oryza sativa"
                     /mol_type="rRNA"
                     /db_xref="taxon:4530"
     gene            1..996
```

**FIGURE 4.4**

Nucleotide sequence format structure of GenBank.

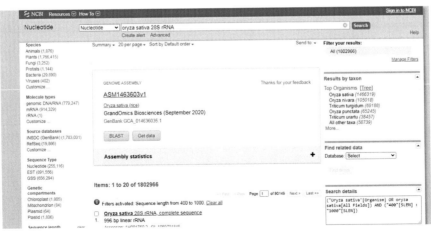

**FIGURE 4.5**

Retrieval of nucleotide sequence of a given gene.

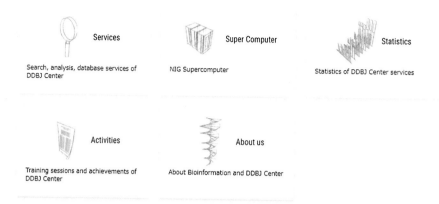

**FIGURE 4.6**

An overview of DDBJ's sharing and analysis services.

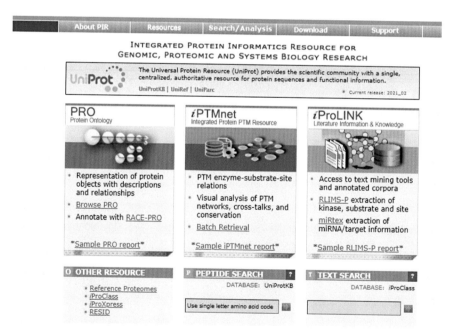

**FIGURE 4.7**

PIR resources.

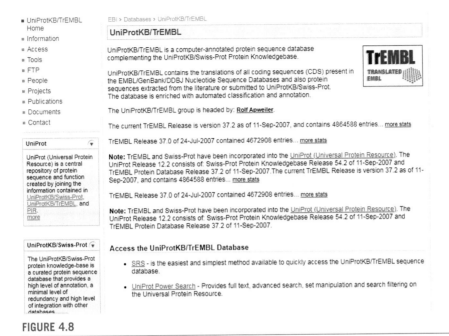

**FIGURE 4.8**

Webpage of UniProtKB/TrEMBL.

in the early 1980s to store data produced by new sequencing techniques at that time. EMBL and GenBank comprise of the first nucleotide databases that were compiled and annotated in 1982. In 1986, DDBJ and the International Nucleotide Sequence Database (INSD) were launched.

Objectives of nucleic acid databases:

- Sequence databases are primarily used to store and retrieve information.
- Provide abundance of data to molecular biologists.
- Offer a one-of-a-kind opportunity for computer analysis of existing sequences.
- Make comparisons to newly determined sequences easier.
- Serve as a repository for data that can be used to generate and test theories about molecular sequence and evolution.

## 4.3 **EMBL**

The European Bioinformatics Institute's (EBI) primary nucleotide sequence resource is the EMBL Nucleotide Sequence Database (also known as EMBL-Bank). It was released to the public for the first time in June 1982, with 568 entries. The EMBL Nucleotide Sequence Database (www.ebi.ac.uk/embl/) is the European member of the International Nucleotide Sequence Database Collaboration (INSDC), which is composed of the three organisations DDBJ/EMBL/GenBank. The EBI provides bioinformatics resources, including various sequencing functions for database searches, sequence and homology searches. An extensive sequence similarity algorithm set is maintained in the EBI, accessible via the EMBL-EBI website. This database incorporates data from genome sequence centres, individual scientists, the European Patent Office (EPO) and INSD collaborators. The information is available online. In February 2004, 30,351,263 entries representing 150,000 species were in the database (dominated by model organisms). The vast majority of data are transmitted from main centres, and the database is expanding at breakneck pace.

## 4.4 EBI's mission

The organisation's various objectives are as follows:

- Opening of data and methods in bioinformatics for all science sectors.
- Making biology more available through research based on fundamental research.
- To educate scientists at all levels in advanced bioinformatics.
- To assist industry in disseminating cutting-edge innovations.
- To coordinate the provision of biological data in Europe.

## 4.5 The EMBL entry structure

The database's entries are arranged in such a way that they are both human and machine readable. For easy access by computer programmes, free-text definitions are saved in organised information fields. Each line of data in an entry is preceded by a two-character code indicating the type of data found in that line. There are over 20 distinct line forms. Several of them include the following:

> **ID line**: includes the name of the entry, the taxonomic division and the length of sequence.
> **AC line**: a unique accession number.
> **DE**: an inventory of the sequence containing the gene names that it codes for, its derived genome region and all other details that help to classify the sequence.
> **DR**: cross-references within a database which point to other similar information.
> **CC**: free-text comments.
> **KW**: abbreviations for key terms/words that emphasise functional, structural or other distinguishing characteristics.
> **FT**: feature table that stores sequence annotations, protein coding sequences position, i.e. CDS, and features discovered during data preparation.

## 4.6 GenBank

GenBank is the most extensive and annotated collection, which is part of the INSDC, of public DNA sequences. The National Library of Medicine was set up in 1988 by the National Health Institutes of the United States (NIH) (USA). The data set is progressively developing, principally through the consideration of EST and other elite information from sequencing centres. Shown records are isolated into segments which are generally ordered yet in addition partitioned into EST, GSS and HTG by the document size and the assortment of the information sources, among different segments. Data from the genome mapping database, phylogenetic expression, gene expression and protein structure, as well as DNA and protein sequence databases can be used as an interface to GenBank data by using NCBI Entrez' Recovery Method. In addition, it includes links to the MEDLINE database, the primary source of quotations and abstracts. This integrated architecture greatly improves the wealth of GenBank as a biological data repository, through its direct linkages to the literature and other sequence sources. GenBank also has the opportunity to scan the BLAST suite of programmes using the NCBI Web Interface for query sequences.

A released GenBank sequence file has indices for different fields of database (e.g. author, reference) and database data (e.g. GenPept).

## 4.7 The GenBank entry structure

Every entry contains a rundown of keywords, their comparing sub-keywords and a discretionary feature table. The broad nucleotide sequence file format structure of this information base is as per the following:

1. **Locus**: This is a term that alludes to the title allotted by GenBank to the sequence entry. It contains information such as the name of locus, length of sequence, molecule type and modification date.
2. **Definition**: This is a brief overview of the nucleotide sequence.
3. **Accession**: This section includes information about the accession number, the accession version and the GI number.
4. **Keyword**: This segment contains a rundown of brief phrases allocated by the creator portraying the products of gene and other related entry details.
5. **Source**: This refers to the organism from which the sequences were derived.
6. **Citation**: Specifies how the sequence was retrieved, as sequences were originally exclusively obtained from established literature.
7. **Features**: These are the sequence's attributes like organic source, coding area, exon, intron, promoters, alternative splice patterns and mutations.
8. **Series**: Contains the count of each nucleotide present in the sequence as well as the complete nucleotide sequence.

## 4.8 Access to GenBank

GenBank data can be searched and retrieved in a variety of ways.

- Use Entrez Nucleotide to search GenBank for sequence annotations.
- Using BLAST, GenBank sequences are searched and matched in a series

- NCBI's anonymous FTP server offers ASN.1 and flatfile formats.
- NCBI e-utilities can be used to Search, link and download various sequences.

## 4.9 Protocol: retrieval of nucleotide sequence of a given gene from GenBank

1. Access GenBank through www.ncbi.nlm.nih.gov.
2. On NCBI homepage select nucleotide database in drop-down menu.
3. Search for the organism you are looking for, e.g. *Oryza sativa.*
4. Left side of the website will show number of filters, you can select any of the filters, e.g. molecule type can be selected as rRNA.
5. After activating filters you will get a number of results for rRNA of a given organism.
6. Select any of the RNA sequence as required.
7. Open the flat file and save it in FASTA format.

## 4.10 DDBJ

The Mishima National Institute of Genetics founded the DNA Data Bank of Japan in 1986. At present, DDBJ is Asia's only database of nuclear sequence. Although DDBJ is predominantly composed of Japanese researchers, data of researchers from other countries are also accepted. It is a member of the INSDC. The majority of DDBJ's information originates in a number of sequence centres, particularly the international consortium on human genome sequence. Therefore, the database is constantly growing – in 1999 alone, the number of entries processed was more than doubled during the preceding 10 years and between July 2000 and July 2001. In order to better handle the growing size of the database, it is divided into species-based divisions, which makes it possible to obtain more productive information about species. In addition, the database has a separate patent data division which the Japanese Patent Office, the United States Patent and Trademark Office and the EPO have received and processed. Its interpretations are naturally added to the Japan International Protein Information data set.

## 4.11 Tasks of DDBJ

The DDBJ Centre's primary responsibilities are as follows:

1. INSDC establishes and operates, which in association with the patent application offers nucleotide and amino acid sequence data.
2. Conducts biological data searches and analyses.
3. A training session and a journal.

## 4.12 Workflow of DDBJ

The submission of data to DDBJ follows a specific workflow.

1. **Submission of Data:** In general, DDBJ accepts submissions of nucleotide sequences through the Nucleotide Sequence Submission System or the Mass Submission System. After processing submitted data, DDBJ assigns accession number to each sequence.
   a. Nucleotide Sequence Submission System
      DDBJ suggests that you use the Nucleotide Sequence Submission System in general.
   b. Mass Submission System or MSS: The MSS is recommended only if submission contains an increased number of sequences (>1024), long nucleotide sequences or it contains multiple features (>30 in an entry).
2. **Annotation:** Annotation is performed in compliance with the DDBJ/ENA/GenBank consortium's rules and international standards.
3. **Accession Number Assignment and Notification:** The INSDC will allocate a unique number to a Contact Person whose e-mail address is entered in the field "Contact person". Normally, this notice is sent within five working days.
4. **Notification of Data Release:** DDBJ data are accessible through getentry and anonymous FTP. The data are transmitted to GenBank and ENA, and are also accessible via GenBank and ENA. The data also include DDBJ, Search and Analysis services and ARSA services. Essentially, the data published by DDBJ are open to the public.

## 4.13 The INSD

Sequence information is produced in huge size that individual groups were not able to compile it. Thus, EMBL and GenBank united with DDBJ in 1987 fully intent on disentangling and normalising measures for data collection and annotation. They are presently assembling a segment of the worldwide recorded sequence information and trade new and changed passages consistently through the Internet to guarantee ideal synchronisation. This triangular collaboration is the product of the INSD. This implies that the amounts shared by participating databases are nearly and users need to submit only their sequence to one of the tools to represent it in the others. DNA sequences from more than 150 000 unique life forms have been saved in libraries, predominantly by individual labs and large-scale sequence projects, and new species are presented at a pace of more than 1400 every month. The essential objective of INSD was to foster a common element table organisation and annotation practise standards to improve information quality and dependability, just as to advance interoperability and data sharing.

## 4.14 Protein sequence databases

Protein sequence databases range in complexity from simple to complex. Some are briefly discussed in the sections below.

## 4.15 Swiss-Prot

The Department of Medical Biochemistry at the University of Geneva and EMBL have been working together since 1986 to develop Swiss-Prot. The database was transferred to EBI, the UK's external station, after 1994, and transferred to the Swiss Institute for Bioinformatics (SIB) in April 1998. The SIB and EBI therefore now co-keep the database. By connecting to more than 30 different databases, which store sequences of nucleic acid or protein, family of proteins, structures or advanced data collections, Swiss-Prot adds value. Details on the associated genetic disorders (OMIM) and the three-dimensional structures of protein in order to obtain the nucleic acid sequence (EMBL) encoding the protein, information specific to its protein family (PROSITE, PRINTS, InterPro) (PDB). Therefore, Swiss-Prot acts as a hub for the communication of databases. Prot's annotations distinguishes it from other protein sequence methods and has developed it for most research purposes as a database of choice.

The characteristics of Swiss-Prot include the following:

1. **Annotations**: bibliography, taxonomy, protein function, PTM, domain structure, functional sites, associated conditions and similarity in relation and with other proteins are included in the annotations.
2. **Minimum redundancy**: simplified and combined data seem more succinct and consistent. Data conflicts are mentioned for each data entry.
3. **Interoperability with other databases**: interoperability with sequence-related databases of the three different types, i.e. nucleic acid sequences, protein sequences and protein tertiary structures. Cross-references to external data repositories are also maintained by Swiss-Prot.
4. **Documentation**: indexing and registering of all files is included in the documentation.

## 4.16 PIR

The National Biomedical Research Foundation founded Protein Information Resource (PIR) initially, in 1984. A joint partnership was created by PIR-PSD (IASRI, ND), a public bioinformatics resource in genomics and proteomics research by PIR and by the Munich Protein Sequences Information Center and the Japan International Protein Information Base. It is very useful for identifying and analysing protein sequences. It has been a member of UniProtKB since 2002. This database contains non-redundant information, is comprehensive and employs object-oriented databases (Database Management System). This database is unique by classifying protein sequences by superfamily. Thus, the information base is coordinated progressively around the idea of family, with its constituent proteins consequently grouped dependent on sequence similarity. Sequences inside super families have a typical architecture and overall length. A manual comment supplements the automated classification system by integrating new components into existing super families and characterising new bunches dependent on boundaries, for example, sequence identity, overlap length, area course of action — this incorporates superfamily names, brief descriptions, bibliographies, representative listings and seed components, and architectural domains and motives typical of the family. By combining sequences with experimentally validated data from the literature, the precision of annotation can be increased and errors that could occur in large-scale genome sequence projects prevented.

## 4.17 TrEMBL

The TrEMBL database contains computer-generated entries that result from the translation of all coding sequences found in the DDBJ/EMBL/GenBank databases. TrEMBL contains a variety of protein sequences mined from existing literature or presented directly by users to ensure its completeness. This database allows you to quickly access data from the protein sequence. When a match is made, the significance can be checked using a series of secondary patterns determined using the eMotif algorithm.

Two major types of TrEMBL:

1. **SP-TrEMBL (Swiss-Prot-TrEMBL)**, which includes entries that have not yet been annotated which will eventually be integrated into Swiss-Prot.
2. **REM-TrEMBL (REMaining-TrEMBL)**, containing non-Swiss-Prot sequences (e.g. immunoglobulins, T-cell receptors, etc.) which do not code for real proteins.

## 4.18 UniProt

The EBI, SIB and the PIR are the founding consortium in UniProt. Each is deeply involved in the maintenance and annotation of protein. This database includes high-quality data as well as information on protein function.

UniProt has three elements, each adapted for particular applications:

- The UniProt Knowledgebase is the primary source of annotated protein information such as protein's function, classification, cross-references, etc.
- Non-redundant Reference (UniRef) databases combine sequences closely linked to a single record.

- UniProt Archive (UniParc) is a detailed archive that represents all protein sequences accurately. It is assisted by grants from the European Commission, the NIH, the NCI-caBIG, the Department of Defense and the Swiss Government.

## Further reading

Chaturvedi, V.K., Mishra, D., Tiwari, A., Snijesh, V.P., Ahmad Shaik, N., Singh, M.P., 2019. Chapter 3 Sequence Databases. Springer Science and Business Media LLC.

Higgs, P.G., Attwood, T.K., 2013. Information Resources for Genes and Proteins. In: Bioinformatics and Molecular Evolution.

Khandelwal, I., Sharma, A., Agrawal, P.K., Shrivastava, R., 2017. Chapter 4 Bioinformatics Database Resources. IGI GlobaL.

# Pairwise sequence alignment

## 5.1 Definition

The heart of bioinformatics research is sequence comparison. This is a critical first step in studying newly discovered sequences with structural and functional properties. Comparisons between sequences are becoming increasingly significant because new biological sequences have been created exponentially, enabling a new protein to be found in the database with a functional and evolutionary inference. In this kind of examination, sequence arrangement is by a wide margin, the most essential methodology. This is the way to compare sequences through the search for common patterns of character and to establish a link between similar sequences among residences. The two sequence alignment approach is called the pairwise sequence alignment and forms the basis for searching for similarities in the database.

## 5.2 Bio-significance

In general, the more identical two sequences are, the more similar their functions should be and the more phylogenetically close they should be. The more phylogenetically distant a group of species is, the more distinct the sequences for the same gene would be. Sequences will undergo mutations over time, because the more two organisms have existed, the more mutations will have occurred in their sequences, and the more distinct their sequences will be. Residue (nucleotide or amino acid) substitutions and indels are all examples of mutations. Biological sequences are generally identical since they are homologous, meaning they came from the same ancestor. Two sequences can or cannot be homologous but 50% cannot be homologous. Homology is not a numerical concept. They either share or do not share an ancestor.

How do we tell if two sequences are identical? We usually deduce it from their resemblance. We prefer to assume that two biological sequences are identical since they are homologous.

Bioinformatics for Everyone. https://doi.org/10.1016/B978-0-323-91128-3.00013-6

## 5.3 Utility

Alignments may be used to

- Calculate the evolutionary distance between two sequences.
- Keep an eye out for functional domains.
- Examine the genomic region of an mRNA.
- Look for polymorphisms and mutations among different sequences.

## 5.4 Developmental basis

Evolution has created DNA and proteins. The natural molecules like structure blocks, atomic bases and proteins (amino acids) are straight groupings that shape the essential design of particles. Throughout this time frame, molecular sequences undergo spontaneous shifts, the majority of which have been selected for by evolution. Due to the mutations and variations in the known sequences over time, evolutionary signals can still be detected in some regions of the sequences to determine their shared ancestry. The fact that natural selection tends to retain residues which perform important functional and structural functions, while less important residues for the structure and function are more commonly associated with evolutionary traces. For instance, in light of the fact that the dynamic area deposits in the group of proteins will in general be safeguarded since they are liable for catalytic capacities. Consequently, conservation patterns and variance can be determined by comparing sequences by orientation. For instance, the dynamic area deposits in the group of enzymes will in general be protected since they are answerable for catalytic capacities. As an outcome, by looking at arrangements by direction, examples of conservation and variety can be set up. The sequence conservation evaluation of the arrangement demonstrates the transformative linkage of different sequences, while the variety fit as a fiddle during improvement reflects changes. It helps to define evolutionary connections between them to characterise the position of unknown sequences. In the event that the sequence arrangement is altogether comparative among them, a gathering of groupings can be viewed as a component of a similar family. If one family member has a given structure and function experimentally characterised, the knowledge can be transferred to the other. Sequence alignment can also be used to predict uncertain sequences structure and function. The relativity of the two investigated sequences is inferred from sequence alignment. If the two sequences share important similarities, the substantial similarity between them is highly unlikely to be acquired by chance and implies that both sequences have common developmental origin. At the point when a sequence arrangement is effectively made, it mirrors the transformative connection between the two groupings: the adjusted yet not indistinguishable locales address buildup replacement, while those areas where residues in one sequence do not equal anything in the other are inserts or deletions that took place in one sequence of evolution.

## 5.5 Evaluating the alignments

We will score the various potential alignments in order to compare them. We may devise a scoring scheme that rewards biologically more rational alignments with more points. In an ideal world, we would devise a scoring system that rewards alignments that align homologous positions with more points.

A naive score system may be used to calculate the number of matching positions or number of matching positions for 100 residues. Normally, scoring systems take into consideration the number of hole. Depending upon the number and duration of gaps present, the allocations are penalised. Therefore, in the development of a scoring system, the most important considerations generally are

- Number of residues that match (considering the similarity if they are amino acids)
- Mis-match number
- Gaps
- Gap length

With these steps we can design various scoring schemes. For instances,

- scoring pattern 1: match $+1$, mis-match: 0, gap creation: $-1$ gap extension: $-1$
- scoring pattern 1: match $+1$, mis-match: $-1$, gap creation: $-1$ gap extension: 0

Of course, various scoring systems can give one alignment a different score. If we do not take into account the scoring schema used, the score of an alignment is meaningless. It's also of no use to compare the results of different alignments which are performed under various schemes.

Once we have settled on a scoring pattern, the alignment algorithm should aim to establish the alignment with the highest possible score under that scoring schema.

Almost every algorithm's software implementation would have certain default values for its parameters. The software developer has calibrated these default values to fit in a specific issue. The bioinformatician must know how well those principles relate to the problem at hand. If the issue is similar to the one that inspired the software's development, the default value will normally suffice since the software's original developer usually knows how to customise his software for that role.

## 5.6 Methods

The ultimate objective of pairwise sequence alignment is to determine the best pairing of two sequences in order to maximise residue correspondence. To do this, one series must be moved relative to the other in order to find the location with the most matches. There are two different types of alignment methods, i.e. global alignment and local alignment.

## 5.7 Global alignment

The two sequence arrangements are regularly viewed as something very similar over the entire length of its global arrangement. The best alignment is done from the beginning of the two sequences over the entire duration. This approach works best when the two sequences are aligned closely, with the same duration. For differences in sequences and sequences of variable lengths, this approach does not provide the best possible result because the local regions between the two sections are not considered extremely similar.

## 5.8 Local alignment

Local alignment does not really mean that the two sequences over their entire range are similar. The only lineup that takes into consideration the alignment of the rest of the sequential regions is to the highest degree of similarity of the two sequences. This approach can be used in order to align more divergent sequences in DNA or protein sequences to find conserved patterns. The length of the two aligned sequences will vary. This methodology is more qualified for adjusting natural sequences that contain just similar modules, otherwise called domains or motifs (Fig. 5.1).

## 5.9 Algorithms for alignment

The only differentiation among global and local algorithms is the technique of optimisation used to align similar residues. The dot matrix method, dynamic

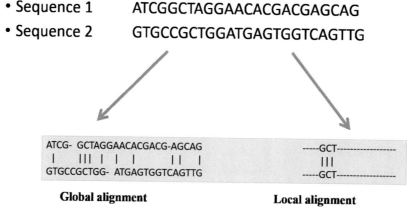

- Sequence 1    ATCGGCTAGGAACACGACGAGCAG
- Sequence 2    GTGCCGCTGGATGAGTGGTCAGTTG

| ATCG- GCTAGGAACACGACG-AGCAG | -----GCT----------------- |
| I    III I I  I      II  I   | III |
| GTGCCGCTGG- ATGAGTGGTCAGTTG | -----GCT----------------- |

**Global alignment**          **Local alignment**

FIGURE 5.1

Exhibits the contrasts among global and local pairwise arrangement.

programming method and word methods are all methods which can be used with any algorithm. In this segment we will discuss the methods of dot matrix and dynamic programming.

## 5.10 **Dot matrix method**

The dot matrix method, which is otherwise called the dot plot method, is the most central technique for sequence alignment. It's a two-dimensional matrix comparison tool that compares two sequences graphically. In a dot matrix, all sequences are written in the x and y axis of the matrix that are comparable. The thing that matters is delivered by discovering the relationship between the lingering and the buildups in the other arrangement in one grouping. A dot is positioned inside the graph if a residue match is identified. The matrix positions are otherwise left unmarked. At the point when the two sequences are fundamentally indistinguishable, a few focusses are arranged to shape touching slanting lines, which show the arrangement of the order. The centre of the diagonal line interferences mean additions or deletions. The repeated regions of the sequences represent parallel diagonal lines within the matrix. When using the dot matrix approach to compare large series, there is an issue called the high noise level. Dots are plotted all over the graph in most of the dot plots, making it difficult to identify the true alignment. The issue is particularly extreme in DNA sequences since there are four potential characters in DNA, giving every buildup a one-in-four possibility of coordinating with a buildup in another sequence. Instead of scanning for similarities with a single residue, a filtering method must be used, which uses a "window" of fixed length spanning a stretch of residue pairs to minimise noise. Filtering compares all possible stretches by sliding windows between the two sequences. Focusses must be situated if a bunch of residues equivalent to the size of the window fit into a sequence. This technique has proved effective in reducing levels of noise. Also known as a tuple, the window can be adapted to produce a consistent sequence pattern. The sensitivity of the alignment is lost, however, if the window size is too large.

The dot matrix method provides a description of two sequences and aims to classify the areas that have the highest connections. The benefit of this procedure is that repeated sequences dependent on the presence of equal boundaries of a similar dimension, in an upward direction or on a level plane, in the matrix are recognised. The approach is therefore used in genomics. It can be used to find repeats of chromosomes and to compare gene preservation between two closely associated genomes. It can also be used in a series to detect auto-complementarity and classify secondary nucleic acid structures.

All possible sequence matches are shown using the dot matrix process. It is also the responsibility of the user to create a full alignment by linking adjacent diagonals with inserts and removals. Another disadvantage of this method to visual analysis is that the assessment of alignment precision lacks analytical rigour. In addition, the procedure is limited to pairwise alignment. The method has a hard time scaling up to multiple alignments. Some examples of web servers using dot plots to compare sequences in pairs are given below:

- **Dotmatcher and Dottup** are two EMBOSS applications that have been made available online as part of the EMBOSS package. Dotmatcher aligns and displays dot plots of two FASTA-formatted input sequences, which can be either DNA or proteins. A scoring scheme and a window of a certain length are used. If the resemblance between the positions of the windows is greater than a certain threshold, diagonal lines are drawn over them. In order to coordinate sequences, Dottup uses a word approach and can handle sequence length genome only if diagonal lines match the same word length.
- **Dothelix** is a dot matrix software used to analyse sequences of different macromolecules like DNA or protein. The programme implements matrices for protein sequences and offers a range of threshold options (similar to window size). The programme shows true pair alignment, besides drawing the diagonal line over a certain threshold with similarity scores.
- **MatrixPlot** is a more advanced matrix alignment programme for protein and nuclear acid. Consumers may add details such as sequence logo profiles or remote matrices from recognised 3D protein structures or nucleic acids. The programme uses coloured grids to display an orientation or other user-defined information instead of points and lines.

## 5.11 Dynamic programming method

It is a technique for accomplishing the best alignment by contrasting two groupings for each conceivable pair of characters. It works similarly as the dot matrix, creating a two-dimensional arrangement matrix. It finds alignment, however, by converting a dot matrix to a scoring matrix that is responsible for series matches and maladjustments in a quantitative way. The best match can be found by searching the highest scores in this matrix.

## 5.12 Dynamic programming for global alignment

The Needleman–Wunsch algorithm is a global pairwise alignment algorithm that is dynamically programmed. This algorithm provides the best alignment for all sequence lengths. It should reach out from the start to the furthest limit of the two sequences to accomplish the most noteworthy complete focus. As such, the matrix's arrangement course should run from the correct lower corner to one side image. The inconvenience of relying solely upon the full-length sequence alignment score is that you risk passing up the main local similarity.

GAP is a pairwise global alignment programme that runs on the Internet. It aligns two sequences without taking into account terminal distances, enabling the alignment of similar sequences of varying lengths. To consider their incorporation, long gaps in the arrangement are treated with a consistent penalty. This job can be utilised to fit exons in genomic DNA that contain a similar gene to cDNA.

## 5.13 **Dynamic programming for local alignment**

In 1981, Temple F. Smith and Michael S. Waterman first suggested the Smith—Waterman algorithm. The algorithm describes local sequence alignment, gives conserved sections between the two sequences, and one can align two sequences, which are partly overlapping. Dynamic programming is a technique of algorithm widely used in sequence analysis. In the event of recursion, dynamic programming is used, but ineffective, because it solves the same sub-problems over and over again. The differences between the two sequences are not easily understood in standard sequence alignment. The length can also be different for both sequences. In such cases, it may be less necessary than identifying regional sequence similarity to identify a match that includes all residues. The first use of dynamic programming for a local alignment is the Smith—Waterman algorithm. For corresponding residues and zeros for flaws in this algorithm, positive scores are assigned. No negative assessments are included. A similar tracing technique is used for dynamic programming. On the other hand, the alignment course will begin and finish in the main diagonal. It starts at the highest score point and moves diagonally to the left until a zero-filled cell is reached. Gaps are formed if necessary. In this case, the affinity distance penalty is also applied. Several segments with the highest ratings can often be found perfectly balanced. As it is in the global alignment, the final outcome depends on the scoring systems used. The goal of local alignment is to achieve local alignment results at the highest possible level, even if this means sacrificing the maximum overall alignment. It can be helpful to align divergent sequences of multiple domains from various sources. The most popular web servers such as SIM, SSEARCH and LALIGN for the local alignment technique are described below

- **SIM** is a web-based programme which finds the best scoring non-overlapping local alignments among two sequences using the Smith—Waterman algorithm. It can accommodate genomic sequences of tens of kilobases. A scoring matrix and gap penalty scores may be set by the user. A set number of the highest-scoring alignments is created.
- **SSEARCH**, for pairwise alignment of sequences, search is a simple web-based programme that employs the Smith—Waterman algorithm. Only one of the highest-scoring alignments is awarded. There are no scoring matrices or gap penalty scores available.
- **LALIGN** is a web-based programme which can align two sequences in a Smith—Waterman version. In contrast, LALIGN gives a list of best scored alignments only as SSEARCH is the best scored. Even the user can adjust the scoring matrice and gap penalty ratings. The ALIGN programme's global synchronisation is also available via the same web interface (Table 5.1).

**Table 5.1** Bioinformatic programmes and their links.

| Programme | Link |
|-----------|------|
| Dotmatcher | bioweb.pasteur.fr/seqanal/interfaces/dotmatcher.html |
| Dottup | bioweb.pasteur.fr/seqanal/interfaces/dottup.html |
| Dothelix | www.genebee.msu.su/services/dhm/advanced.html |
| MatrixPlot | www.cbs.dtu.dk/services/MatrixPlot/ |
| GAP | http://bioinformatics.iastate.edu/aat/align/align.html |
| SIM | http://bioinformatics.iastate.edu/aat/align/align.html |
| SSEARCH | http://pir.georgetown.edu/pirwww/search/pairwise.html |
| LALIGN | www.ch.embnet.org/software/LALIGN form.html |

## 5.14 Some other programmes for pairwise sequence alignment

FFAS — it is known as The Fold and Function Assignment System. A client's protein profile would now be able to be connected to a sum of 20 extra profile information bases. Various outcomes pages can be explored through a progression of tabs, and novel highlights, for example, a dotplot graph viewer, displaying programming, an improved 3D arrangement watcher, and connections to the primary similarities information base are incorporated.

LAST — offers a lot of data handling power, as well as dotplots and coloured alignments.

Wasabi — is a web-based framework for visualising and analysing molecular sequence data with multiple alignments.

Pairwise nucleotide sequence alignment for taxonomy for nucleotide sequences which are less than 5 kb. It gives colour alignments and a similarity score.

GeneWise — it compares protein sequence and introns and frame-shift errors to the genomic DNA sequence.

WebPRANK — the webprank server matches DNA, protein and codon sequences, as well as protein-translated cDNAs, and provides structural models for integrated genome sequence alignment. The resulting alignments are commonly used for the study of evolutionary sequences in different formats.

BLAST2 — BLAST can also be used to compare DNA sequences. Provides a tiny graphic that can only be used for proteins or DNA sequences that are short.

EMBOSS matcher — it identifies the top local alignments between two sequences.

zPicture — it is a DNA or genome arrangement and perception tool. It focusses on the blastz arrangement programming. Arrangements can be submitted to rVista 2.0 naturally to characterise transformative safeguarding factor sites.

FOLDALIGN — it aligns and folds the RNA structures with lightweights and sequence similarities (making a fold alignment). The new version produces alignments in pairs.

# Further reading

Batzoglou, S., 2005. The many faces of sequence alignment. Briefings Bioinf. 6, 6—22.

Brenner, S.E., Chothia, C., Hubbard, T.J., 1998. Assessing sequence comparison methods with reliable structurally identified distant evolutionary relationships. Proc. Natl. Acad. Sci. U. S. A 95, 6073—6078.

Chao, K.-M., Pearson, W.R., Miller, W., 1992. Aligning two sequences within a specified diagonal band. Comput. Appl. Biosci. 8, 481—487.

Henikoff, S., Henikoff, J.G., 1992. Amino acid substitution matrices from protein blocks. Proc. Natl. Acad. Sci. U. S. A 89, 10915—10919.

Huang, X., 1994. On global sequence alignment. Comput. Appl. Biosci. 10, 227—235.

Hull Havgaard, J., Lyngsø, R.B., Stormo, G.D., Gorodkin, J., 2005. Pairwise local structural alignment of RNA sequences with sequence similarity less than 40%. Bioinformatics 21 (9), 1815—1824.

Jaroszewski, L., Li, Z., Cai, X.H., Weber, C., Godzik, A., 2011. FFAS server: novel features and applications. Nucleic Acids Res. 39 (Web Server issue), W38—W44.

Löytynoja, A., Goldman, N., 2010. webPRANK: a phylogeny-aware multiple sequence aligner with interactive alignment browser. BMC Bioinf. 11, 579.

Pagni, M., Jongeneel, V., 2001. Making sense of score statistics for sequence alignments. Briefings Bioinf. 2, 51—67.

Pearson, W.R., 1996. Effective protein sequence comparison. Methods Enzymol. 266, 227—258.

Rost, B., 1999. Twilight zone of protein sequence alignments. Protein Eng. 12, 85—94.

States, D.J., Gish, W., Altschul, S.F., 1991. Improved sensitivity of nucleic acid database searches using application-specific scoring matrices. Methods 3, 66—70.

Valdar, W.S., 2002. Scoring residue conservation. Proteins 48, 227—241.

Vingron, M., Waterman, M.S., 1994. Sequence alignment and penalty scores. J. Mol. Biol. 235, 1—12.

# Multiple sequence alignment

## 6.1 Introduction

### 6.1.1 What is multiple sequence alignment?

In multiple sequence alignment (MSA), we attempt to coordinate two or more identical sequences with the aim of ensuring the best possible match between them. MSA's goal is to arrange a number of sequences to fit as numerous characters from every sequence with a certain score (Fig. 6.1).

While there are many similarities between DNA and protein sequences, there are usually many unique ones as well. This is because the various organisms that share similar genes have similar or completely different functions, or because they are shifted due to natural selection based on differing functions. Many genes and patterns do not change much because of the simplicity of design. In order to investigate this form of conservation, several sequences must be compared and aligned at the same time. MSA has been necessary, and that is why it was created.

MSA is the process of aligning more than two sequences simultaneously. For an illustration, let us have four hypothetical protein sequence, i.e. SeqA, SeqB, SeqC and SeqD. The MSA of these sequences is shown below with the substitution of (F/Y) and deletion of (L) and insertion of (K) (Fig. 6.2).

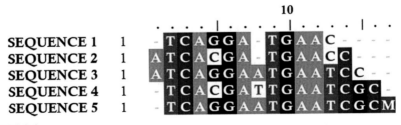

**FIGURE 6.1**

Result of multiple sequence alignment of five different sequences.

Bioinformatics for Everyone. https://doi.org/10.1016/B978-0-323-91128-3.00011-2

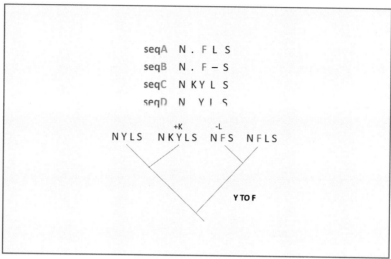

**FIGURE 6.2**

Multiple sequence alignment evolutionary tree.

### 6.1.1.1 Sequences
SeqA: NFLS
SeqB: NFS
SeqC: NKYLS
SeqD: NYLS

### 6.1.1.2 Multiple sequence alignment
SeqA: N * F L S
SeqB: N * F–S
SeqC: N K Y L S
SeqD: N * Y L S

## 6.2 Scoring

The MSA scoring method depends on the sum of scores in a multi-line scoring matrix for all possible pairs of sequences.

Score of MSA $= \sum$ score (A, B), where score (A, B) = pair-wise alignment score of A, B.

Let us look at an example.

Seq (1): G K N

Seq (2): T R N

Seq (3): S H E

Sum of pairs: $-1 + 1 + 6 = 6$.

Sum of second Col = score (K, R) + score (R, H) + score (K, H) = $2 + 0 + -1 = 1$.

## 6.3 Multiple sequence alignment — types

It can be difficult to coordinate three or more sequences which almost always take time to align. Therefore, these alignments are generated and analysed with computational algorithms. Dynamic and heuristic approaches are used in most MSA algorithms.

The techniques for MSA that use heuristic methods are listed below.

1. Progressive Alignment Construction
2. Iterative Alignment Construction
3. Block-Base Alignment

These techniques are fit for finding arrangements among every conceivable solution; however, they do not have the best arrangement. They are thus regarded as approaches, but in a short span of time we will quickly find a solution that is similar to the real one.

### 6.3.1 Progressive Alignment Construction

In 1984, Paulien Hogeweg and Ben Hesper invented this approach, also called as the hierarchical method or tree method. It constructs a final MSA by integrating pair-like alignment from the pair that is the most similar to the pair that is the furthest apart.

#### 6.3.1.1 Advantages

- Fast
- Efficient
- In many instances, the resulting alignments are fair.

#### 6.3.1.2 Disadvantages

- Heuristic
- Accuracy is very important
- Errors in progressive steps are propagated.

At the moment, two of the most widely recognised progressive alignment methods being used are

1. Clustal Omega
2. T-Coffee

### 6.3.2 Iterative Alignment Construction

This methodology comprises of various techniques for creating MSAs while eliminating progressive method errors. They function in similar ways with progressive approaches, but re-align the initial sequences again and again and introduce new sequences to increasing MSA (Fig. 6.3).

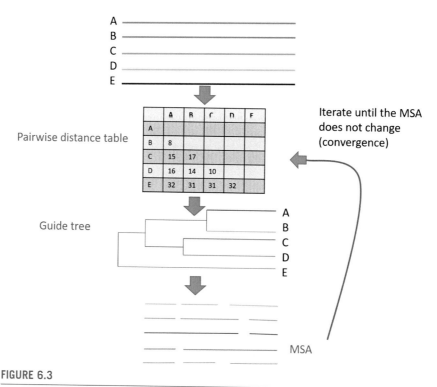

Pairwise distance table

Guide tree

Iterate until the MSA does not change (convergence)

MSA

**FIGURE 6.3**

Steps in iterative alignment.

### 6.3.2.1 Advantages
- Alignment of the profile illustrates conservation in a population (biologically relevant).
- It is easy and can handle a large number of sequences.

### 6.3.2.2 Disadvantages
- Imprecise target feature.
- Any misalignments generated during the process are preserved.

### 6.3.3 Block-base alignment

This methodology divides sequences into squares and endeavours to discover ungapped blocks of arrangements. DIALIGN2 is a typical technique for block alignment.

## 6.4 Methods for multiple sequence alignment

MSA is entirely a computer problem with various computer task aspects. The standard Dynamic Programming Model, suitable for pair alignment of sequences, can be expanded into more sequence alignment. However, this problem is really very difficult, since only a small number of relatively short sequences can be evaluated in more than three sequences. As a consequence, various approximation models are used, some of them are provided below.

### 6.4.1 Dynamic programming-based models

Progressive Global Alignment is an optimum alignment procedure that uses dynamic programming. The pair alignment of the most similar sequences is achieved first in this process. Alignment is then constructed by adding additional sequences. Another approach to find optimum alignment is called the Iterative Model, which uses the dynamic programming. Alignments for many groups or classes are first made in the iterative model. And this alignment is used to align itself with much better alignments.

The main issue with the above-mentioned progressive alignment approach is that errors are propagated to MSA with initial alignments of the most closely related sequences. This problem becomes more pronounced if the initial alignment is between sequences more remotely linked. Iterative models aim to correct this issue by re-aligning sequence sub-groups and then aligning them into an overall alignment.

But with a dynamic programming model, an underlying difficulty is that a suitable scoring material is found, which becomes more difficult if two sequences are concurrently involved. It is exponentially growing in sizes (as the power of number of sequences). As a consequence, the requirements for computational complexity and storage are increasing and becoming impractical for more sequences. Three sets with lower sequence lengths are suitable for dynamic programming. The challenge for this approach is therefore to use a suitable combination of sequence weighting, scoring matrix and distance penalties.

### 6.4.2 Statistical methods and probabilistic models

The MSA model is approximated by various statistical and probabilistic methods. The Hidden Markov (HMM), which includes any possible combination of matches, mis-matches and lacunas to produce an alignment of a series of sequences, was the most commonly used statistical and probability model. HMMs are sometimes as strong, if not better than some, as a several-sequence alignment. A variety of sequences have been trained in the model. The learned model is then used for posterior information in order to achieve the most likely MSA. This model is modelled upon an entirely theoretical probability, no sequence ordering is necessary, no penalties are required for inserting/deleting and experimental information is available.

## 6.5 Usage of multiple sequence alignment

The sequence pair alignment or DNA sequence alignment represents the relationship between two sequences, while MSA provides sequence information on the areas or groups in which it can be related. Protein may provide preserved functional and structural domains with such details and the data for evolutionary relationships are shown for the DNA sequence.

The evolutionary background for sequences is MSA. If the sequences are well aligned with the Multiple Alignment Series, the sequences would probably come from a similar ancestor sequence. They may be distant evolutionary links for poor alignment. This results in evolutionary relations among the sequences being discovered.

The objective is to detect structural or functional similarities between proteins in the comparison of protein sequence. Biologically related proteins can show no clear sequence resemblance, but even when the sequences share only weak similarities, we still want to see resemblance to them. When the sequence similarity is low, biologically related sequences could not be identified in pairs, as poor similarities in pairs could fail statistical tests. Simultaneous comparisons of several sequences can also be found with sequence comparisons where similarities are invisible.

## 6.6 Applications of multiple sequence alignment

MSA can be used for

- Identifying sequence similarities (closely or distinctly related).
- Detecting sequences of preserved areas or motifs.
- Detecting structural homology.
- Enhanced prediction of secondary and tertiary protein structures.
- Making patterns or models which can be used further in order to predict new family sequences.
- Inferring or linking evolutionary trees.

**NOTE: The various Multiple Sequence Alignment tools, software's and protocols are described in Chapter 7.**

## Further reading

Altschul, S.F., 1989. Gap costs for multiple sequence alignment. J. Theor. Biol. 138, 297–309.

Ravi, R., Kececioglu, J.D., 1997. Approximation algorithms for multiple sequence alignment under a fixed evolutionary tree. Discrete Appl. Math. 88, 355–366.

Raghava, 2001. GPS A graphical web server for the analysis of protein sequences and alignment. Biotech Softw. Internet Rep. 2 (6).

Simossis, V.A., Heringa, J., 2005. Praline: a multiple sequence alignment toolbox that integrates homology-extended and secondary structure information. Nucleic Acids Res. 289−294.

Suplatov, D.A., Kopylov, K.E., Popova, N.N., Voevodin, V.V., Švedas, V.K., 2018. Mustguseal: a server for multiple structure-guided sequence alignment of protein families. Bioinformatics 34 (9), 05.

Wheeler, T.J., Kececioglu, J.D., 2007. Multiple alignment by aligning alignments. Bioinformatics 13, 559−568.

# Multiple sequence alignment tools — software and resources

## 7.1 Introduction

Multi-sequence alignment (MSA) is one of the oldest computational biology issues. It has more than two DNA, RNA or protein sequences that are associated with it. One frequently employed technique is to eliminate misplaces, inserts and deletions in the alignments, and an optimal alignment can be calculated using the Dynamic Programming (DP) algorithm. Unfortunately only a limited number of sequences can computerise the DP algorithm, and DP is thus only used for calculating alignments in pairs. The complexity of the computation of pair sequences is O $(n_2)$, however, and thus, while computationally costly, still can be calculated optimally. We must use various heuristic methods to construct multiple sequence alignments (MSAs). The computer complexity is O $(2^k n^k)$, where k is the sequence number and n the length. It takes around $2^8$ to $100^8 = 3$ to $10^{18}$ s, slightly longer than the predicted universe Age, in other words to align eight DNA sequences of 100 bases each.

Sequence comparison, data quality evaluation, protein and RNA-structure prediction, database quest and phylogenetic analyses can be used to compare different sequence alignments. Therefore, depending on the function, different approaches are used. The most commonly used MSA software's and tools are well-described here.

### 7.1.1 Kalign

Kalign is a rapid and precise multi-sequence protein, RNA and DNA sequence alignment algorithm. It is locally focussed and adaptable to large alignments.

**Steps to use:**

(1) Open Kalign on your browser using link https://www.ebi.ac.uk/Tools/msa/kalign/.
(2) Select type of sequence whether DNA or protein that needs to be analysed.
(3) Paste sequences in any suitable format.
*For example, using two sequences, i.e. Sequence1 and Sequence2 of Brassica oleraceae variety* (Fig. 7.1).

Bioinformatics for everyone. https://doi.org/10.1016/B978-0-323-91128-3.00012-4

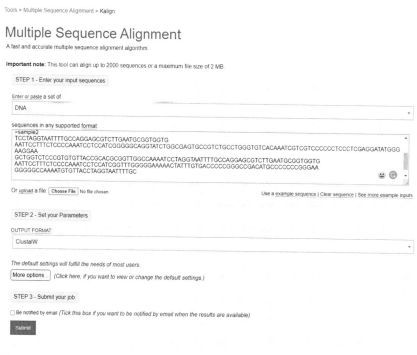

**FIGURE 7.1**

Kalign-Multiple sequence alignment.

**(4)** Submit your sequences.
**(5)** Download alignment file (Fig. 7.2).
**(6)** You can also download phylogenetic tree of submitted sequences (Fig. 7.3).

## 7.1.2 MView

MView reformats sequence database search results (BLAST, FASTA, etc.) or multiple alignments (MSF, PIR, CLUSTAL, etc.) and optionally adds HTML to the page design and layout power. MView is neither a multi-alignment application nor a general-purpose alignment editor.

**Steps to use:**

**(1)** Open MView on your browser using link https://www.ebi.ac.uk/Tools/msa/mview/.
**(2)** Select the type of sequence (DNA or protein) that need to be analysed.
**(3)** Paste sequences in any suitable format.
   *For example, pasting two sequences, i.e. Sequence1 and Sequence2 of Brassica oleraceae variety* (Fig. 7.4).
**(4)** Submit.
**(5)** Download alignment file (Fig. 7.5).

```
CLUSTAL multiple sequence alignment by Kalign (2.0)


sample1    ----------------------------------------------------------
sample2    TCCTAGGTAATTTTGCCAGGAGCGTCTTGAATGCGGTGGTGAATTCCTTTCTCCCCAAAT


sample1    --------GGGGGCAGGTATCTGGCGAGTGCCGTCTGCCTGGGTGTCACAAATCGTCGTC
sample2    CCTCCATCGGGGGCAGGTATCTGGCGAGTGCCGTCTGCCTGGGTGTCACAAATCGTCGTC


sample1    CCCCCTCCCTCGAGGATATGGGAAGGAAGCTGGTCTCCCGT------CCGCACGCGGTTG
sample2    CCCCCTCCCTCGAGGATATGGGAAGGAAGCTGGTCTCCCGTGTGTTACCGCACGCGGTTG


sample1    GCCAAAATGTGTTACCTAGGTAATTTTGCCAGGAGCGTCTTGAATGCGGTGGTGAATTCC
sample2    GCCAAAAT------CCTAGGTAATTTTGCCAGGAGCGTCTTGAATGCGGTGGTGAATTCC


sample1    TTTCTCCCCAAATCCTCCATCGGTTTGGGGGAAAAACTATTTGTGACCCCCGGGCCGACA
sample2    TTTCTCCCCAAATCCTCCATCGGTTTGGGGGAAAAACTATTTGTGACCCCCGGGCCGACA


sample1    TGCCCCCCCGGGAAGGGGGGGCCCCC---TTGAGTTAAAGACACAATAG--AA------
sample2    TGCCCCCCCGGGAAGGGGG------CCAAAATGTGTT----AC-C--TAGGTAATTTTGC
```

**FIGURE 7.2**

Clustal alignment by Kalign.

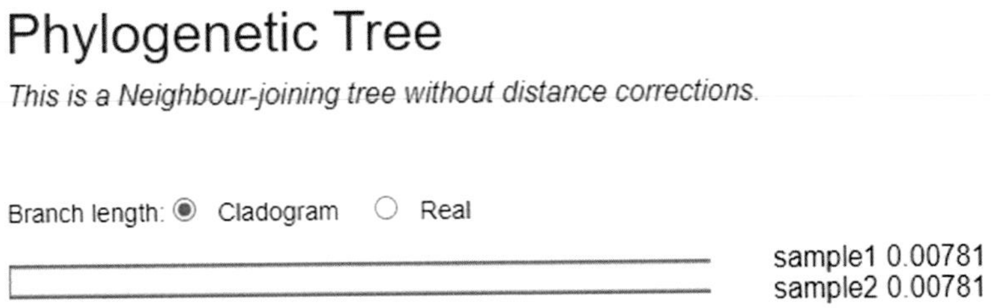

# Phylogenetic Tree

*This is a Neighbour-joining tree without distance corrections.*

Branch length: ● Cladogram    ○ Real

sample1 0.00781
sample2 0.00781

**FIGURE 7.3**

Phylogenetic tree by Kalign.

## 7.1.3 WebPRANK

WebPRANK is a modern MSA programme with phylogenics which uses progressive information to help insert and delete information. The WebPRANK server facilitates genome sequencing with DNA, protein and codon sequences, as well as protein-translated DNA alignment. The resulting alignments are commonly used in the evolutionary sequence analysis in different formats. In order to visualise and post-processing the findings in a server-related cladogram, a web-based alignment browser provides the webPRANK server for removal of low reliably alignment columns. In addition to de novo alignments, WebPRANK can be used to deduce the age sequences with phylogenetically feasible distance patterns, as well as annotation and post-processing of existing alignments.

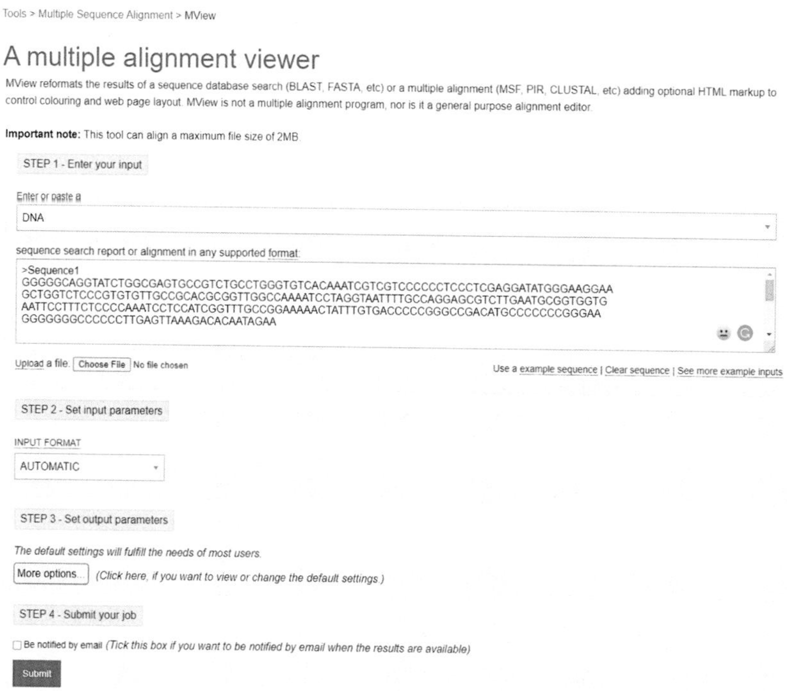

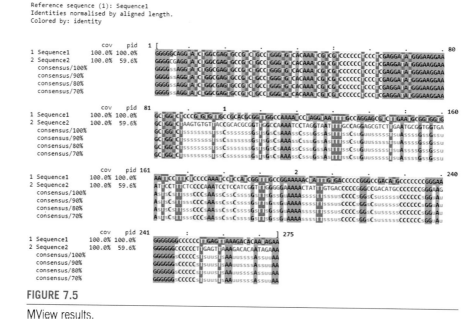

Tools > Multiple Sequence Alignment > MView

## A multiple alignment viewer

MView reformats the results of a sequence database search (BLAST, FASTA, etc) or a multiple alignment (MSF, PIR, CLUSTAL, etc) adding optional HTML markup to control colouring and web page layout. MView is not a multiple alignment program, nor is it a general purpose alignment editor.

**Important note:** This tool can align a maximum file size of 2MB.

STEP 1 - Enter your input

Enter or paste a

DNA

sequence search report or alignment in any supported format:

>Sequence1
GGGGGCAGGTATCTGGCGAGTGCCGTCTGCCTGGGTGTCACAAATCGTCGTCCCCCCTCCCTCGAGGATATGGGAAGGAA
GCTGGTCTCCCGTGTGTTGCCGCACGCGGTTGGCCAAAATCCTAGGTAATTTTGCCAGGAGCGTCTTGAATGCGGTGGTG
AATTCCTTTCTCCCCAAATCCTCCATCGGTTTGCCGGAAAAACTATTTGTGACCCCCGGGCCGACATGCCCCCCCGGGAA
GGGGGGGGCCCCCCTTGAGTTAAAGACACAATAGAA

Upload a file: Choose File  No file chosen                    Use a example sequence | Clear sequence | See more example inputs

STEP 2 - Set input parameters

INPUT FORMAT

AUTOMATIC

STEP 3 - Set output parameters

*The default settings will fulfill the needs of most users.*

More options  *(Click here, if you want to view or change the default settings.)*

STEP 4 - Submit your job

☐ Be notified by email *(Tick this box if you want to be notified by email when the results are available)*

Submit

## FIGURE 7.4

MView- Multiple alignment viewer.

---

Reference sequence (1): Sequence1
Identities normalised by aligned length.
Colored by: identity

FIGURE 7.5

MView results.

**Steps to use:**

**(1)** Open webPRANK using link https://www.ebi.ac.uk/goldman-srv/webprank/.
**(2)** Paste the sequences that needs to be aligned in FASTA format.
  *For example, pasting two sequences viz., Sequence1 and Sequence2 of a Brassica oleraceae variety* (Fig. 7.6).
**(3)** Submit and start alignment.
**(4)** Download results (Fig. 7.7).

**FIGURE 7.6**

WebPRANK- Data input.

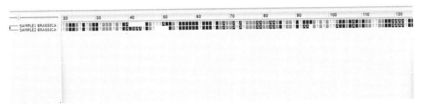

**FIGURE 7.7**

WebPRANK results.

## 7.1.4 TM-aligner

An online method for aligning the transmembrane proteins with an algorithm matching string Wu-Manber. In different colour schemes, the tool can display multiple sequence lines. TM-align is a sequence-independent algorithm for comparison of the protein structure. TM-align first produces an optimised residue-to-residue alignment with structural similarity, using heuristic DP iterations, in respect of two protein structures of unknown equivalence. The two structures based on the detected alignment are returned with an ideal superimposition, along with a TM score that measures the structural resemblance. The TM-score is in (0, 1), where 1 means the two structures fit perfectly. Scores below 0.2 refer to the unrelated randomly selected protein, while those above 0.5 typically take on the same fold in SCOP/ CATH, based on strict statistics for structures in the PDB.

**Steps to use tm-aligner:**

**(1)** Open TM-Aligner using link https://zhanglab.dcmb.med.umich.edu/TM-align/.
**(2)** Input Structure 1 and Structure 2 in PDB format or PDBx/mmCIF format (mandatory):
   *Example, Structure 1 and Structure 2 of random sequences* (Fig. 7.8).
**(3)** Run TM-Aligner.
**(4)** Protein visualisation (Protein-1 in blue and Protein-2 in red) (Fig. 7.9).

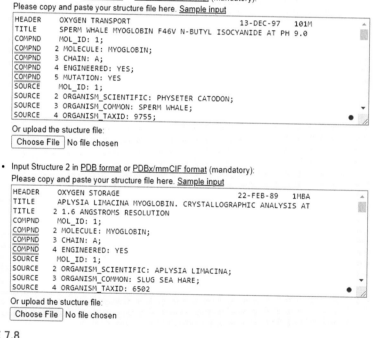

FIGURE 7.8

TM-Aligner Sequence Input page.

### 7.1.5 Mustguseal (multiple structure-guided sequence alignment)

It is a multi-sequence protein family alignment web application. The programme builds structural and other information-based alignments in public databases.

**Visualization (Protein-1 in blue and Protein-2 in red)**

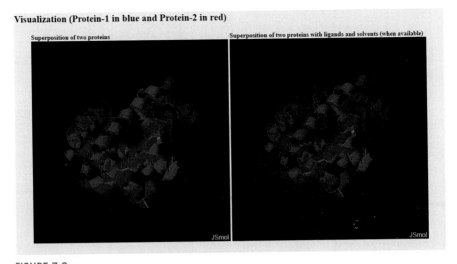

FIGURE 7.9

Protein visualization in TM-Aligner.

Bioinformatic protocol designed to create a wide arrays of functionally diverse protein families. Mustguseal is a web-based platform. Mustguseal can be used in a superfamily to create a concentrated alignment in the selected family of proteins or to superimpose a wide collection of similar proteins.

## 7.2 How does mustguseal function?

The Mustguseal Protocol conducts a similarity structure quest to evolvingly collect remote family members who are supposed to represent various protein groups. Then, Mustguseal carries out a sequence quest for similarities to collect closely linked relatives — members of the respective families — for each evolutionarily distant relative gathered. In order to achieve a range of functionally diverse homologous proteins, Mustguseal takes into account variation of sequences and structures within a broad superfamily. The final multiple alignment is then applied by a combination of structure and sequence alignment procedures.

**Steps to use:**

**(1)** Open Mustguseal using link https://mustguseal.belozersky.msu.ru/#scenario=1.
**(2)** Submit a Query code in PDB database, e.g. **1r3c**.
**(3)** Submit Query chain, e.g. A.
**(4)** Choose a PDB structure, e.g. X-ray structures only or the entire PDB database.
**(5)** Select sequence similarity search database.
**(6)** Submit.
**(7)** Download results.
**(8)** Showing annotation based on protein 0_1r3c_A (Fig. 7.10).

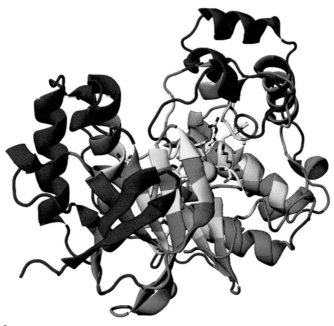

**FIGURE 7.10**

Annotation based on protein (Mustguseal).

## 7.2.1 PSAweb

PSAweb is a web server that is designed to analyse protein alignment and amino acid sequence. This is a comprehensive Internet online tool that enables the quick visualisation of an analysis in GIF format through output. It helps the user to analyse and present the primary protein structure and protein alignment.

Protein sequence analysis: The server enables users to map the proprieties of amino acids along the basic protein (e.g. plot for flexibility and hydrophilicity). Up to four properties can be selected out of 36 server features available, in a single window or in several windows at a time.

**Steps to use:**

**(1)** Open PSAweb server.
**(2)** Click on Analysis of Single Sequence or MSA.
**(3)** Run analysis.
   *For example, amino acid sequence of Insulin (Homo sapiens)* (Fig. 7.11).
**(4)** View analysis of submitted protein sequence (Fig. 7.12).

**Analysis of a Protein Sequence (Result in A Graphical Form)**

Paste your amino acid sequence:

```
malwmrllpl lallalwgpd paaafynghl cgshlvealy lvcgergffy tpktrreaed
lqasalslss ststwpegld atarappalv vtanigqagg sssrqfrqra
lgtsdspvlfihcpgaagta qgleyrgrrv ttelvweevd sspqpqgses lpaqppaqpa
pqpepqgare pspevsccgl wprrpqrsqn
```

or Submit your sequence  [ Choose File ]  No file chosen

**Select Format of your Sequence** [ Amino Acids only (single letter code)  ⌄ ]
Select Parameters (**Maximum Four,Defauly % Exposed Residues**):

| Barrell, Bankier and Drouin (1979) | ▲ |
| Signature for rapidly degraded proteins | |
| Charge of amino acids (example scale) | |
| Local concentration of aromatic amino acids | ▼ |

**Moment Method:** [ Direct/No Moment ⌄ ] **Window Size (Default Size 7):** [ 7 ⌄ ]
**Averaging Method:** [ Mean Over Window ⌄ ] **Window Size (Default Size 7):** [ 7 ⌄ ]
**Width of graph :** [ Variable ⌄ ] **Presentation of Properties in** [ Multiple Graphs ⌄ ]

[ Clear All ]

[ Run Analysis! ]

**FIGURE 7.11**

PSAweb- Sequence input.

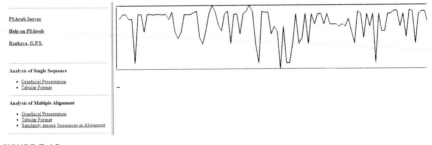

**FIGURE 7.12**

Protein analysis in PSAweb.

## 7.2.2 PVS (protein variability server)

In order to calculate sequence variability in a multi-protein sequence alignment, the PVS web server uses several variability metrics. The tool will map the sequence variability to the supplied 3D structure, map the variability, serial variability, predict t-cell epitopes, find preserved 3D structured sequences and return retention fragments. The PVS measures are very straightforward. Only enter your order in the box and perform analysis (Fig. 7.13).

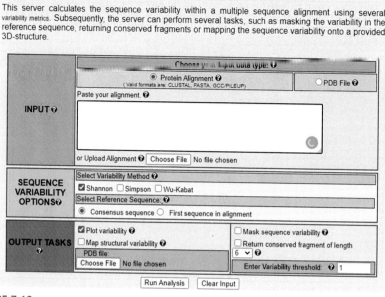

**FIGURE 7.13**

PVS homepage.

### 7.2.3 PRALINE

Praline is an MSA programme with various alignment approaches, such as structural information integration into the alignment process. It also offers an overview of the various alignment of the sequences.

**Steps to use:**

**(1)** Open PRALINE on your browser using link https://www.ibi.vu.nl/programs/pralinewww/.

**(2)** Paste in your PROTEIN sequences in FASTA format (MAX 500 sequences, length 2000).

**(3)** Submit and run.

*For example, if there are two protein sequences viz., Sample1 and Sample 2. The result will be like (Fig. 7.14).*

### 7.2.4 PROMALS3D

It's a web-based tool for creating MSAs. The databases are being scanned and structured and used with user limitations.

**Steps to use:**

**(1)** Open link for PROMALS3D viz., http://prodata.swmed.edu/promals3d/promals3d.php.

The PRALINE alignment process was completed in 112.0 seconds

Alignment score = 2308.00
Alignment score per aligned residue pair = 17.10
Sequence identities = 119
Percent sequence identity = 0.88
Number of sequences = 2
Alignment length = 166
Number of residues = 301
Number of gaps = 31

Save all data for this job (tar and gzipped file)

Download the final alignment [alignment.fasta_ali]
Download PRALINE raw output file [results.out]
Download PSI-BLAST output files
Download Secondary structure prediction files

**Results colour-coded for amino acid conservation**

The current colourscheme of the alignment is for **amino acid conservation**.

Residue Type    Hydrophobicity    Sec.Structure    Make PDF

The conservation scoring is performed by PRALINE. The scoring scheme works from 0 for the least conserved alignment position, up to 10 for the most conserved alignment position. The colour assignments are:

Unconserved  0 1 2 3 4 5 6 7 8 9 10  Conserved

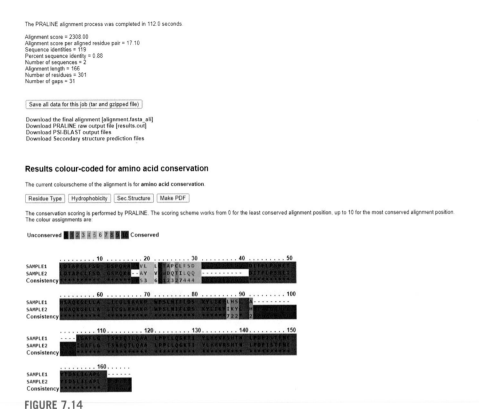

**FIGURE 7.14**

PRALINE Sequences submit.

**(2)** Enter two sequences or more than two sequences of protein in FASTA format that needs to be aligned. For example, sequences of insulin, isoform 2 precursor [*Homo sapiens*] and MicE [*Microbacterium arborescens*] (Fig. 7.15).
**(3)** Submit sequences.
**(4)** Check alignment results (Fig. 7.16).

### 7.2.5 MAFFT (CBRC)

MAFFT is a nucleotide and protein sequence alignment software. It enables users to choose sequences and visualisations interactively.

**Steps to use:**

**(1)** Open link for MAFFT on your browser https://mafft.cbrc.jp/alignment/server/.
**(2)** Paste protein or DNA sequences in FASTA format.
**(3)** Submit.
**(4)** Check results (Fig. 7.17).
**(5)** Check phylogenetic tree of submitted sequences (Fig. 7.18).

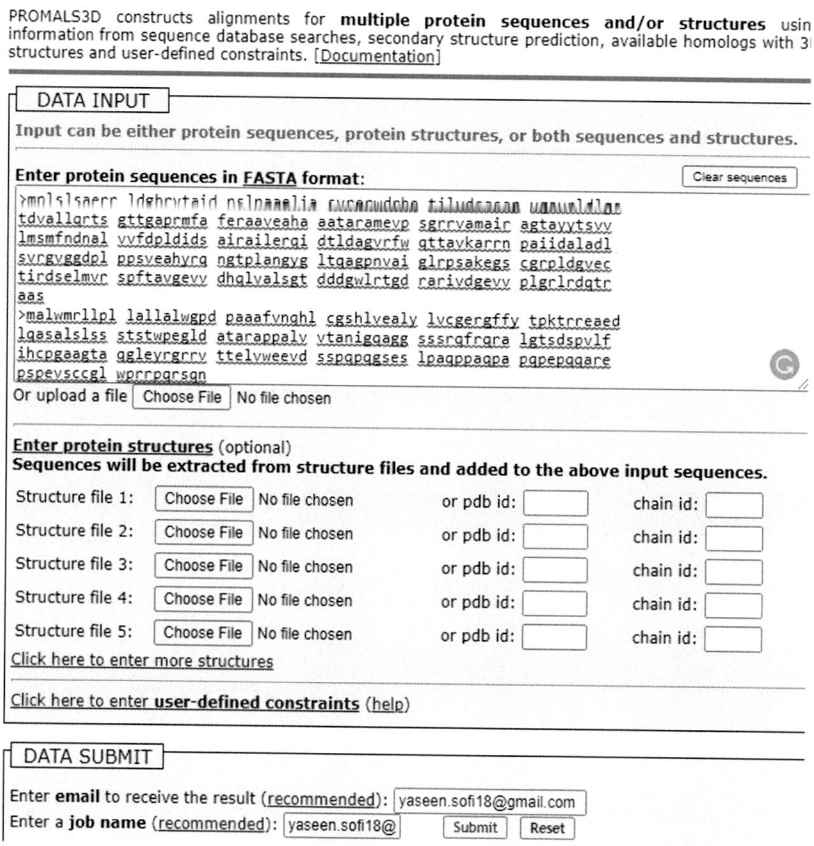

PROMALS3D constructs alignments for **multiple protein sequences and/or structures** usin information from sequence database searches, secondary structure prediction, available homologs with 3 structures and user-defined constraints. [Documentation]

---

**DATA INPUT**

Input can be either protein sequences, protein structures, or both sequences and structures.

**Enter protein sequences in FASTA format:** | Clear sequences |

```
>mplslsaerr ldghrvtaid nslnaaelia cvcaovdebe tiludcaaan uaaueldlaa
tdvallgrts gttgaprmfa feraaveaha aataramevp sgrrvamair agtayytsvv
lmsmfndnal vvfdpldids airailergi dtldagvrfw qttavkarrn paiidaladl
svrgvggdpl ppsveahyrq ngtplangyg ltqagpnvai glrpsakegs cgrpldgvec
tirdselmvr spftavgevv dhqlvalsgt dddgwlrtgd rarivdgevv plgrlrdgtr
aas
>malwmrllpl lallalwgpd paaafvnghl cgshlvealy lvcgergffy tpktrreaed
lqasalslss ststwpegld atarappalv vtanigqagg sssrqfrqra lgtsdspvlf
ihcpgaagta qgleyrgrrv ttelvweevd sspqpqgses lpaqppaqpa pqpepqqare
pspevsccgl wprrpqrsqn
```

Or upload a file | Choose File | No file chosen

---

**Enter protein structures** (optional)
**Sequences will be extracted from structure files and added to the above input sequences.**

Structure file 1: | Choose File | No file chosen    or pdb id: [    ]    chain id: [    ]

Structure file 2: | Choose File | No file chosen    or pdb id: [    ]    chain id: [    ]

Structure file 3: | Choose File | No file chosen    or pdb id: [    ]    chain id: [    ]

Structure file 4: | Choose File | No file chosen    or pdb id: [    ]    chain id: [    ]

Structure file 5: | Choose File | No file chosen    or pdb id: [    ]    chain id: [    ]

Click here to enter more structures

---

Click here to enter **user-defined constraints** (help)

---

**DATA SUBMIT**

Enter **email** to receive the result (recommended): | yaseen.sofi18@gmail.com |
Enter a **job name** (recommended): | yaseen.sofi18@ |   | Submit |  | Reset |

**FIGURE 7.15**

Data input-PROMALS3D.

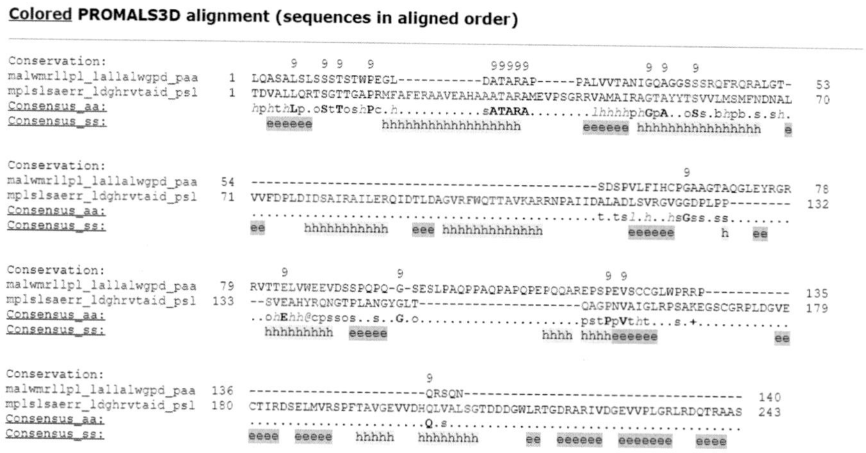

---

Colored **PROMALS3D alignment** (sequences in aligned order)

```
Conservation:
malwmrllpl_lallalwgpd_paa   1 LQASALSLSSSTSTWPEGL-----------DATARAP-----PALVVTANIGQAGGSSSRQFRQRALGT-   53
mplslsaerr_ldghrvtaid_psl   1 TDVALLQRTSGTTGAPRMFAFERAAVEAHAAATARAMEVPSGRRVAMAIRAGTAYYTSVVLMSMFNDNAL   70
Consensus_aa:                 hphthLp.oStToshPc.h..........sATARA.......lhhhhphGpA..oSs.bhpb.s.sh.
Consensus_ss:                     eeeeee       hhhhhhhhhhhhhhhhhh      eeeeee hhhhhhhhhhhhhhh  e

Conservation:                                                         9
malwmrllpl_lallalwgpd_paa  54 -------------------------------------------SDSPVLFIHCPGAAGTAQGLEYRGR   78
mplslsaerr_ldghrvtaid_psl  71 VVFDPLDIDSAIRAILERQIDTLDAGVRFWQTTAVKARRNPAIIDALADLSVRGVGGDPLPP--------  132
Consensus_aa:                 .............................................t.tsl.h..hsGss.ss........
Consensus_ss:                 ee    hhhhhhhhhh     eee hhhhhhhhhhhh            eeeeee      h   ee

Conservation:                   9               9           9 9
malwmrllpl_lallalwgpd_paa  79 RVTTELVWEEVDSSPQPQ-G-SESLPAQPPAQPAPQPEPQQAREPSPEVSCCGLWPRRP-----------  135
mplslsaerr_ldghrvtaid_psl 133 --SVEAHYRQNGTPLANGYGLT---------------------QAGPNVAIGLRPSAKEGSCGRPLDGVE  179
Consensus_aa:                 ..ohEhh@cpssos..s..G.o....................pstPpVt.ht...s.+...........
Consensus_ss:                 hhhhhhhh eeeee                   hhhh hhheeeeee                ee

Conservation:                                    9
malwmrllpl_lallalwgpd_paa 136 ---------------------QRSQN------------------------------------  140
mplslsaerr_ldghrvtaid_psl 180 CTIRDSELMVRSPFTAVGEVVDHQLVALSGTDDDGWLRTGDRARIVDGEVVPLGRLRDQTRAAS  243
Consensus_aa:                 .....................Q.s...........................
Consensus_ss:                 eeee  eeeee  hhhhh  hhhhhhhh    ee  eeeeee eeeeeee  eeee
```

**FIGURE 7.16**

Colored PROMALS3D alignment result.

MAFFT-<u>L-INS-i</u> Result

CLUSTAL format alignment by MAFFT (v7.475)

```
1LYLA       FNDELRNRREKLAALRQQGVAFPNDFRRDHTSDQLHEEFDAKDN------QELESLNIEV
1B8AA       ----------------------MYRTHYSSEITEELNGQK----------------V
1ASZB       -EDTAKDNYGKLP------------LIQSRDSDR-----TGQKRVKFVDLDEAKDSDKEV
1ADJA       ------------------------------------------------------------


1LYLA       SVAGRMMTRRIMGK-ASFVTLQDVGGRIQLYVARDSLPEGVYNDQFKKW----DLGDIIG
1B8AA       KVAGWVWEVKDLGG-IKFLWIRDRDGIVQITAPKKK-----VDPELFKLIPKLRSEDVVA
1ASZB       LFRARVHNTRQQGATLAFLTLRQQASLIQGLVKANK--EGTISKNMVKWAGSLNLESIVL
1ADJA       ------------------------------------------------------TARA


1LYLA       ARGTLFKTQ-------TGELSIHCTELRLLTKALRPLP--------------------D
1B8AA       VEGVVN-----FTPKAKLGFEILPEKIVVLNRAETPLP--LDPTGKVKA----------E
1ASZB       VRGIVKKVDEPIKSATVQNLEIHITKIYTISETPEALPILLEDASRSEAEAEAAGLPVVN
1ADJA       VRGTKD------------------------------------------------LFG
            ..*


1LYLA       QEVRYRQRYLDLIANDKSRQTFVVRSKILAAIRQFMVARGFMEVETP-------------
1B8AA       LDTRLNNRFMDL-RRPEVMAIFKIRSSVFKAVRDFFHENGFIEIHTP-------------
1ASZB       LDTRLDYRVIDL-RTVTNQAIFRIQAGVCELFREYLATKKFTEVHTP-------------
1ADJA       KELRMHQR-------------------IVATARKVLEAAGALELVTPIFEETQVFEKGVG
            :  *   *               :    *. :      *: **


1LYLA       --------MMQVIP--GGASARPFITHHNALDLDMYLRIAPELYLKRLVVGGFERVFEIN
1B8AA       --------KIIATATEGGTELFPM----KYFEEDAFLAESPQLYKEIMMASGLDRVYEIA
1ASZB       --------KLLGAPSEGGSSVFEV----TYFKGKAYLAQSPQFNKQQLIVADFERVYEIG
1ADJA       AATDIVRKEMFTFQDRGGRSLTLR-PEGTAAMVRAYLEHGMKVWPQPV------RLWMAG
            :  **.      .     :*  : .   .:      *::


1LYLA       RNFRNEGISV-RHNPEFTMMELYMAYAD-YHDLIELTESLFRTLAQEV-------LGTTK
1B8AA       PIFRAEEHNTTRHLNEAWSIDSEMAFIEDEEEVMSFLERLVAHAINYVREHNAKELDIL-
1ASZB       PVFRAENSNTHRHMTEFTGLDMEMAFEEHYHEVLDTLSELFVFIFSELPKRFAHEIELVR
1ADJA       PMFRAERPQKGRY-RQFHQVNYEALGSE--NPILD--AEAVVLLYECL-----KELGLRR
            ** *  .  *:  :    ::      :   . ::.      .   . :        :
```

**FIGURE 7.17**

MAFFT Results.

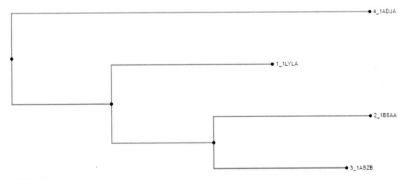

**FIGURE 7.18**

Phylogenetic tree by MAFFT.

## 7.3 Some other MSA tools

### 7.3.1 OPAL (progressive-iterative alignment)

It is a 'Shape and Polish Technique' method for MSA. It can align protein and DNA sequences, and expects FASTA inputs. The authors say that OPAL is more accurate in protein sequence alignment than the muscle and comparable to Muscle and that its accuracy is similar to that of MAFFT and Muscle in DNA sequence alignments.

### 7.3.2 DIALIGN-TX

It is the most recent release of the MSA tool. It generates substantially better alignments on locally and globally linked sequence sets than previous versions of DIALIGN due to several algorithmic improvements. However, DIALIGN-T uses a straightforward greedy method, as in the original implementation of the programme, to combine various alignments from local pairs of similarities. The most important algorithm in DIALIGN-T is the use of a guide tree.

### 7.3.3 CHAOS and DIALIGN web server

It is a web-based framework using an application that searches from the CHAOS database to find a list of similarities in local sequences. These similarities are used by DIALIGN as anchor points for several alignments of series.

### 7.3.4 UniProt align

An MSA web interface in Uniprot using Clustal Omega.

### 7.3.5 Phylo

Phylo is the most used platform by people to refine DNA's MSA with patterns. It is very easy to use as there is no need for detailed biological expertise in this platform.

### 7.3.6 PRANK

PRANK has been planned to create several lines representing the progressive homology and phylogenetic details for inserts and deletions.

### 7.3.7 CRASP

In order to identify associated residues the method analyses many Protein Sequence alignments. The algorithm takes the position that residues are the product of functional inventions. Estimates are dependent on physicochemical properties.

### 7.3.8 ProbCons

Multiple alignment of amino acid sequences based on probabilistic consistency. In the alignment construction it employs probabilistic modelling and consistency technique. In comparison with T-Coffee, Clustal W and Dialign, the authors say this method has enhanced alignments.

### 7.3.9 DIALIGN

DIALIGN is a platform for MSAs. DIALIGN-TX is an enhanced variant, a switch that improves on DIALIGN-T, combining selfish, egalitarian approaches.

### 7.3.10 Muscle (WS jabaws)

Jalview is a command-line user interface that you can use to JABAWS or install and run JABAWS on your own device.

### 7.3.11 R-Coffee

R-Coffee is a packet that is extracted from the T-coffee package for several alignments of RNA sequences. It uses structural information to build sequence alignments, and a special T-Coffee version builds several sequence alignments with structural information. Specifications: RNAlppold, Mafft, Muscle, ProbCons and ConSan from Vienna kit.

### 7.3.12 PRANK API

An MSA method for the sequence of nucleic acid and amino acids at EBI for PRANK. In order to prevent overestimating insert/delete events, the core algorithm varies from 'standard ones'. The evolutionary gap between sequences is taken into consideration.

### 7.3.13 OD-seq

OD-seq is an MSA tool to identify outliers. It works by identifying sequences in the multiple alignment with an inconsistent average distance from sequences.

### 7.3.14 BARCOD

By using the Vronique Barriels process, BARCOD creates a character matrix that codes each input/deletion event for a single event, regardless of its duration, and maintains common indels.

### 7.3.15 Edialign

Edialign is an EMBOSS variant of DIALIGN 22 MSA tool. It provides an MSA and takes nucleic acid or protein sequences as input. The sequences do not have to be identical over the full duration, since the software builds alignments from pairs of gapless sequence segments. Such pairs of segments are called diagonals. If (possibly) coding nucleic acid sequences are to be matched, edialign can alternatively convert the compared 'nucleic acid segments' to 'peptide segments', or even perform comparisons at both the nucleic acid and protein levels to improve sensitivity.

### 7.3.16 MAFCO

MAFCO is Multiple Alignment Format Compression tool specially built to compress MAF files.

### 7.3.17 MAFFT (REST)

It is an MSA tool at EBI with REST interface.

### 7.3.18 MSAprobs

It is a tool for analysis of protein sequences using MSA. It uses a mix of hidden Markov models, weighted probabilistic accuracy, weighted profile to profile alignments.

### 7.3.19 Clustal Omega (EBI)

The multiple interfaces of EBI Clustal Omega include web interface, REST API, SOAP API and Open API.

### 7.3.20 T-Coffee (EBI)

It is the most widely used MSA programme. The T-Coffee programme pre-processes the data by pairing all sequences and incorporates this information into the gradual alignment procedure. Different sources may obtain structural sequence information. Amino acid and nucleotide sequences may be aligned. The programme brings together various methods of alignment.

### 7.3.21 Biojs-io-clustal

It is one of the important tools used for parsing Clustal files in web browser.

### 7.3.22 PASTA

PASTA is also known as Practical Alignment using Sate and TrAnsitivity. It uses a guide tree for MSA.

### 7.3.23 SARA-Coffee

SARA is an MSA web server resource of various three-dimensional structure-driven RNA sequences. The SARA software combines pair-wise structural alignments in multiple RNA alignments with another R-Coffee resource.

### 7.3.24 Staccato

Staccato is an MSA, combining three-dimensional probabilities of structure alignment and the normal probabilities of amino acid replacement.

### 7.3.25 MARS

MARS is a method developed specifically for the alignment of circular genome sequences, like mitochondria and viral genome sequences.

### 7.3.26 Malakite

Malakite (Multiple Alignment Automatic Kinship Tiling Engine) is a web-based method for the study of aligned blocks in several alignments in the protein chain.

### 7.3.27 trimAl

It is a tool available online for removing incorrectly matched MSA sequences. To maximise the signal-to-noise ratio, you can automatically detect and pick different parameters.

### 7.3.28 Multi-LAGAN

Multi-LAGAN is a multi-genomic sequence alignment tool. It is also known as MLAGAN.

### 7.3.29 Pro-Coffee

A component and implemented for multiple alignment of the promoter areas, the T-Coffee Kit includes Pro-Coffee.

### 7.3.30 R3D-2-MSA

R3D-2-MSA is a web-based application for connecting 3D structures with a range of RNA sequence alignments. The R3D-2-MSA is a tool for the RNA 3D structures.

### 7.3.31 ProDA

ProDA is a method that first identifies repeatedly homologous regions in a series of protein sequences for local multiple sequence (MSAs).

### 7.3.32 MSAProbs-MPI

It is a Multiple Sequence MSAProbs parallel edition. The process is based on Markov's secret models.

### 7.3.33 HmmCleaner

It is used in conjunction with hidden Markov profile models to remove alignment and sequencing errors from different sequence alignments (pHMM). The tool is built upon and incorporates.

### 7.3.34 MSA-PAD 2.0

It is an MSA DNA web-based tool. The algorithm uses PFAM or user-supplied profiles. Registration and login are needed for the web interface.

### 7.3.35 PnpProbs

It operates in two groups with a sequence assignment distant and 'normally' and uses only a guideline tree for 'normally' linked sequences. A non-progressive approach for multiple sequences for remotely linked sequences is used.

### 7.3.36 ANTICALIgN

An instrument developed specifically for combinatory protein engineering. Based on a reference sequence template and global sequence alignment, ANTICALIgN can create MSA.

### 7.3.37 FAMSA

FAMSA is designed to quickly align large protein families with multiple sequences. It first identifies the longest common sequences and is able to calculate the gap costs in a specific way. It continues to apply a new iterative approach gradually to the alignments. The authors say that Clustal Omega and MAFFT are superior to FAMSA.

### 7.3.38 KMAD

KMAD is a particular platform that has been developed to construct multiple aligned proteins (IDPs). IDPs differ from globular proteins because they lack tertiary structure and have less sequence conservation.

### 7.3.39 VerAlign

VerAlign is a software that compares the accuracy of a test alignment to the quality of a reference version of the same alignments. It uses SPdist scoring, which calculates a distance between malfunctioned pairs of amino acid.

# Further reading

Cabanettes, F., Klopp, C., 2018. D-GENIES: dot plot large genomes in an interactive, efficient and simple way. PeerJ 6, e4958.

Frazer, K.A., 2004. VISTA: computational tools for comparative genomics. Nucleic Acids Res. 32 (Web Server issue), W273–W279.

Garcia-Boronat, M., Diez-Rivero, C.M., Reinherz, E.L., Reche, P.A., 2008. PVS: a web server for protein sequence variability analysis tuned to facilitate conserved epitope discovery. Nucleic Acids Res. 1 (35–41), 36.

Junier, T., Pagni, M., 2000. Dotlet: diagonal plots in a web browser. Bioinformatics 16 (2), 178–179.

Katoh, K., Rozewicki, J., Yamada, K.D., 2019. MAFFT online service: multiple sequence alignment, interactive sequence choice and visualization. Briefings Bioinf. 20 (4), 1160–1166.

Noé, L., Kucherov, G., 2005. YASS: enhancing the sensitivity of DNA similarity search. Nucleic Acids Res. 33, W540–W543.

Pei, J., Tang, M., Grishin, N.V., 2008. PROMALS3D web server for accurate multiple protein sequence and structure alignments. Nucleic Acids Res. 36 (Web Server issue), W30–W34.

Raghava, G.P.S., 2001. A graphical web server for the analysis of protein sequences and alignment. Biotech Softw. Internet Rep. 2 (6).

Simossis, V.A., Heringa, J., 2005. PRALINE: a multiple sequence alignment toolbox that integrates homology-extended and secondary structure information. Nucleic Acids Res. 33 (Web Server issue), W289–W294.

Suplatov, D.A., Kopylov, K.E., Popova, N.N., Voevodin, V.V., Švedas, V.K., 2018. Mustguseal: a server for multiple structure-guided sequence alignment of protein families. Bioinformatics 34 (9).

Lassmann, T., Sonnhammer, E.L.L., 2006. Kalign, Kalignvu and Mumsa: Web servers for multiple sequence alignment. Nucleic Acids Res. 34 (Suppl. 1_2), W596–W599.

Troshin, P.V., Procter, J.B., Barton, G.J., 2011. Java bioinformatics analysis web services for multiple sequence alignment-JABAWS: MSA. BMC Bioinf. 27 (14), 2001–2002.

Wheeler, T.J., Kececioglu, J.D., 2007. Multiple alignment by aligning alignments. Bioinformatics 23 (13), i559–i568.

Robert, X., Gouet, P., 2014. Deciphering key features in protein structures with the new ENDscript server. Nucleic Acids Res. 4, W320–W324.

Zhang, Y., Skolnick, J., 2005. TM-align: a protein structure alignment algorithm based on TM-score. Nucleic Acids Res. 33, 2302–2309.

# CLUSTALW software

Multiple Sequence Alignment of DNA, RNA and protein sequences is one of the most crucial techniques of the fields of molecular biology, computer science and bioinformatics. The sequencing technologies of the next generation change the biological landscape and flood the databases with huge quantities of raw sequence data. The number of algorithms for multiple sequence alignment increases almost monthly and one to two new algorithms are published every month. There is continuous improvement in the computing complexity and precision of alignments, but there is still no biologically perfect solution.

Clustal is a number of popular computer programmes for the alignment of multiple sequences that are used in bioinformatics. The programme Clustal has changed several times, all of which are described below:

- **Clustal:** the original multi-sequence alignment programme developed in 1988 by DES HIGGINS based on a pair-wise derivation of amino acid and nucleotide phylogenetic trees.
- **ClustalV:** the Clustal Programme of the second generation was published in 1992. It implemented the phylogenetic reconstruction of the tree with the final alignment; the capability to establish alignments from already existing alignments; and it opted for the development of trees with a neighbouring approach.
- **ClustalW:** the third generation of nucleotides or protein sequences, published in 1994, is a widely used method. The best alignment sequences are initially aligned with multi-sequence alignment. ClustalW uses progressive alignment techniques. The more distant sequence groups are aligned gradually until a global alignment has been achieved.
- **ClustalX:** the first edition to include a graphical user interface, published in 1997.
- **Clustal Omega**: a new software that uses seeded guide trees and HMM profile technique to produce aligns among three or more sequences.
- **Clustal2:** the ClustalW and ClustalX versions are revised with increased precision and performance.

Bioinformatics for Everyone. https://doi.org/10.1016/B978-0-323-91128-3.00003-3

The most common multiple sequence alignment algorithm is probably ClustalW. It has been introduced in 1994 by Thompson and co-workers. It rapidly became the tool for the generation of multiple sequence alignments as the alignment accuracy, sensitivity and speed were dramatically increased in comparison with other algorithms. ClustalW has a novel location specific scoring scheme and an over-represented sequence weighting scheme, 'W' represents 'weights'.

## 8.1 ClustalW history

ClustalW's invention has a lot of folklore. The most famous is Des Higgins, the founder, in a smoky Dublin pub in the early 1990s, designed the original concept of Clustal behind an envelope. Actually Paula Hoggeweg defined the Clustal algorithm at the beginning of the 1980s, so the Clustal algorithm was not invented by Des Higgins in reality. However, Des Higgins packed it and organised it for easy use and turned it into one of the most popular bioinformatics programmes: the X Window Implementation of ClustalV, ClustalW and ClustalX. He was also the one who created all the right modules so that anybody could use the software on almost any device. So it could be said Paula, Higgins and EMBL co-authored this brilliant software.

## 8.2 ClustalW method

In ClustalW initially the algorithm aligns all sequences (nucleotide or amino acid) with either Wilbur and Lipman's k-tuple method or Needleman–Wunsch method (Whole Dynamic Programming Method). These methods measure a matrix that demonstrates the similarity of each sequence pair. The parameter score(s) are translated to remote score(s) and then, using the neighbour joining (NJ) form, the algorithm uses the distances to create a guide tree. The last step of the algorithm is to construct the multiple sequence alignment. The multiple sequence alignment is constructed by gradually aligning the sequences that are closely related to the guidance tree given by the NJ method. Precisely using the progressive method ClustalW aligns by a global sequence alignment.

The main steps are as follows:

**(a)** Aligns all sequences in pairs by dynamic programming.
**(b)** Phylogenetic tree construction using alignment scores through neighbouring joining.
**(c)** Align sequences, led by a phylogenetic tree.

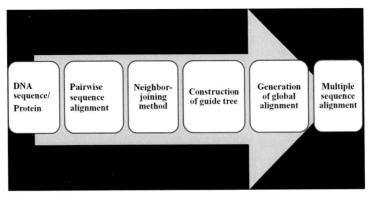

**FIGURE 8.1**

Outline of progressive alignment.

So the sequences that are closer to each other are lined up first and further sequences and sequence groups are added and led by the initial alignments producing a multiple sequence alignment which shows sequence changes between the sequences in each column. Sequences are measured by their relationships in the forecast evolutionary tree for the multiple sequence alignment. Weight is dependent on the distance from the root of every sequence. The alignment results between two places in the multi-sequence alignment are then determined by multiplication factors with the resulting weights. As more sequences are added to the profile, differences accumulate and affect sequence alignment. ClustalW novelly measures gaps within conserved domains. Initial gaps remain fixed in the alignment. When more sequences have been inserted, new gaps can then be entered in the Multiple Alignment (Fig. 8.1).

## 8.3 Pros and cons of ClustalW

### 8.3.1 Pros

- ClustalW is fitted for redundancy and provides very good alignments.
- ClustalW can handle many input formats, including FAST, Swiss-Prot and PIR, as well as the most popular formats for multiple alignment of sequences.
- The most modules are more rapid to implement compared to other programmes, with a large number of details.
- A list of DNA and protein sequences will function with ClustalW2.

### 8.3.2 Cons

- The progressive alignment algorithm uses all the sequences in the set but all the information it contains is not used. This may be a waste if two sequences have any valuable knowledge not used by the software.
- ClustalW will not eliminate existing gaps in a number of already aligned sequences.
- The alignment you input will affect the alignment of the ClustalW.

## 8.4 ClustalW contribution to research

Many Molecular Biology researchers have used the modules of ClustalW during their original research for building multiple sequence alignment. ClustalW is one of the most frequently cited scientific programmes in the history of biology with over 35,000 quotations. In these days, ClustalW is being hit instantly for several reasons. Besides its rapid results capability, the freeware licence and its efficient modules make it one of the most frequently used programmes for multiple sequence alignments.

## 8.5 Steps for retrieving multiple sequence alignment of mRNA sequences of various species using ClustalW

- Alignment sequences should be included in a single file. The following formats must be included in this file: EMBL/SwissProt, NBRF/PIR, FASTA, GCG/MSF, GDE, GCG/RSF, or CLUSTAL.
- Go to the browser, in one tab open NCBI and in another tab open CLUSTALW.
- In NCBI homepage search for the sequences you need to align, e.g. here we search for mRNA sequences of various organisms viz., Wheat, *Oryza* and *Arabidopsis*. The mRNA sequences of Wheat, *Oryza* and *Arabidopsis* are shown below (Fig. 8.2A–C):
- On opening their flat files, open the sequences in FASTA format and copy their sequences.
- Paste sequences from NCBI or load your query sequence from disc into the 'Query Sequence' field. Only the FASTA format as query entry is accepted by the application. You can adjust the parameters for your query once the right CLUSTAL software has been selected.

**FIGURE 8.2**

(A) NCBI results of mRNA sequences of *Oryza sativa* in FASTA format. (B) NCBI results of mRNA sequences of Wheat in FASTA format. (C) NCBI results of mRNA sequences *Arabidopsis* in FASTA format.

- The sequences can be pasted in the space provided in the following way:

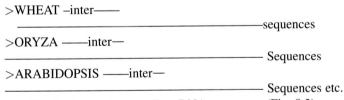

You can align both protein as well as DNA sequences (Fig. 8.3).

- Then Hit the 'Execute Multiple Alignment' button when finished or you can reset the query field if you feel there is some error.
- A page displays indicating that your query is running. If you would like to return to your CLUSTAL results later, you can store the displayed query link. For 1 week results are stored (Fig. 8.4).

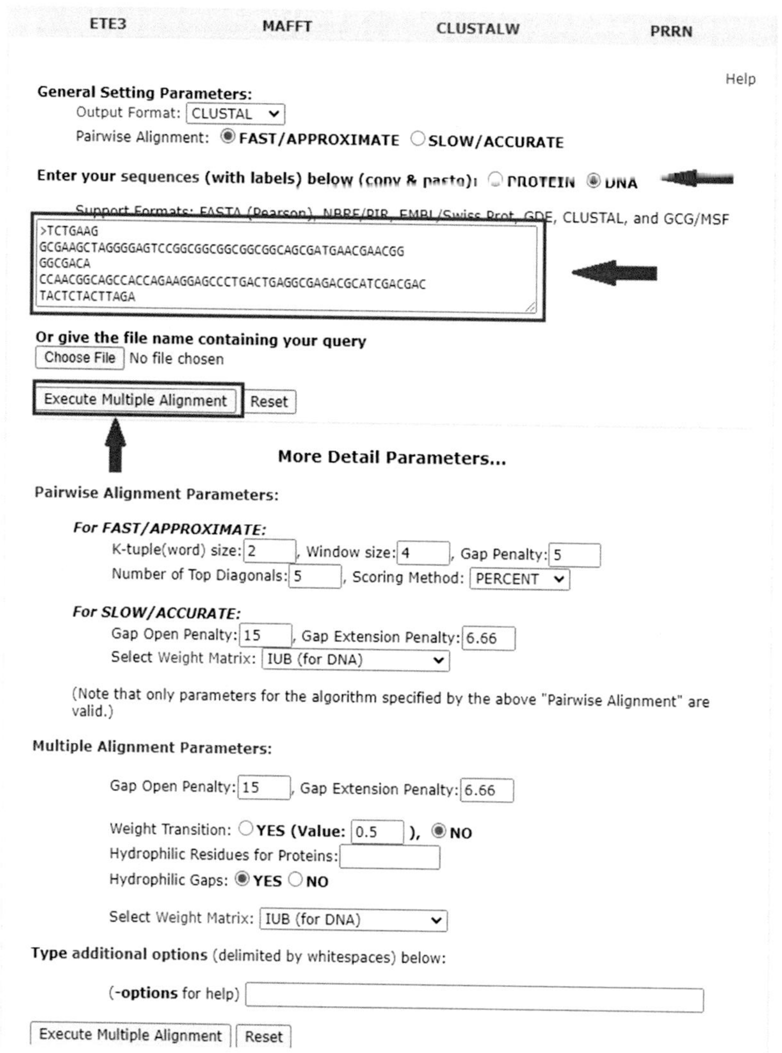


**FIGURE 8.3**

CLUSTALW webpage.

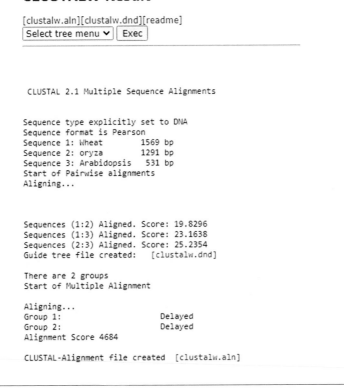

**CLUSTALW Result**

[clustalw.aln][clustalw.dnd][readme]

| Select tree menu ∨ | Exec |

```
CLUSTAL 2.1 Multiple Sequence Alignments


Sequence type explicitly set to DNA
Sequence format is Pearson
Sequence 1: Wheat          1569 bp
Sequence 2: oryza          1291 bp
Sequence 3: Arabidopsis     531 bp
Start of Pairwise alignments
Aligning...


Sequences (1:2) Aligned. Score: 19.8296
Sequences (1:3) Aligned. Score: 23.1638
Sequences (2:3) Aligned. Score: 25.2354
Guide tree file created:   [clustalw.dnd]

There are 2 groups
Start of Multiple Alignment

Aligning...
Group 1:                   Delayed
Group 2:                   Delayed
Alignment Score 4684

CLUSTAL-Alignment file created  [clustalw.aln]
```

**FIGURE 8.4**

CLUSTALW aligning the sequences.

- When the CLUSTAL programme has finished, your results will be displayed.
- You can easily download the alignment file (shown in 'Report Details', phylo-genetic tree, if available) and submission details including parameters used in this query from the option 'Download'.
- Finally, we will get alignment sequences of various organisms which is shown in both zoomed in and zoomed out view as follows (Figs. 8.5, 8.6) (Table 8.1).
- Phylogenetic tree of organisms of which sequences have been used for the purpose of multiple sequence alignment can also be displayed by choosing the option 'Select tree menu Execute' below the alignments as shown below (Figs. 8.7, 8.8).

## CLUSTALW Result

[clustalw.aln][clustalw.dnd][readme]

Select tree menu ⌄ | Exec

```
CLUSTAL 2.1 Multiple Sequence Alignments


Sequence type explicitly set to DNA
Sequence format is Pearson
Sequence 1: Wheat        1569 bp
Sequence 2: oryza        1291 bp
Sequence 3: Arabidopsis   531 bp
Start of Pairwise alignments
Aligning...



Sequences (1:2) Aligned. Score: 19.8296
Sequences (1:3) Aligned. Score: 23.1638
Sequences (2:3) Aligned. Score: 25.2354
Guide tree file created:   [clustalw.dnd]

There are 2 groups
Start of Multiple Alignment

Aligning...
Group 1:                Delayed
Group 2:                Delayed
Alignment Score 4684

CLUSTAL-Alignment file created  [clustalw.aln]
```

```
clustalw.aln

CLUSTAL 2.1 multiple sequence alignment


oryza           ------------------------------------------------------------
Arabidopsis     ------------------------------------------------------------
Wheat           GGAGTTCCCGCATTTGCTGGTCCCGGCGAGGTCCGCTCCTCTGCACGCGTGGGTGGCGGC


oryza           ------------------------------------------------------------
Arabidopsis     ------------------------------------------------------------
Wheat           GCCCTCGCCGGCGTCGCGTCGCGCCGGCCCCCGAATCTCCGGCGAGCCGCTCGCGCCCCA


oryza           ------------------------------------------------------------
Arabidopsis     ------------------------------------------------------------
Wheat           AGCCCGAGCCCGGTGAGGCCTACTGCTCTAGGTCTTCCTGCCACCCAGAGTTTTCGATAT


oryza           ----------------------------------------------------CTCCC
Arabidopsis     ------------------------------------------------------------
Wheat           ACTGGTTTTGATATGGAGTGATTGGTGGAGCTGGTCGTCCGGAAGCTCTGCTGGTGAATC


oryza           ATCTCGAAATCAAGCACGAGGACTCCCAAGTCCAGCCATGAAAGCCACGACGACAGCAGT
Arabidopsis     ------------------------------------------------------------
Wheat           CGATGGGGAGCAACGATCCTAGCACGCCGTCTAAGGCTTCGAAGCCACCAGAACAGGAGC


oryza           GGCCCTCCTCGTGGCCGCCGCGGCCATGGTGGCGCAGGTAGTCGCCGAGCAGTGTGGCTC
Arabidopsis     ------------------------------------------------------------
Wheat           AACCTCCG--GCTACTACCTCTGGCACCACAGCTCCAGTTTACCCTGAATGGCCCGGCTT
```

**FIGURE 8.5**

Results showing the alignment of the sequences (zoomed out view).

```
oryza        CGGCGCTGTGGTTCTGGATGACGCCGCAGTCGCCGAAGCCGTCGTGCCACGACGTGATCA
Arabidopsis  CGTGAGGGAGGAGGAGGATACGGTGGTGGTGAAGGAGGAGGTTACGG-AGGAAGCGGTGG
Wheat        AGAGGAAGCTGTCCAACCGGGAATCAGCGCGCAGGTCCCGGCTGCGCAAGCAGGCTGAGT
               *      *  *                    *       *       *     *  *  *  *

oryza        CGAGGCAGTGGACGCCGAGCTCGGGGGACATCGCGGCCGGGCGGGTGCCGGGGTACGGCG
Arabidopsis  TCTGGAG--GATGGTAA--------------------------------------------
Wheat        GTGAAGAGCTCGGGCAGCGCGCTGAGGCTTTGAAGTCAGAGAACTCGTCCCTCAGGATCG
               *    **        *

oryza        TGATCACCAACATCATCAACGGCGGGTTGGAGTGCGGGTTCGGCCCCGACGACCGGGTGG
Arabidopsis  ------------------------------------------------------------
Wheat        AGCTCGACCGGATCAAAAAGGAGTACGAGGAGCTCCTTTCGAAGAACACCTCTCTGAAGG
```

**FIGURE 8.6**

Results showing the alignment of the sequences (zoomed in view).

**Table 8.1** Symbols and their meanings.

| Symbol | Meaning |
|---|---|
| Asterisk (*) | Positions with a single, fully conserved residue |
| Colon (:) | Conservation of highly similar properties between groups With a pam 250 matrix score greater than 0.5 |

```
oryza        CATGCAG-----------
Arabidopsis  ------------------
Wheat        TTCTCACCGCCAAAACTC
```

```
clustalw.dnd

(
Wheat:0.41121,
oryza:0.39049,
Arabidopsis:0.35715);
```

Select tree menu ⌄   Exec   ⬅

**FIGURE 8.7**

Tree formation tab.

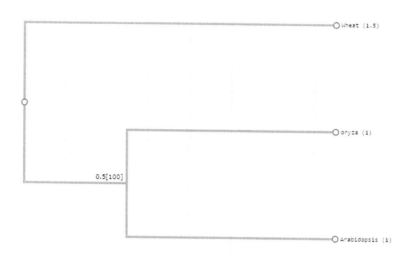

FIGURE 8.8

Phylogenetic tree of the aligned sequences.

# Further reading

Higgins, D.G., Sharp, P.M., 1988. CLUSTAL: a package for performing multiple sequence alignment on a microcomputer (Cluster analysis; phylogenetic tree; protein secondary structure; RNA secondary structure; globin; 5s RNA; dendrogram). Gene 73, 237–244, 237.

Larkin, M.A., Blackshields, G., Brown, N.P., Chenna, R., McGettigan, P.A., McWilliam, H., Valentin, F., Wallace, I.M., Wilm, A., Lopez, R., Thompson, J.D., Gibson, T.J., Higgins, D.G., 2007. Clustal W and Clustal X version 2.0. Bioinformatics 23 (21), 2947–2948.

Thompson, J.D., Higgins, D.G., Gibson, T.J., 1994. Clustal W: improving the sensitivity of progressive multiple sequence alignment through sequence weighting, position-specific gap penalties and weight matrix choice. Nucleic Acids Res. 22 (22), 4673–4680.

# Plant genomic data and resources at NCBI

## 9.1 Introduction

The National Center for Biotechnology Information (NCBI), which aims to develop molecular biology information systems at the National Institute of Health, was set up in 1988. In expansion to keeping up the GenBank nucleic acid grouping database, NCBI gives data collection resources and computational facilities for the examination of GenBank information and assortment of other organic information. The NCBI collects and combines information from a number of different sources with analysis and retrieval processes. Plant Genome Central gives you direct access to this information. The NCBI uses the Entrez search and retrieval system to combine data from more than 20 biological databases. Entrez Nucleotide, a focal information base in Entrez, incorporates GenBank, an essential database of nucleotide sequences created and put away by NCBI and every day facilitated with the DNA Databank of Japan and the European Molecular Biological Laboratory databases. Entrez Nucleotide contains almost 12 million plant-determined sequences. Entrez information bases that are firmly identified with the nucleotide sequences of Entrez Nucleotide incorporate the NCBI Taxonomy, Protein, PubMed and PubMed Central. Over 60,000 plant taxa and 160,000 species are described in the NCBI Taxonomy database. Map Viewer and BLAST are two valuable methods of analysing and examining the molecular basis of biological phenomena, plant genes, structure of genome and function. With the finalisation of the genome programmes for *Arabidopsis thaliana* and *Oryza sativa*, plant scientists are using these genomes for relative plant genomics, with high-performance indefinite arrangement data and delineate markers. NCBI offers a catalogue of delineate and caricature gene databases for arrangement closeness searches with advanced seed genome BLAST sections. The NCBI Map Viewer, which uses the same Entrez database technology, displays genomic maps for several plants and animals and supports boolean logic in text queries. Genomic BLAST scans can be used to locate complete genomic sequences from bacteria to higher plants and animals (Fig. 9.1).

Bioinformatics for Everyone. https://doi.org/10.1016/B978-0-323-91128-3.00019-7

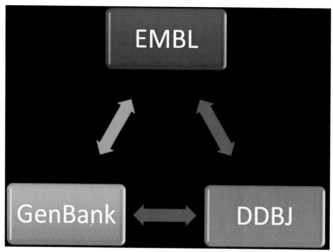

**FIGURE 9.1**

Information from GenBank, EMBL and DDBJ keeps on flowing.

## 9.2 Primary sequence data

Most of NCBI's primary plant genomics are in three categories, representing the types of projects the plant science community is currently undertaking. Examples include genomic assemblies, expressed sequence tags (ESTs) batches and maps of the genomes or physical genomes.

## 9.3 International sequence databases of nucleotides

The principle source of essential sequence information is the nucleotide groupings or sequences communicated by individual agents and sequence centres of the world. These groupings are either reproduced from one of the planning libraries, such as the DNA Databank of Japan and sent straightforwardly to GenBank and put away by NCBI. Assembling of genome include the *Arabidopsis* Genome Initiative and the International Rice Genome Sequencing Project.

## 9.4 Trace archive

Entire genome shotgun sequencing creates most of the information obtained in genome sequencing programmes, coming about in arbitrary short (600–800 nucleotide) fragments. Computer programmes put the pieces together to create a consensus sequence. In 2001, a store for crude grouping vestige created by major sequence project is developed between The National Center for Biotechnology Information and the Wellcome Trust Genome Campus, Hinxton, UK, to recover both the arrangement record and the basic information it creates. Crude grouping information from the trace archive are connected to agreement genomic arrangement by the assembly archive, which was created in 2004 at NCBI. Trace data are currently held in the trace archive at NCBI for about 42 plant sequencing programmes.

## 9.5 Expressed Sequence Tags

ESTs are single-pass sequences peruses from mRNA that are normally short (1000 bp) (cDNA). They are normally made in large parcels. They mirror a preview of qualities communicated in a specific tissue or potentially developmental stage. They are expression tags (some coding, some not) for the cDNA library of interest.

## 9.6 BAC end sequences

Several genome ventures are created from a library of BAC with inserts from 100 to 200 kbp. The adjacent BACs are composed of the FPC. The economical method of collection of any contig sequence data is to identify the nucleotide sequence at the end of the BACs for about 300–500 nucleotides. These bacterial artificial chromosome-end sequences are stored in global nuclear arrangement stores. On standard premise, NCBI extracts data from FASTA format form-specific subsets of the BES plant. The FTP server contains these files.

## 9.7 Probe database

The probe database gives a public register of nucleic acid reagents, reagent distributor's records, sequence similitudes and test execution. Clients of the database approach genetic expression, silencing of gene and planning applications just as to receptive variety research just as probe-based projects. The probe information base is kept up consistently. The current goal of this plant resource database is to organise a few of the information related to mapped loci over a wide extend of species into a framework that can be used for comprehensive computing and data extract.

## 9.8 Derived data/pre-calculated data

In primary sequence data documents, NCBI has designed a variety of methods to arrange the interaction between elements so that users can easily access them. Many of these include calculating the relationship ahead of time and saving the results in a database.

## 9.9 UniGene clusters

UniGene lists species with 70,000 or more available EST sequences. UniGene is an experimental way to partition sequences of GenBank automatically into a non-redundant set of gene-based clusters. Every UniGene cluster contains sequences which show a single gene, as well as data relating to the gene and mapping location of the tissue types. There are currently clusters for over 40 species in the UniGene array, and over 200,000 clusters for 20 plants. However, the UniGene web pages have been retired in July 2019. All UniGene pages now redirect to a new web page post (Fig. 9.2).

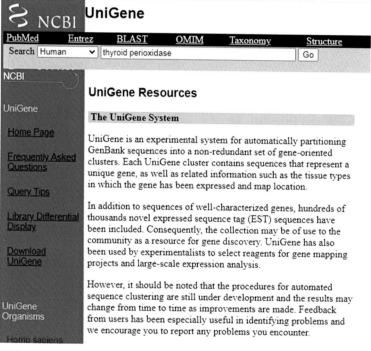

FIGURE 9.2

Homepage of NCBI unigene.

## 9.10 UniSTS

- UniSTS is a powerful information base of STS-based maps and different analyses with tagged sites (STSs).
- PCR essential sets are recognised by STSs, and are connected to additional subtleties, for example, the genomic area, genes and sequences.
- Search by Gene name, Gene depiction, Keywords, etc. To confine the search, utilise the 'limited to' drop-down menu.
- Discover subtleties like primer sequences, size of product and mapping information, just as cross references to LocusLink, dbSNP, RHdb, GDB, MGD and the Entrez Map Viewer.

## 9.11 **Entrez Gene**

Entrez Gene is the NCBI's gene-specific database. Entrez Gene contains records from fully sequenced genomes with the intention of contributing gene-specific knowledge in an active research community or which are scheduled for intensive sequence analysis. NCBI introduced Entrez Gene, which is a key node in the genomic outline nexus, arrangement, gene expression, protein structure, function of protein and homology data. Gene databases for genes observed or anticipated with a nuclear sequence or map position are developed. Entrez is a database retrieval system that uses simple Boolean queries to allow text searching. Entrez Gene is the NCBI's gene-specific database. Entrez Gene contains records from fully sequenced genomes with the intention of contributing gene-specific knowledge in an active research community or which are scheduled for intensive sequence analysis. The Entrez Gene content is the product of curing and automated incorporation of NCBI Reference Sequence (RefSeq), collaborative databases of models and other databases in NCBI. Entrez Gene records are allocated as identifiers to single, stable and tracked integer. Contents of the map and their attributes, markers, phenotyper and connections (including names and mapping locations, genetics) are supported by interactive browsing by the NCBI Entrez framework and through NCBI's Entrez (E-Utilities) programming utilities and for the bulk ftp (Fig. 9.3).

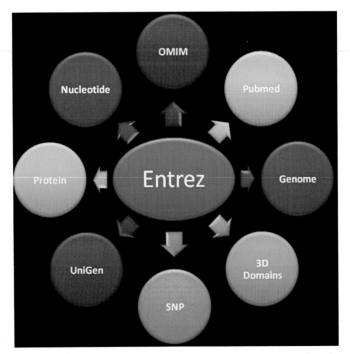

**FIGURE 9.3**

Entrez databases.

## 9.12 HomoloGene

HomoloGene is the automatic homolog identification method of many fully sequenced eukaryotic genomes within the annotated genes. It comprises over a dozen model organisms' clusters of homologous genes, including almost 16,000 clusters for plants. HomoloGene is a homolog detection method for 18 fully sequenced eukaryotic genomes in the annotated genes, including homologues of *Homo sapiens*, *Drosophila melanogaster*, *Saccharomyces cerevisia*, etc. The HomoloGene building process is led by the taxonomic tree and uses preserved genetic order and DNA similarity measures in closely related organisms, while using the protein similarity of more distant organisms.

## 9.13 Conserved protein domains

Conserved Domain Database may be list of grouping alignments and protein profiles that were preserved during molecular development, representing protein domains.

## 9.14 BLink

BLAST Link or Blink shows pre-computed arrangement with the corresponding arrangement for each protein arrangement within the Entrez databases. BLink can view arrangement subgroups based on ordered parameters, origin indices, full genome, COG membership or a 3D structure or protein space relationship. BLink connections for protein records and Gene reports are shown in Entrez.

## 9.15 Gene Expression Omnibus

Gene Expression Omnibus (GEO) is a public vault for functional genomics information that acknowledges MIAME-compliant data submissions. Information as arrays and in form of sequences are recognised. Users may utilise the tools provided to question and import experiments and curated gene expression profiles. The NCBI-created GEO is a public vault for information given by high-throughput microarray tests. Several types of data sets can be sent, processed and retrieved using GEO such as expression of high-throughput genes, genomical hybridisation and testing on the antibody array. The 2005 collection covers over 20 species, counting 38 data groups and more than 600 000 plant tissue expression profiles (Fig. 9.4).

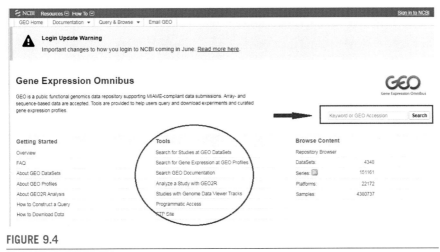

**FIGURE 9.4**

Geo tools.

## 9.16 Plant-specific data resources

The three wide arrangements of information bases that hold information are the Map Viewer database, which contains plant genomic and genetic maps, the Probe data set and UniSTS, which contain probes and primers used to perceive the allelic condition of a locus in a planning attempt, and the PlantBLAST databases, which contain different subsets of GenBank progressions connected with the plant genomic resources at NCBI. Two arrangements of plant-explicit information can be downloaded by means of FTP, the BES and the supplements forming the database basic PlantBLAST.

## 9.17 PlantBLAST databases

NCBI can build BLAST databases by discovering GenBank successions(s) for a particular probe. Every one of these data sets incorporates a subset of progressions to GenBank connected to mapped loci for a distinct organism. Four data sets are used in the personalised databases:

1. Sequences from the GenBank database linked to the probe that is utilised to classify mapped genetic loci in genetic maps.
2. The two rice contig collections produced by the Chinese WGS efforts.
3. *A. thaliana* genome and the *Oryza sativa* genome whole-genome material.
4. A list of NCBI databases containing organism-specific ESTs that can be searched using BLAST.

## 9.18 Genetic map data

The public domain data are used to create genetic map data in Map Viewer. The data came from three different places:

1. Data for soybean, Poaceae and Solanaceae came from non-NCBI databases.
2. A single investigator have generated map data for sorghum, barley, onion, etc.
3. The map results from papers examined by experts for asparagus, almond and walnut met the condition that the count of chromosome pairs does not surpass 110% of the count of chromosome pairs.

## 9.19 Methods for accessing the plant data at NCBI

Plant data can be used in a variety of ways at NCBI. In order to access plant information and resources, the researcher selects a particular route based on the research project emphasis and goal or its level of interest. There are three types of searches:

1. Enter or Map Viewer text searches,
2. Guided searching in Map Viewer, and
3. BLAST search based on similarities between sequences.

A database of single nucleotide polymorphisms (dbSNPs), a single basis nuclear substitution site and brief polymorphisms for erasure and inclusion, has now 10 million human SNPs and a further 10 million, with 5 million added last year from a variety of other organisms. SNP reports use Cn3D, the interactive macromolecular visualiser for NCBI's link to the MMDB's 3D structures to display the amino acid implied variations in the coding regions. Additional validation, community reference information for dbSNP registration as well as additional information on validation of population-specific alleles and human genotypes are provided by dbSNP. These data are accessible in XML-structured genotype reports on the dbSNP FTP database (Fig. 9.5).

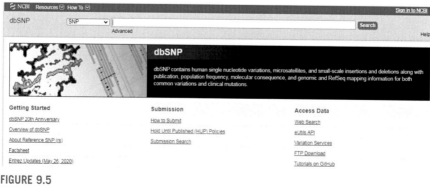

**FIGURE 9.5**

NCBI dbSNP Database.

# Further reading

Balakrishnan, R., Christie, K.R., Costanzo, M.C., Dolinski, K., Dwight, S.S., Engel, S.R., Fisk, D.G., Hirschman, J.E., Hong, E.L., Nash, R., Oughtred, R., Skrzypek, M., Theesfeld, C.L., Binkley, G., Dong, Q., Lane, C., Sethuraman, A., Weng, S., Botstein, D., Cherry, J.M., 2005. Fungal BLAST and model organism BLASTP best hits: new comparison resources at the Saccharomyces genome database (SGD). Nucleic Acids Res. 33, D374—D377.

Benson, D.A., Karsch-Mizrachi, I., Lipman, D.J., Ostell, J., Wheeler, D.L., 2005. GenBank. Update Nucleic Acids Res. 33, D34—D38.

Bourne, P.E., Addess, K.J., Bluhm, W.F., Chen, L., Deshpande, N., Feng, Z., Fleri, W., Green, R., Merino-Ott, J.C., Townsend-Merino, W., 2004. The distribution and query systems of the RCSB Protein Data Bank. Nucleic Acids Res. 32, D223—D225.

Marchler-Bauer, A., Anderson, J., Fedorova, N., DeWeese-Scott, C., Geer, L.Y., Hurwitz, D., Jackson, J.J., Jacobs, A., Lanczycki, C., Liebert, C., 2005. MMDB: entrez's 3D-structure database. Nucleic Acids Res. 33, D192—D196.

Pruitt, K., Tatusova, T., Maglott, D., 2005. Entrez gene. Nucleic Acids Res. 33, D54—D58.

Schuler, G.D., Epstein, J.A., Ohkawa, H., Kans, J.A., 1996. Entrez: molecular biology database and retrieval system. Methods Enzymol. 266, 141—162.

Sherry, S.T., Ward, M.H., Kholodov, M., Baker, J., Pham, L., Smigielski, E., Sirotkin, K., 2001. dbSNP: the NCBI database of genetic variation. Nucleic Acids Res. 29, 308—311.

Sprague, J., Doerry, E., Douglas, S., Westerfield, M., 2001. The Zebrafish Information Network (ZFIN): a resource for genetic, genomic and developmental research. Nucleic Acids Res. 29, 87—90.

Tatusov, R.L., Fedorova, N.D., Jackson, J.D., Jacobs, A.R., Kiryutin, B., Koonin, E.V., Krylov, D.M., Mazumder, R., Mekhedov, S.L., Nikolskaya, A.N., 2003. The COG database: an updated version includes eukaryotes. BMC Bioinf. 4, 41.

Wang, Y., Geer, L.Y., Chappey, C., Kans, J.A., Bryant, S.H., 2000. Cn3D: Sequence and structure views for Entrez. Trends Biochem. Sci. 25, 300—302.

Wheeler, D.L., Smith-White, B., Chetvernin, V., Resenchuk, S., Dombrowski, S.M., Pechous, S.W., Tatusova, T., Ostell, J., 2005. Plant genome resources at the national center for Biotechnology information. Plant Physiol. 138 (3), 1280—1288.

Wu, C.H., Yeh, L.S.L., Huang, H., Arminski, L., Castro-Alvear, J., Chen, Y., Hu, Z., Kourtesis, P., Ledley, R.S., Suzek, B.E., 2003. The protein information resource. Nucleic Acids Res. 31, 345347.

# NCBI BLAST

## 10.1 Definition

While data from nucleotide strings and sequences of protein are valuable to cells, no human being is able to collect information from those series without the assistance of computer and bioinformatics tools. BLAST resource at NCBI portal is a rapid and straightforward programme whose work is to match every sequence with those in a tremendous database and subsequently surveys the reasonability of alignment. The BLAST is a simple and quick programme. A simple BLAST search normally gives adequate data to perform two basic tasks while working with genes or whole genome sequences.

**(1)** To determine the putative role of the DNA or protein sequence that are newly identified; and

**(2)** Whether a genome (or the other large sequence database) has a comparable sequence with a recognised gene.

## 10.2 Introduction

BLAST search at NCBI is the most generally utilised programming in bioinformatics and biotechnology-related research. The primary role of this search engine is to compare a sequence of interest and the query sequence, to sequence in a large database. The protein, the RNA or DNA sequence is a window of its set of experiences and capacity. The particular order, length and organisation of protein subunits (their 'main structure') are primarily responsible for their binding and catalytic properties. The protein it encodes, in essence, dictates these same characteristics of nucleic acid. The validity of enzymes and their phenotypical effects change very little over time. There are two principle applications in this simple programme. In the first place, if the query sequence function is known, it tends to be surmised that it works based on recognised sequence functions. Secondly, if one has a query sequence with a known function, sequences with comparable functions might be identified in the database. One of the establishments of bioinformatics is the capacity to surmise the properties of new proteins and genes through the correlation of sequences.

Bioinformatics for Everyone. https://doi.org/10.1016/B978-0-323-91128-3.00021-5

The BLAST is a programme which seeks sequence areas similar to two different sequences of nucleotides or protein. The BLAST compares a sequence of the researcher in a vast database (the 'Query' sequence), such as a whole genome sequence or a list of all the GenBank sequences. The BLAST search announces the best matches or hits in the database to the researcher. Since the determining of complex relationships between two sequences can be so many different conclusions, BLAST whether for nucleotide or protein searches are likewise a fast and proficient approach to find a scope of the gene and protein properties.

## 10.3 BLAST — alignments and scoring

To decide the level of identity of a query, sequencing shares in each sequence, the BLAST programme should adjust the sequences properly first. Few out of every databases, sequence is of similar length or starts with a similar query sequence. Clearly, it relies first upon appropriately figuring out which residues ought to be looked at and on surveying how close two residues are to each other to score the quantity of nucleic acids or amino acids that are shared by two sequences. Over the years, a number of scoring systems were used to decide the best alignment among two sets of residues. For each column containing the same nucleotide or amino acid, the simplest possible system will achieve the highest possible score of one point; the line placing the maximum number of the same residues side by side would be highest. A very similar method for the comparison of nucleotide sequences is still used today. For amino acids this score system is too naïve — proteins comprise of 20 distinct amino acid subunits that have altogether different chemical characteristics. While amino acid identity alignments alone can be estimated, a few amino acids can be substituted, with little effect on protein function. Though not strictly defined, the substitution of the same amino acids offers further information for each other which is suitable for the most effective alignment.

See the alignments of two proteins in Fig. 10.1 as an example. The two proteins are comparable apart from the second alignment position. In Fig. 10.1A, the second column that you can see has an Alanine amino acid in the first sequence and an Arginine amino acid in the second. While as in Fig. 10.1B, there is an Alanine amino acid

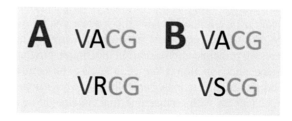

FIGURE 10.1

Alignment of two proteins.

in the second column in the alignment, while the second sequence has a Serine amino acid. It reveals that Alanine is much more similar to Serine than it is to Arg.

As there are numerous approaches to portray the similarities and the contrasts between amino acids, for example, hydrophobicity, size, chemical-related composition, and so on, a variety of matrices for the proper alignment of protein sequences have over the years been designed. In 1978, by using close-linked sequences that were easily aligned, Margaret Dayhoff created a simple score matrix and calculated the frequency where of each amino acid substituted one in real sequences. The selection of a matrix by using this method is entirely avoided. Two amino acids which often evolutionarily substitute each other are considered identical, whereas amino acids which are almost unlike any other. PAM matrices were also commonly used through their efforts. Another series of matrices, i.e. BLOSUM matrices, was created by Henikoff and Henikoff in 1992, who were also focussed on the observed biological sequence replacement frequencies of amino acids. These matrices are derived not within the framework of the unit, but since every PAM and BLOSUM matrix has a totally different technique, such matrices can be more suitable for either diverging or related sequences.

A number is followed, e.g. PAM250 or BLOSUM62, for each PAM or BLOSUM matrix. While the value of these numbers exceeds the reach of this unit, it must be recognised that the large numbers of PAM matrices are more appropriate for the coordination of divergent sequences and the larger numbers of BLOSUM matrices are better suited for a near sequence alignment.

Needleman and Wunsch (1970), taking into account a methodology which is called as dynamic programming, have established a mathematically rigorous method to ensure the best possible alignment in between two sections given a certain replacement matrix. Their approach aligns all two sequences, but then Smith and Waterman in 1981 changed the procedure so that similar regions could be identified between two sequences. The algorithm Smith−Waterman, instead of aligning the whole chain, compares all segments and returns the most similar segments. This approach could be theoretically used to look for similar sequences to the one of interest in a database. In reality, the algorithm of Smith−Waterman would need much of computing time in view of the enormous amount of sequences in the databases usually queried in a BLAST search. Thus, the BLAST programmes, including the non-redundant (nr-) database held by GenBank, will take just a few seconds to scan even for the largest databases. By using certain approximations (heuristics), the BLAST achieves this in order to maintain computer management time. Although these approximations do not mean that the best hit in the database can be demonstrated by the BLAST mathematical, the BLAST algorithm works very easily and can detect sequences identical very quickly and accurately in the database.

The algorithm does everything else and gives sequences in this score-scheme the best possible alignment. The only thing we have to worry in the Smith−Waterman method is about a parameter and the substitution matrix. Since BLAST utilises heuristics to attain its pace, it implements several optimised parameters.

Normally, these additional parameters do not need us to worry because the BLAST server default values function for most applications and the software can also modify the parameters to achieve better outcomes. Therefore, a few of these specific parameters are not discussed, and the BLAST is instead used in this device with default settings.

## 10.4 To compare BLAST search results

When a sequence is submitted to a BLAST search server, firstly, the programme does a 'target match search' by doing a sequence comparison. The software first decides quickly whether sequences have a similarity region; otherwise, the target sequence is really not analysed in greater detail. If the query is sequence-like, the target is matched to the chosen matrix, and the system is complex that contemplates the number and the partition of shared residues. The score for the query alignment with the principal string is saved and BLAST goes on to the following string. The researchers can see the highest scoring sequences at the end of the BLAST search, the BLAST shows two kinds of scores for each goal series, which is also defined as a BLAST hit. To start with, the bit score is controlled by summing up the scores of every segment of the arrangement directly first from alignment of the query to the target sequence. The BLAST search reports E value or 'expected' value for the second result.

The expected value (E) defines the amount of hits one might 'expect' when searching for a specific database. The match's Score (S) decreases exponentially as it increases. The E value represents essentially the random background noise. An E value of 1 assigned to a hit, for example, can be interpreted as meaning that in a database of the current size, one would expect to see 1 match with a similar score by chance. The more 'important' the match, the lower the E-value, or the closer it is to zero. Bear in mind, however, that almost identical short alignments have relatively high E values. This is because the E value equation takes the length of the query sequence into account. These high E values are meaningful as shorter sequences are purely by chance more likely to occur in the database. As a simple way to establish a threshold for reporting data, the expected value may also be used. On most BLAST sites, you can modify the Expect value threshold. When the expect value is raised from default of 10, a list of more low-scoring hits is reported. For more data on the most proficient method to direct BLAST search and how to utilise the different information bases accessible at the NCBI, see Chapter 11.

## 10.5 Selecting a BLAST programme

Check for one of five main BLAST systems for several different sequence databases at the NCBI. These programmes equate nuclear sequences or protein sequences with previously mentioned scoring matrices. Some programmes often convert the query sequence or nuclear database sequences before protein alignments are performed. This flexibility helps a researcher to compare sequences with any database, and several questions can be answered using a simple tool like the BLAST. Various inquiries may, in any case, require diverse search techniques. In case you are attempting to decide if another primate gene you have sequenced is more like a chimp or a human sequence, you can analyse nucleotide sequences directly; generally human and chimp protein sequences are comparative, however encoded with various codons. A comparison of the protein sequence is also required when looking for gene counterparts of very distant organisms. Not exclusively can indistinguishable amino acids be customised with various codons, yet proteins in various species may have advanced over the long run to produce distinctive amino acids. Nucleotide sequences encoding remotely related proteins may contain little proof of their basic heritage. Since protein coding selections primarily affect protein sequences, nucleotide sequences which encode homologous proteins may be very different in different species. That means it is generally easier to be using the protein sequence alone rather than the nucleotide sequence when looking for homologs for a protein coding sequence.

There are five major nucleotide or protein sequence BLAST programmes that are described in the sections below.

## 10.6 BLASTN (nucleotide BLAST)

This web search engine compares at least one nucleotide query sequences (sequences submitted) to a subject nucleotide sequence or an information database of nucleotide sequences. This programme can be used to

- Identify RNA genes that are not coded (e.g. rRNA, Trna and snRNA).
- To find the conserved promoter elements.
- Locate complementary DNAs that lead to the sequence of the genome.
- Determine the presence of a polymorphism as well as mutations in a sequence.

## 10.7 BLASTX

This programme compares query of nucleotide sequence to a protein sequence database by converting it into six reading frames thereby providing sequences of six proteins. BLASTX is particularly useful because it reads the query sequence through all six reading frames and provides cumulative significance statistics for hits to different frames. This programme can be used to

- Assess the protein-encoded role for a cloned fragment of cDNA or genomic DNA.
- Assess introns position inside a genomic DNA sequence.
- Recognise the errors of the frame shift DNA sequence.

## 10.8 BLASTP

This BLAST type matches one or more sequences of the protein query to the protein sequence of a subject or the database of protein sequences. This programme can be used

- To check for putative genomically encoded proteins for a particular homolog, and
- To recognise protein domains or motifs.

## 10.9 TBLASTN

This BLAST software contrasts a sequence of protein queries with the six framework translations of nucleotide sequence databases. In unnoticed nucleotide sequences such as expressed gene tags (ESTs), and draft genome records (HTG) registering regions located in the BLAST database est and htgs, tblastn may be helpful in determining homologous protein encoding areas. Single-reading cDNA sequences are short ESTs. They comprise several organisms' largest pool of sequence data, and include sections of transcripts from several unspecific genes. Since ESTs do not have annotated sequences of coding, BLAST Protein Databases are not matched by protein translations. A tblastn scan is therefore the only way of finding certain potentially protein-level coding regions.

## 10.10 Tblastx

The BLAST translates all the six read frameworks into a nucleotide query in this kind of search and translates all sequences in all readable frames to a nucleotide database. It then searches for all database translations using all query translations. This kind of search is valuable in the event that you have a nucleotide sequence from which you realise the protein code and are searching for comparable sequences in genome EST or an unexplained nuclear sequence database.

## 10.11 Database selection

You can use the above-mentioned BLAST programmes for searching several databases with NCBI. The nucleotide and protein 'nr' (non-redundant) databases are two of the largest and perhaps most important. These databases contain every one of the nucleotides or protein sequences uploaded to the most widely used three international sequence stores, i.e. GenBank, EMBL and DDBJ. Many students and researchers scan a new sequence for the first database. However, while the 'nr' information base could be the lone data set containing the successions that you are looking for, it might likewise contain far enough firmly related sequences to return significant outcomes for your BLAST scan. A BLAST search, for example, may be used to classify protein amino acids that are conserved and variable. The quest nr with an organism with a large number of some well relatives like *Drosophila* and *Saccharomyces* can therefore return 100 almost similar sequences of these relatives without giving any latest details. The choice of a database is therefore becoming more critical because the number of sequences in databases such as nr is growing. It also takes longer than necessary to search a large database, and waste computing resources on community servers. As the search for large databases may lead to issues like this, it is also an effective strategy to restrict size of your BLAST database. RefSeq database has been developed by NCBI to delete the most similar sequences arising from sequencing errors and mutational analysis.

Entrez is the search engine for the selection of entries from all NCBI databases. Each entry is marked with details such as source organisms, sequence length, sequence molecule type and more in an NCBI sequence database. The quest can only return sequences satisfying the search term by entering an entering term in a BLAST search. Due to the fact that an organism restricts a database, the BLAST website also has a different search word, recognising the taxonomic and common name of several organisations and automatically completing it.

Most of the databases that can be searched at NCBI are listed in the section below.

## 10.12 **Nucleotide-related databases**

**Nucleotide collection (nr/nt):** Both sequences that are included in resources like GenBank and RefSeq databases are included in this comprehensive database.

**Reference RNA sequences:** The Reference Sequence database cloned cDNA entries (fully contained in nr). It is also called refseq_rna.

**Reference genomic sequences:** Reference Sequence Database Genomic Entries (fully contained in nr). It is also called as refseq_genomic.

**Expressed sequence tags:** ESTs are short forms of sequences of DNA ranging from 200 to 500 nucleotides that are produced by sequencing of an expressed gene from ends of one side or both sides. Its aim is to sequence pieces of DNA that reflect genes communicated in different organic entities.

**Genomic survey sequences:** Genome survey sequences, similar to expressed sequences, are nucleotide sequences that are different from mRNA, since the majority of sequences are genomic in origin.

**Whole-genome shotgun contigs:** It is also called as wgs as it contains all the genome assembly readings. The WGS approach involves sequencing several parallel overlapping DNAs and then mounting little fragments into larger contiguities and ultimately chromosomes by using the computer.

## 10.13 Protein-related databases

**Reference proteins:** Reference Sequence Database Protein Sequences.

**Non-redundant protein sequences:** It includes GenBank code sequences, as well as the RefSeq Protein array and PDB sequences.

**Protein Data Bank:** It is a 3D structural data database for major biological molecules, for example, proteins and nucleic acids. Very helpful unless one is curious to find a three-dimensional structure.

## Reference

Needleman, S.B., Wunsch, C.D., 1970. A general method applicable to the search for similarities in the amino acid sequence of two proteins. J. Mol. Biol. 48, 443−453.

## Further reading

Altschul, S.F., Gish, W., Miller, W., Myers, E.W., Lipman, D.J., 1990. Basic local alignment search tool. J. Mol. Biol. 215, 403−410.

Altschul, S.F., Madden, T.L., Schaffer, A.A., Zhang, J., Zhang, Z., Miller, W., Lipman, D.J., 1997. Gapped BLAST and PSI−BLAST: a new generation of protein database search programs. Nucleic Acids Res. 25, 3389−3402.

Chang, W.-J., Zaila, K.E., Coppola, T.W., 2016. Submitting a sequence to GenBank. Curr. Protoc. Essen. Lab. Tech. 12, 11.2.1−11.2.24.

Dayhoff, M.O., Schwartz, R.M., Orcutt, B.C., 1978. A model of evolutionary change in proteins. In: Atlas of Protein Sequence and Structure, vol. 5. National Biomedical Research Foundation, Washington, D.C, pp. 345−352.

Henikoff, S., Henikoff, J., 1992. Amino acid substitution matrices from protein blocks. Proc. Natl. Acad. Sci. U. S. A 89, 10915−10919.

Smith, T.F., Waterman, M.S., 1981. Identification of common molecular subsequences. J. Mol. Biol. 147, 195−197.

# BLAST: protocols

## 11.1 Protocol 1: how to select a sequence using entrez

Entrez is a search engine that searches various National Biotechnology Information Centre (NCBI) databases for keywords. Nucleotide and protein databases such as GenBank, as well as non-sequence databases like PubMed, and OMIM are part of these database packages. You would need to know what sequence you are interested in to implement this protocol.

### 11.1.1 Step by step method details

- Visit the NCBI website http://www.ncbi.nim.nih.gov, there is only one text box on this page in which you can type keywords. You can specify a search index using a pull-down menu, too (Fig. 11.1).

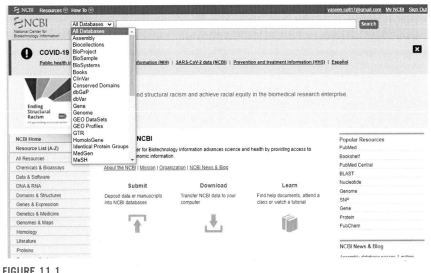

**FIGURE 11.1**

NCBI website

Bioinformatics for Everyone. https://doi.org/10.1016/B978-0-323-91128-3.00023-9

- Choose a nucleotide from the pull-down menu/the sequence database, depending on what you are doing.

Consider, however, that the database is not mandatory in the search process. All-Databases option will display the number of hits in all NCBI databases.

- Type a term you want to search in the text box.
- For example. Here we are selecting a SACCHAROMYCES [ORGANISM] (Fig. 11.2).
- Toggle on the download link that is next to sequence that you would like to download; this one will take you directly to the sequence's entrance page (Fig. 11.3).
- Choose format of sequence like FASTA or GTF that you want to download (Fig. 11.4).
- Download the complete sequence and open up in Notepad (Fig. 11.5).

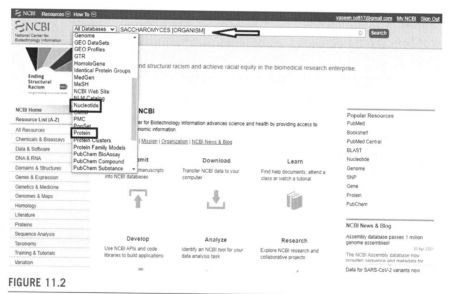

**FIGURE 11.2**

Search selection

**FIGURE 11.3**

Sequence entrance page

**FIGURE 11.4**

Sequence format selection

**FIGURE 11.5**

Sequence in Notepad

## 11.2 Protocol 2: how to search for a nucleotide database using a nucleotide query: BLASTN

In a nucleotide database sequence that is similar to the nucleotide query sequence, the first search protocol will allow you to locate sequences. You can start by using BLASTP and the protein sequence if you can determine this nucleotide sequence code for a protein and protein sequence. This is because the genetic code has degenerated, which means that the same protein can be coded in different nucleotide sequences.

NOTE: You will need a FASTA or GenBank nuclear sequence or an accessory number for the sequence of your interest to perform this protocol.

### 11.2.1 Step by step method details

- Navigate to the NCBI BLAST as already shown in protocol 1, a screen like this is shown in (Fig. 11.6).
- Select a Nucleotide BLAST programme. This page can be seen in (Fig. 11.7).
- In one of the following formats, add interested nucleotide sequence in the text box (Fig. 11.8).

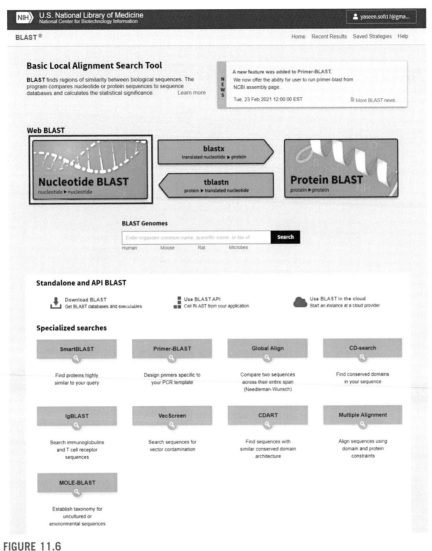

**FIGURE 11.6**

Nucleotide BLAST

**FASTA**: Copy the sequence formatted by FASTA, including the > description section. Alternatively, just add your series and you could skip the description line. This will be used to title the quest if a definition line is included.

**GenBank**: Copy paste the GenBank input sequence field. GenBank: BLAST will delete and apply only the sequence of numbers and spaces. Ensure that you only paste the GenBank entry sequence; otherwise query will not succeed.

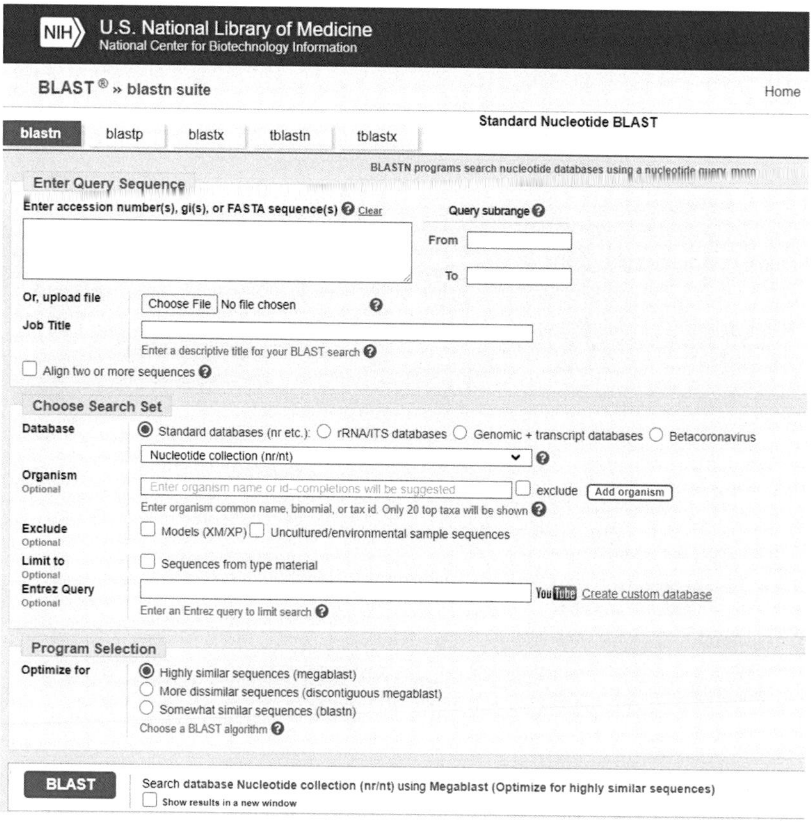

FIGURE 11.7

BLASTN main page

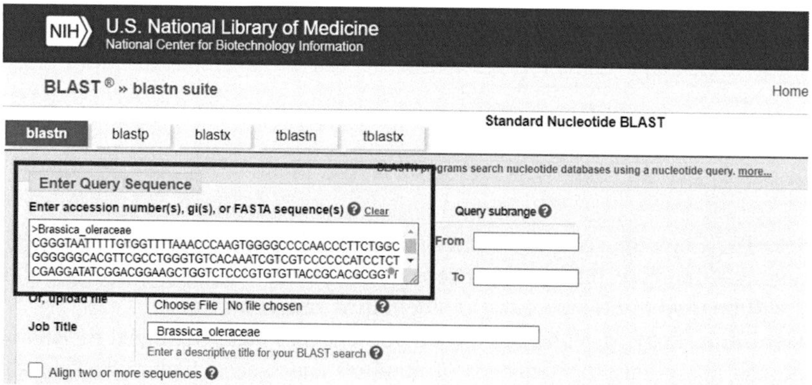

FIGURE 11.8

Enter Query Sequence

**GI** (Accession no): Put GI Number on the search window to BLAST, and the query sequence will be given for BLAST already in GenBank.

- Select the database which needs to be searched (Fig. 11.9).
- Choose the sort of BLAST search to run.
- Set advanced search parameters if desired.
- Usually you do BLAST by default but, often, by changing these parameters, you can boost search performance.

**Max sequences of targets**: since the series has grown so large, it is common for it to become one of the top 100 hits. You can get many more hits on your question by using this very helpful option.

**Short queries**: the default marker for this checkbox is to let the marked checkbox show BLAST to set its parameters so they can find hits in a short series. Rather it does not normally yield meaningful hits, as random sequences happen easily by chance.

**Expect threshold**: only E-value hits smaller than expected thresholds are returned by BLAST. This is adjusted to 10 by default. This increase would bring in a larger number of fewer hits. Reducing this value will lead to fewer, greater hits.

- Hit the BLAST search option.
- Wait while it finishes the scan and displays result page of the BLAST server (Fig. 11.10).

*It may take a few minutes to search BLAST. After the search is complete, the search ID (RID) applied to your search may return to the search results page at this time.*

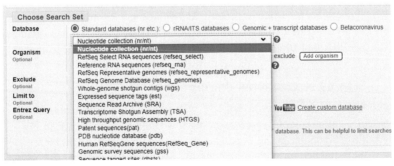

**FIGURE 11.9**

Database selection

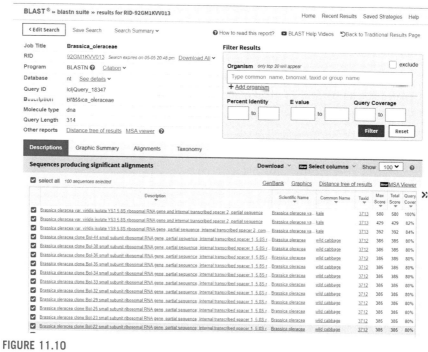

**FIGURE 11.10**

BLAST server result page

## 11.3 Protocol 3: how to search a protein database using a translated nucleotide query: BLASTX

One can enter the nucleotide sequence to BLASTX if having a sequence of nucleotide which codes for a particular protein, and you do not know what frame reading encodes it. This programme translates the sequence into a protein database in the six different possible read frames then searches for sequences identical to those.

### 11.3.1 Step by step method details

- Point your navigator onto the BLAST web page whose link is already given in protocol 1 and protocol 2, you are going to see a screen as shown in Fig. 11.6.
- Click blastx. You are going to see a page as shown in Fig. 11.11.
- Insert the sequence of nucleotides into the textbox.
- If needed, restrict sequence area that is utilised to search a database by entering in the question subrange boxes 'From' and 'To'.
- To translate the nucleotide sequence, choose the Genetic Code (Fig. 11.12).
- Choose a query database.
- To run a search with default setting, click BLAST.
- For most searches these settings work well and usually must not be modified.
- Wait while it finishes the scan and displays result page of the BLAST server.

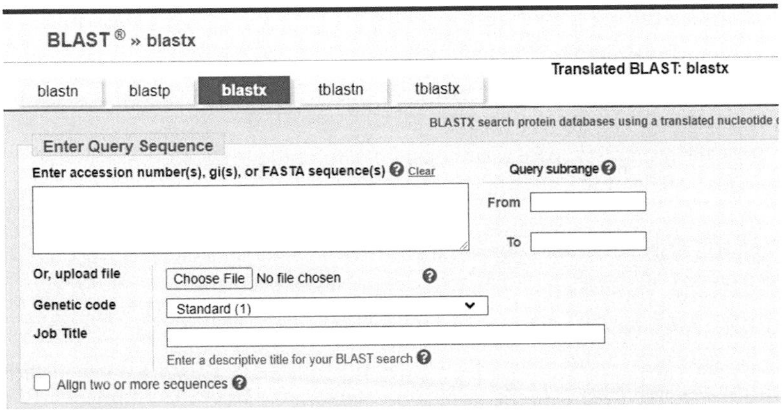

FIGURE 11.11

BLASTX main page

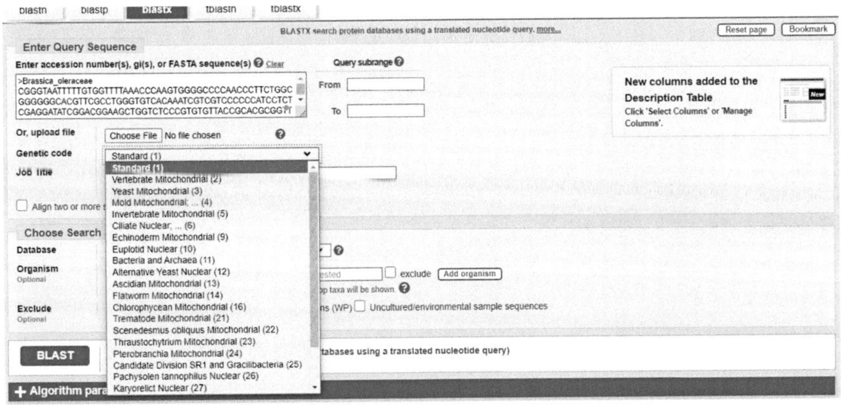

FIGURE 11.12

Genetic code selection

## 11.4 Protocol 4: how to search a translated nucleotide database using a protein query: TBLASTN

Often in a genome or other broad nucleotide base, a protein sequence of concern was not annotated. This is typical during the initial phases of a genome sequencing. You can scan for the nucleotide database using your protein sequence. The BLAST programme will translate the database in all six read frames and thus searches for protein-like sequences in all frames.

## 11.4.1 Step by step method details

- Navigate to the NCBI BLAST web page as already shown in above protocols. You are going to see a screen as shown in Fig. 11.6.
- Select tblastn.
- Copy your protein sequence and paste it into the textbox.
- Example: Selecting a protein sequence of glutaredoxin (*Oryza sativa*) (Fig. 11.13).
- If needed, restrict sequence area that is utilised to search a database by entering in the question subrange boxes 'From' and 'To'.

IMPORTANT NOTE: Genetic code is not mandatory for the use of TBLASTN. For each sequence in the database, the genetic codes required to translate it have already been established. To perform the translation, BLAST automatically uses the correct genetic code.

- Choose the database you want to search.
- To start searching with the default settings, select BLAST. These defaults are sufficient and should not be changed for most searches.
- Wait for the BLAST server to finish the scan till it displays the results page (Fig. 11.14).

**FIGURE 11.13**

Protein sequence of glutaredoxin (*Oryza sativa*)

**FIGURE 11.14**

Result page

## 11.5 Protocol 5: how to compare two or more sequence
### 11.5.1 Step by step method details

Example: In the NCBI database, first select on Nucleotide and then type the following in search box: **Human [organism] AND mitochondrion [title]**

It will look for human nucleotide sequence with the term 'mitochondrion' (Fig. 11.15).

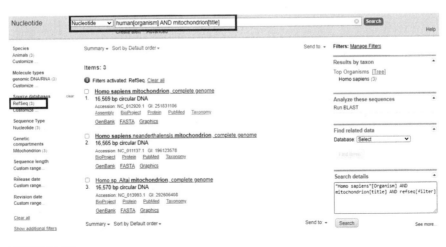

**FIGURE 11.15**

Searching a nucleotide

- Select RefSeq option underneath databases in the filter menu on left side to limit the results to NCBI Reference Sequences. It will show sequences of high quality that are curated and annotated by NCBI personnel's (Fig. 11.15).
- There are three mitochondrial genome Reference Sequences in humans which are shown in figure below. On the right side, there is sub-option under 'analyze these sequences', Search using 'Run BLAST option' (Fig. 11.16).

There will be launch of Nucleotide BLAST, and it will add the accession numbers of reference sequences to the box of query sequence automatically.

- Select the 'Align two or more sequences' box in the query sequence box to compare sequences.
- Paste the two accession numbers in the subject sequence box that will open after clicking on 'align two or more sequences'.
- Copy and paste the sequence of modern human mitochondrial genome (NC 012920.1) in 'Query Sequence' (Fig. 11.17).
- Enter name for the job title and press on the BLAST, without touching rest of the settings.

Two findings can be found in comparison of the sequence of the questionnaire (modern human) with one of the sequences, Neanderthal or Denisovan. Please keep in mind 99% is identical to the sequence of Neanderthal, while 98% to Denisovan sequence.

Follow these steps to check the variation among sequences and their biological significance:

- Switch to Alignments tab and pick Pairwise with dots for identities from the Alignment view drop-down display (Fig. 11.18).
- Choose the CDS function by checking the box next to it (Fig. 11.18).

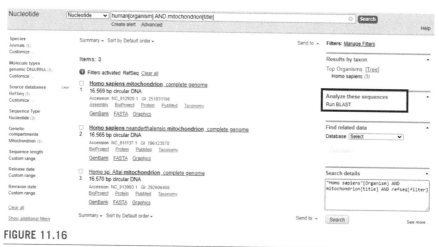

**FIGURE 11.16**

Run Blast

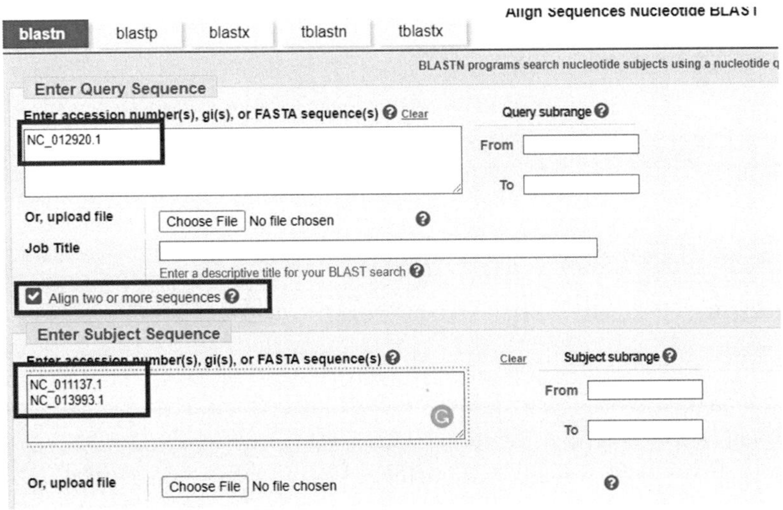

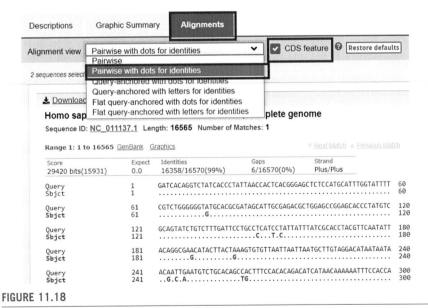

**FIGURE 11.17**

Enter Query Sequence

**FIGURE 11.18**

Pairwise with dots for identities

- Click the first result name, i.e. *Homo sapiens* Neanderthals. In two lines, you can check base-to-base comparison between two sequences. In the second line, the sequence of the subject, i.e. an ancient human sequence is replaced by points for bases where the sequence of the subject is similar to the sequence of the question and the sequence of the subject varies in the red sequence

```
CDS:NADH dehydrogena  1               M  P  M  A  N  L  L  L  L  I  V  P  I  L  I  A  M  A
Query                 3301    AACAACATACCCATGGCCAACCTCCTACTCCTCATTGTACCCATTCTAATCGCAATGGCA  3360
Sbjct                 3296    .......C...........................G........................  3355
CDS:NADH dehydrogena  1               M  A  N  L  L  L  L  V  V  P  I  L  I  A  M  A

CDS:NADH dehydrogena  19      F  L  M  L  T  E  R  K  I  L  G  Y  M  Q  L  R  K  G  P  N
Query                 3361    TTCCTAATGCTTACCGAACGAAAAATTCTAGGCTATATACAACTACGCAAAGGCCCCAAC  3420
Sbjct                 3356    ...........................................G.............T......  3415
CDS:NADH dehydrogena  17      F  L  M  L  T  E  R  K  I  L  G  Y  M  Q  L  R  K  G  P  N

CDS:NADH dehydrogena  39      V  V  G  P  Y  G  L  L  Q  P  F  A  D  A  M  K  L  F  T  K
Query                 3421    GTTGTAGGCCCCTACGGGCTACTACAACCCTTCGCTGACGCCATAAAACTCTTCACCAAA  3480
Sbjct                 3416    ............................................................  3475
CDS:NADH dehydrogena  37      V  V  G  P  Y  G  L  L  Q  P  F  A  D  A  M  K  L  F  T  K

CDS:NADH dehydrogena  59      E  P  L  K  P  A  T  S  T  I  T  L  Y  I  T  A  P  T  L  A
Query                 3481    GAGCCCCTAAAACCCGCCACATCTACCATCACCCTCTACATCACCGCCCCGACCTTAGCT  3540
Sbjct                 3476    ..A.................................C.......................  3535
CDS:NADH dehydrogena  57      E  P  L  K  P  A  T  S  T  I  T  L  Y  I  T  A  P  T  L  A
```

**FIGURE 11.19**

CDS

- Scroll all the way bottom to the CDS. Their regions are shown in four lines. The line of first of the query sequence, i.e. modern human is shown on the second line as an amino acid translation. The third line, i.e. ancient human, and the line after it indicates the translation of amino acid for the subject sequence (Fig. 11.19).

## 11.6 Troubleshooting guide

| Issues in BLAST | Causes and quick fix |
|---|---|
| E-values display weak results or if shows no hits. | Obtain additional sequence information and re-run the scan. Some databases may not contain the sequence you are searching for. Use a wider database, like the nr or EST databases, to conduct the search. The sequence cannot be maintained between species. |
| Query led to many hits, but not an interesting species hit. | Enter the text box to limit your question by entering your species name. It is likely that the gene species of interest has not yet been sequenced. |
| The top hits result in organisms that are either unexpected or distantly related. | In several different organisms, the sequence can be similar and the search results in the same values. No important order is shown in these sequences on the results tab. The gene can be passed horizontally between remote species. The vector sequence, which is sometimes present at the start to the last of a DNA sequence, is still available. |
| Just a portion of the series will be aligned by the hits. | A well-preserved domain may be present in the series. Delete the domain from the sequence and perform the scan. The sequence portion used in the query may also be restricted. The vector sequence may still be attached which is frequently present at the start or end of a DNA sequence read. |

# Further reading

Altschul, S.F., Gish, W., Miller, W., Myers, E.W., Lipman, D.J., 1990. Basic local alignment search tool. J. Mol. Biol. 215, 403−410.

Altschul, S.F., Madden, T.L., Schaffer, A.A., Zhang, J., Zhang, Z., Miller, W., Lipman, D.J., 1997. Gapped BLAST and PSI−BLAST: a new generation of protein database search programs. Nucleic Acids Res. 25, 3389−3402.

Bateman, A., Pearson, W.R., Stein, L.D., Stormo, G.D., Yates III., J.R. (Eds.), 2017. Current Protocols in Bioinformatics. John Wiley & Sons, Hoboken, N.J. Chapter 3.

Chang, W.-J., Zaila, K.E., Coppola, T.W., 2016. Submitting a sequence to GenBank. Curr. Protoc. Essen. Lab. Tech. 12, 11.2.1−11.2.24.

Dayhoff, M.O., Schwartz, R.M., Orcutt, B.C., 1978. A model of evolutionary change in proteins. In: Atlas of Protein Sequence and Structure, vol. 5. National Biomedical Research Foundation, Washington, D.C, pp. 345−352.

Eddy, S.R., 2004a. Where did the BLOSUM62 alignment score matrix come from? Nat. Biotechnol. 22, 1035−1036.

Eddy, S.R., 2004b. What is dynamic programming? Nat. Biotechnol. 22, 909−910.

Engel, S.R., MacPherson, K.A., 2016. Using model organism databases (MODs). Curr. Protoc. Essen. Lab. Tech. 13, 11.4.1−11.4.22.

Henikoff, S., Henikoff, J., 1992. Amino acid substitution matrices from protein blocks. Proc. Natl. Acad. Sci. U. S. A 89, 10915−10919.

Korf, I., Yandell, M., Bedell, J., 2003. BLAST. O'Reilly Media, Inc., Sebastopol, Calif.

Ladunga, I., 2009. Finding similar nucleotide sequences using network BLAST searches. Curr. Protoc. Bioinform. 26, 3.3.1-3.3.26.

Leonard, S.A., Littlejohn, T.G., Baxevanis, A.D., 2006. Common file formats. Curr. Protoc. Bioinform. 16. A.1B.1-A.1B.9.

Needleman, S.B., Wunsch, C.D., 1970. A general method applicable to the search for similarities in the amino acid sequence of two proteins. J. Mol. Biol. 48, 443−453.

Smith, T.F., Waterman, M.S., 1981. Identification of common molecular subsequences. J. Mol. Biol. 147, 195−197.

Stover, N.A., Cavalcanti, A.R., Li, A.J., Richardson, B.C., Landweber, L.F., 2005. Reciprocal fusions of two genes in the formaldehyde detoxification pathway in ciliates and diatoms. Mol. Biol. Evol. 22, 1539−1542. https://doi.org/10.1093/molbev/msi151.

Wheeler, D., 2003. Selecting the right protein− scoring matrix. Curr. Protoc. Bioinform. 00: 3.5.1-53.5.6.

Zufall, R.A., 2017. Beyond simple homology searches: multiple sequence alignments and phylogenetic trees. Curr. Protoc. Essen. Lab. Tech. 1, 11.3.1−1.3.17.

# ExPASy portal

## 12.1 Introduction

The Swiss Bioinformatics Institute (SIB) is a non-profit academic foundation that promotes scientific research, database creation and computer technology, education and service activities in the bioinformatics sector. The server of ExPASy is one of the SIB windows in the world that focusses on proteins and protection systems and offers access to a range of databases and analytics tools. Swiss Institute of Bioinformatics provides ExPASy (expert protein analysis system) a global web server for the community of life sciences (SIB). ExPASy began operating in 1993 as first World Wide Web, i.e. www server in life science field. The high degree of integration and interconnectedness between all available databases and facilities is one of ExPASy's main assets.

## 12.2 History

In August 1993, ExPASy was created as one of the first biological science web servers to operate. It has constantly changed and improved since that date. The SIB ExPASy bioinformatics portal was launched in June 2011. The prototype server ExPASy was developed by Amos Bairoch who is the founder of SWISS-PROT and is now the leader of the SIB group, and Ron Appel who is a popular computer proteome specialist, the developer of melanie software and now also the executive director of the SIB. The first two open access databases were SWISS-PROT and SWISS-2DPAGE.

ExPASy was originally conceived and developed as a web server for life science that allowed proteomic data analysis. ExPASy has increased and strengthened on many occasions over the past 20 years. ExPASy has been planned, created and maintained by the SIB web team in cooperation with several other SIB groups and ExPASy users.

## 12.3 Resource of the SIB

The updated ExPASy edition of the 'ExPASy: SIB Bioinformatic Resource Portal' was released in June 2011. The notion of 'server proteomics' is no longer employed,

Bioinformatics for Everyone. https://doi.org/10.1016/B978-0-323-91128-3.00017-3

it is included in the new portal, as the new edition covers all scientific areas of SIB (such as proteomics and genomics, phylogeny/evolution, system biomy and populating genetics, and transcriptomics, among other things). Artimo and co-workers provide details of the latest web portal update (2012).

As regards the previous edition, key revisions are as follows:

- Unified SIB resources Entry Point.
- The actual database and software tools generally managed at various online servers at the different places of the Swiss Bioinformatics Institute Community, while the Portal gives a feeling that they host all of their resources.
- Advanced resource detection and remote database querying function.
- Visual guide to text-oriented search interfaces as an alternative.
- Active management of featured services and quality control. The refurbishment was carried out in order to keep existing users of ExPASy in the 'proteomics' category with their proteomic tools.

## 12.4 Databases available at ExPASy

ExPASy is the main host for partially or entirely established databases in Geneva.

- **SWISS-PROT:**
  The knowledgebase SWISS-PROT which gives high-quality data like the function of a protein, structure of a domain, modifications after translation and variants, a reduced redundancy level and a high degree of incorporation in other databases is a curated protein sequence database. The SIB and the European Institute of Bioinformatics are co-operating between SWISS-PROT and TrEMBL (EBI).
- **SWISS-2DPAGE:**
  It is an information base of proteins known for 2D polyacrylamide gel electrophoresis (2D PAGE). SWISS-2DPAGE contains information from an assortment of natural examples, including human and mouse tests, just as *Arabidopsis thaliana*, *Escherichia coli*, *Saccharomyces cerevisiae* and *Dictyostelium discoideum*.
- **PROSITE:**
  PROSITE includes sites, trends and profiles that are biologically important and help accurately classify the known protein family. It is a database of protein domains and families.
- **ENZYME:**
  ENZYME can be accessed at ExPASy homepage. It gives data on enzyme nomenclature.
- **SWISS-MODEL:**
  The SWISS-MODEL Repository is an automatically created database of structural protein models.

## 12.5 ExPASy tools for sequence analysis

BLAST offers high-speed search similarity to a protein or nucleotide sequence against a database. The ExPASy BLAST operation on the specific hardware is maintained in a joint effort with the Swiss EMBnet node.

- **ScanProsite:**
  ScanProsite scans a PROSITE pattern or a profile or rules sequence against all SWISS-PROT, TrEMBL and/or PDB sequences, as well as all PROSITE patterns, profiles and laws.
- **SWISS-MODEL:**
  SWISS-MODEL can develop models for three-dimensional protein structure, the sequence of which is connected with that of 3D-structured proteins. It is a knowledge-based automatic protein modelling server.
- **ProtParam:**
  ProtParam measures physio-chemical sequence parameters such as the structure of amino acids, Pl, atomic composition, coefficient of extinction, etc.
- **ProtScale:**
  ProtScale calculates and reflects the profile that is formed on a selected protein by any amino acid scale. There are about 50 scales which are already defined, such as the hydrophobicity scale in Doolittle and Kyte.
- **RandSeq:**
  RandSeq is a tool which creates an irregular protein grouping based on the composition and sequence length defined by the user.
- **Sulfinator:**
  In protein sequences, the sulfator predicts tyrosine sulfation sites.

## 12.6 ExPASy proteomics tools

There are various types of instruments for analysing protein and proteomic data from two-dimensional polyacrylamide gel electrophoresis and mass spectrometric studies. ExPASy provides access to all of these tools:

- **AACompIdent** — This tool helps in identification of a protein by the composition of its amino acid.
- **AACompSim** — This tool is used to compare the amino acid composition of a SWISS-PROT entry with different entries in the database.
- **Compute pI/MW** — It calculates entry of a SWISS-PROT, TrEMBL or molecular weight (MW) for a theoretical isoelectrical point (pI) and a theoretical consumer sequence.
- **FindMod** forecasts post-translation potential protein and the possible replacement of peptides to single amino acids.
- **FindPept** recognises peptides resulting from non-specific protein cleavage by its experimental weights considering artifactual chemical modifications and post-translation changes.

- **Glycan Mass** — The density of an oligosaccharide structure is calculated by Glycan Mass.
- **GlycoMod** forecasts potential structures of oligosaccharides on proteins from their experimental masses. The mass of a potential glycan is contrasted with a rundown of pre-registered glycan masses.
- **PeptideCutter** — The sites of protease cleavage and those sites that are cleaved in provided protein sequence are predicted by PeptideCutter.
- **PeptideMass** — PeptideMass figures the hypothetical masses of peptides created by the substance or enzymatic cleavage of proteins to aid the translation of peptide mass fingerprinting.
- **PeptIdent, TagIdent, MultiIdent** — These programmes are used for classification of proteins using various experiments such as PI, TheMW, the structure of amino acids and partial sequences and peptide fingerprinting results.

## 12.7 Protocol: using ExPASy's 'translate' tool

Example: Translation of a given gene sequences, e.g. rice (*Oryza sativa*) to amino acid sequence using ExPASy software.

Steps involved in the translation of gene sequences of rice to amino acid sequences are as follows:

- Go to NCBI website, search the sequence of a waxy gene of rice and copy its sequence in FASTA format (Fig. 12.1).

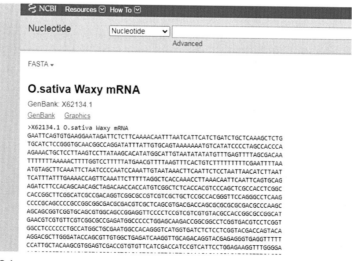

**FIGURE 12.1**

Oryza sativa Waxy mRNA sequence.

- In another tab to go ExPASy, its homepage will display a number of resources, select translate tools amongst various resources or directly go ExPASy translate tool via https://web.expasy.org/translate/(Fig. 12.2).
- Paste the sequence of given gene in the DNA/RNA field given (Fig. 12.3).
- In the output format, you can customise your results, e.g. include Met in place of M (methionine) amino acid in the translated frame. You can also include both

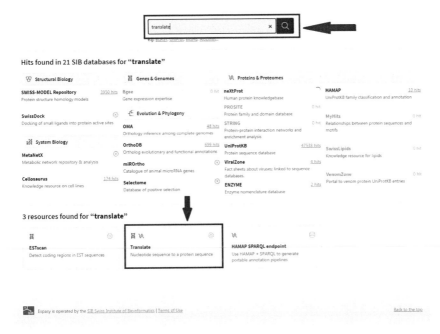

**FIGURE 12.2**

ExPasy homepage.

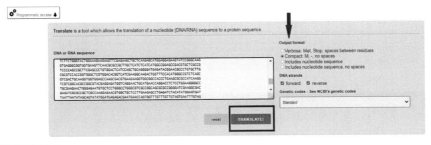

**FIGURE 12.3**

Translate tool.

the nucleotide sequences as well as the amino acid translated for easy understanding (Fig. 12.4).

- Then click on the option translate, and results of the sequence, i.e. open reading frames of sequences will get displayed which will be highlighted in red colour (Fig. 12.5).
- You can also download all the translated reading frames.

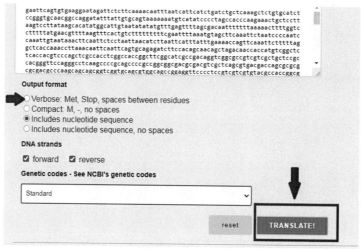

**FIGURE 12.4**

Customizing query sequence.

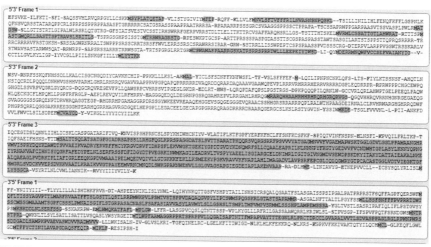

**FIGURE 12.5**

ORF's of sequence displayed.

# Further reading

Bridge, A., Lane, L., Stockinger, H., Appel, R., Xenarios, I., 2014. Databases and data sources at SIB, Swiss Institute of bioinformatics. In: Comprehensive Biomedical Physics.

Gasteiger, E., 2003. ExPASy: the proteomics server for in-depth protein knowledge and analysis. Nucleic Acids Res. 32 (13), 3784–3788. https://doi.org/10.1093/nar/gkg563, 12824418.

Schneider, M., 2004. The Swiss-Prot protein knowledgebase and ExPASy: providing the plant community with high quality proteomic data and tools. Plant Physiol. Biochem. 42, 1013–1021. https://doi.org/10.1016/j.plaphy.2004.10.009, 15707838.

# Primer designing tools

# 13

## 13.1 FastPCR

- The FastPCR programme is an integrated tool environment that offers broad and expert facilities for designing of PCR primers for ordinary, significant distance, inverse, realtime, multiplex PCR, Xtreme Chain Reaction, group-specific or special, overlap extension PCR (OE-PCR), Loop-mediated Isothermal Amplification (LAMP) and many other applications.
- Oligonucleotide 'in silico' research is useful to detect sites of target binding for calculating the annealing temperature of PCR.
- Microarray analysis of dual labelled oligonucleotides for samples like molecular beacons can be designed with a long oligonucleotide.
- All primary secondary structures like the alternate Watson–Crick base combination of hydrogen, wobble base pairs, hairpins, self-dimers and cruciferous dimers are tested for all primary structures.
- The software uses regular and degenerated primers for all tools, and based on the closest thermodynamic parameters for the estimation of the melting temperature.
- The software is used to detect effectively and completely the different types of repeats that have been developed and used for the visioning programme (Fig. 13.1).

## 13.2 AutoPrime

AutoPrime allows for the rapid design of real-time primers for the expression of eukaryotes and their analysis. These primers are typically chosen so that they can amplify cDNA derived from mRNA but will not produce a product on genomic DNA. This is refined by utilising the eukaryotic splicing mechanism for mRNA.

The Primer pairs are chosen such that one among the primer matches an exon-exon border sequence that does not exist in the genomic sequence. The primer pair can also be designed by placing each primer in a different exon, thereby, resulting in a genomic product that includes a long intronic sequence. This software adds these features to the primer3 primer-design app (Fig. 13.2).

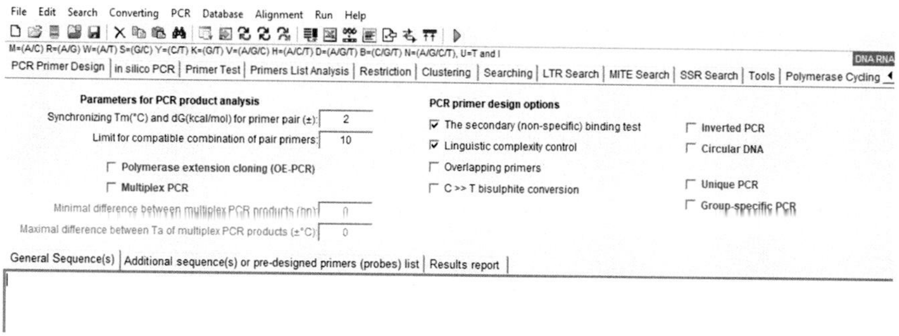

File Edit Search Converting PCR Database Alignment Run Help

M=(A/C) R=(A/G) W=(A/T) S=(G/C) Y=(C/T) K=(G/T) V=(A/G/C) H=(A/C/T) D=(A/G/T) B=(C/G/T) N=(A/G/C/T), U=T and I

PCR Primer Design | in silico PCR | Primer Test | Primers List Analysis | Restriction | Clustering | Searching | LTR Search | MITE Search | SSR Search | Tools | Polymerase Cycling

**Parameters for PCR product analysis**

Synchronizing Tm(°C) and dG(kcal/mol) for primer pair (±): 2

Limit for compatible combination of pair primers: 10

☐ Polymerase extension cloning (OE-PCR)

☐ Multiplex PCR

Minimal difference between multiplex PCR products (bp): 0

Maximal difference between Ta of multiplex PCR products (±°C): 0

**PCR primer design options**

☑ The secondary (non-specific) binding test          ☐ Inverted PCR

☑ Linguistic complexity control                              ☐ Circular DNA

☐ Overlapping primers

☐ C >> T bisulphite conversion                            ☐ Unique PCR

☐ Group-specific PCR

General Sequence(s) | Additional sequence(s) or pre-designed primers (probes) list | Results report |

**FIGURE 13.1**

FastPCR 6.7.

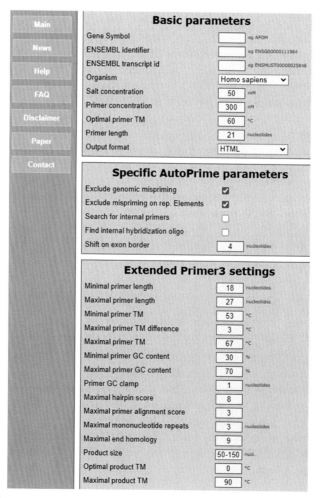

**FIGURE 13.2**

AutoPrime software.

## 13.3 **MethPrimer**

MethPrimer is a software for creating Methylation PCR Primers based on bisulphite conversion. It can design primers for two forms of bisulphite PCR:

**(1)** The Methylation-Specific PCR and
**(2)** The Bisulphite-Sequencing PCR.

MethPrimer is also capable of predicting CpG islands in DNA sequences (Fig. 13.3).

### 13.3.1 **Step by step method**

- DNA sequences can be inserted in any format, i.e. there is no need for pre-input editing.
- For example, inserting *Homo sapiens*: chrX (AR promoter −500-+200 with 2 CGIs) in the sequence box (Fig. 13.4).
- Click on submit.
- After clicking on submit, it will show results both in text format and graphical view. It will also display results of CpG island prediction and primer design picking (Fig. 13.5).
- You can also download EPS image.

MethPrimer is an online platform which provides a number of tools and databases to facilitate the study of DNA methylation and epigenetics, including tools for designing primers and probes for various bisulfite conversion based PCRs, predicting CpG islands, and manipulating sequences.

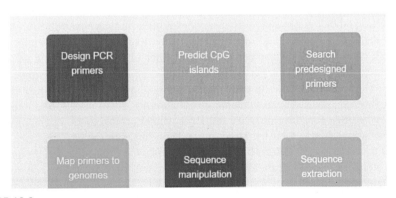

**FIGURE 13.3**

MethPrimer 2.0 version.

MethPrimer allows you to design primers for most bisulfite conversion based PCR primers and to predict CpG islands on an input sequence. It also allow you to search for predesigned primers for human and mouse genes.
- **Design primers on your input sequence:** Paste an ORIGINAL DNA sequence. Input sequence doesn't need virtual bisulfite conversion (e.g. convert 'C' to 'T'). Try this Sample sequence.
- **Search for predesigned primers for human and mouse genes:** Type in the box below gene symbol, RefSeq ID, to search for pre-designed primers for protein coding genes, lncRNAs and miRNAs (e.g., ESR1, NM_000044, mir-1-1, PANDA).
- **CpG island prediction:** You can also use the program to predict CpG islands in a sequence.

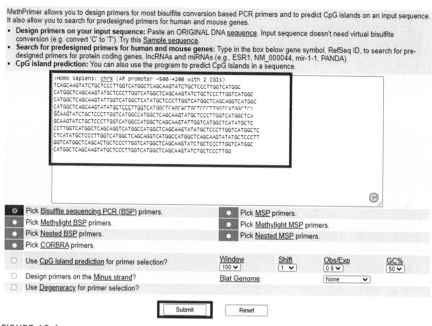

FIGURE 13.4

Sequence of *Homo sapiens*.

## 13.4 Oligo.Net

It is the most basic primer analysis software and is also the most important technique for making and examining sequencing and PCR (polymerase chain reaction) primers, synthetic genes and various sorts of probes like siRNA, miRNA, etc. Oligo's search calculations find ideal PCR primers, like TaqMan, profoundly multiplexed, consensus or degenerate primers, in light of the latest closest neighbour thermodynamic information. It is possible to process several files in a single batch. It's also a great tool for site-directed mutagenesis. Oligo's various investigation windows show an abundance of valuable information for every primer or groundwork pair, including secondary of DNA and RNA, dimer arrangement, bogus preparing and homology, inner security, structure and physical properties. You may utilise Oligo to assess open reading frames down to assessed molecular weight and pKa of proteins, just as search for restriction enzyme sites in DNA and reverse-translated proteins.

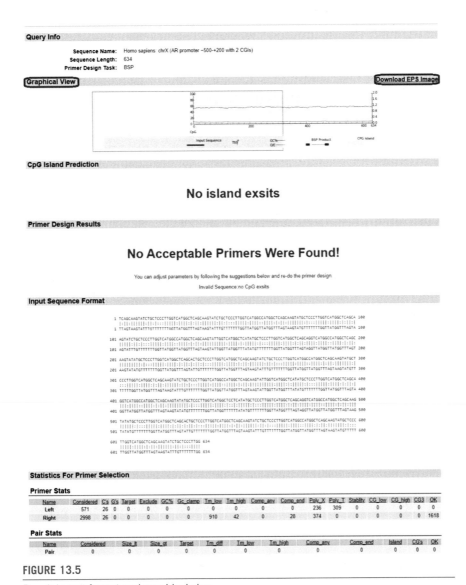

**FIGURE 13.5**

Result in text format and graphical view.

This software firstly came online in 1989. It underwent many changes, the most extensive of which was the upgrade from version 6 to 7. Oligo 7 is the most recent update and can automatically pick multiplex primers, design different PCR-related primers to cover multiple DNA regions in a single scan and also find primer sets for RT-PCR (Fig. 13.6).

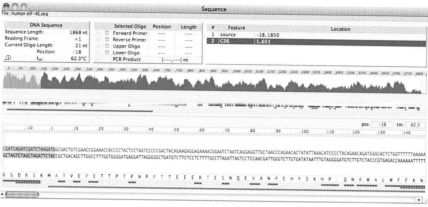

**FIGURE 13.6**

Human elf-4E sequence in Oligo 7 tool.

## 13.5 GeneFisher

The GeneFisher is the most commonly used web-based interactive programme for the creation of degenerate primers. The underlying premise is that genes with a corresponding feature from different species demonstrate a strong sequence similarity. This assumption leads to gene separation by multiple alignments of genes from various species in a target organism. It accepts sequences in these formats as shown in the sections below (Fig. 13.7).

### 13.5.1 AA — consensus backtranslation

Backtranslates an amino acid alignment using the consensus codon table and then the unclear consensus sequence of that alignment. Please keep in mind that the degeneracy of the primer and the 3′ end is likely to be very large when using this function. Please adjust your settings accordingly.

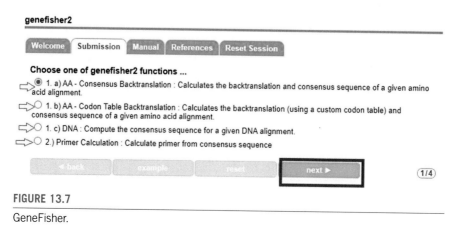

**FIGURE 13.7**

GeneFisher.

### 13.5.2 AA — codon table backtranslation

Calculates the backtranslation of an amino acid alignment using a custom codon table, followed by the alignment's unclear consensus sequence. Please keep in mind that the degeneracy of the primer and the 3' end is likely to be very large when using this function. Please adjust your settings accordingly.

### 13.5.3 DNA

Compute the consensus sequence for a given DNA alignment.

### 13.5.4 Primer calculation

Primers are calculated using the consensus sequence produced in the last steps.

## 13.6 GenomePRIDE 1.0

GenomePRIDE is one of the important tools in bioinformatic analysis. It helps is designing of PCR primers or long oligonucleotides on an annotated sequence. GenomePRIDE has so far been utilised to make deoxyribose nucleotide arrays or chips that contain all ORFs from the listed organisms:

- *Bacillus subtilis* (4100, full ORF primer pairs, >>97% success)
- *Schizosaccharomyces pombe* (~5000, ORF-specific primer pairs, >99% success)
- *Drosophila melanogaster* (Heidelberg FlyArray, 21,000, ORF-specific primer pairs, >99% success)
- *Candida albicans*, etc.

### 13.6.1 Features of GenomePRIDE

- High success rate
- PCR primer and/or oligo computation
- Fast computation
- Specified length of fragment
- Homologies are analysed
- Visualisation (based on the Staden package)
- Development of primers within a given frame

## 13.7 CODEHOP

CODEHOP is a programme which creates PCR primers from multiple sequence alignment of protein. The software is intended for situations in which the protein sequences are far apart and degenerate primers are needed. The MSA should be of protein amino acid sequences in the Blocks Database format. Proper alignments and blocks for the formatting of the databases is available on the website with various methods. The CODEHOP software produces degenerate sequences of DNA primers that can be used for PCR. One should choose suitable primers, synthesise them and conduct the PCR to see how well they function. This software was extremely successful in identifying 'universal degenerate' primers capable of amplifying informative genes from a wide range of bacterial lineages.

## 13.8 Oligos 6.2

'OLIGOS' is simple, easy to use, fast and powerful programme for searching the best primer combinations to use in normal PCR, inverse PCR and single-side PCR. Provided a single set primer, the software assists in the design of primer combinations. The universal DNA code for primary design is used for the software. This programme checks primers to see if they are compatible and calculates the best annealing temperature for an unknown PCR element.

## 13.9 Primo Pro 3.4

It is the one of the important software packages that decreases PCR noise by decreasing the likelihood of random primering. For the p53 gene, for example, ACTACCTGCTGCTGCAC appears to be appropriate because it follows widely used primer design requirements. Since the 3' 8 nucleotides occur in 4800 genes in the human transcriptome, this primer might have a high history. Primo Pro analysed transcriptomes to identify over-represented sequences, allowing users to choose primers with few over-represented sequences at the 3'-end.

## 13.10 Primo degenerate3.4

This software is used to design PCR primers that are based on a single peptide sequence or MSA of proteins or nucleotides. The probability of binding to the target is proportional to the effective concentration of the specific primer for degenerate primers.

## 13.11 RE-specific primer designing

It is a tool for analysing mutations in a sequence. It is mostly used by bioinformaticians and biotechnologists for restriction analysis of sequence mutations.

## 13.12 AlleleID

The AlleleID tool in bioinformatics is designed to address the challenges for identification of different bacteria, pathogens or species.

## 13.13  Array Designer 2

It quickly generates hundreds of individual oligonucleotides for studies related to single nucleotide polymorphism detection, expression analysis and for hundreds of polymorphism chain reaction primer pairs for complementary DNA microarrays. One can easily retrieve, evaluate and store data. It effectively investigates the complete organism by examining each gene or exon in the genome. It also characterizes the transcriptome, discovers and genotypizes SNPs, and compares genome hybridisation between individuals or communities.

Array Designer produces thousands of oligo and cDNA micro-array primers and samples in seconds. It develops single nucleotide polymorphism detection probes, microarray gene expression probes and probes for gene expression profiling.

### 13.13.1  Standard array design

You can create primers and samples to detect SNP and gene expression on multiple sequences in a single search run. Users can normally pick approximately 10,000 sequences.

### 13.13.2  Whole genome array

By detecting any gene or exon in the entire genome with Array Designer, you can easily explore the genes of whole species. Differentiated and alternative transcripts, SNPs, DNA sequence variations and comparative genome hybridisation in individuals and populations can be easily identified (CGH).

### 13.13.3  Tiling arrays

Every basis of a long sequence of genomes, also called gene amplification, is seen and repeated regions are avoided. The design of arrays to define or examine epigenetic changes, methylation patterns and protein binding sites was never easy.

## 13.14  LAMP designer

This software is used to create powerful primers for Loop-Mediated Isothermal Amplification assays, which amplify DNA and RNA sequences at isothermal temperatures without the need for a PCR setup.

## 13.15  Beacon designer

It is a powerful programme that automises the improvement of real time and tests. It is utilised by atomic researcher everywhere on the world to make effective real-time PCR assays. It sets aside time and cash in fruitless analyses. Beacon Designer is a flexible answer for your requirements for real-time printing and test plan and consistently pays for itself. From inside the product, you can BLAST scan sequences and search for layout structures. The consequences of the two ventures are utilised to construct primers and probes. The areas with significant cross-homologations and template structures are consequently avoided during design.

## 13.16 NetPrimer

It is a powerful programme for analysis of primer that is used to determine the features of the secondary structures of generated primer sequences. NetPrimer incorporates the most up-to-date primer analysis algorithms with a web-based interface that allows users to analyse primers over the Internet. The software simplifies primer quantitation by measuring primer molecular weight and optical operation. Each primer is rated on the basis of stability of its secondary structures to aid in the selection of an optimal primer. Individual primers or primer pairs may be printed with a detailed study report.

The main features of NetPrimer tool are as follows:

- It uses an efficient nearest neighbor thermodynamic algorithm to predict primer melting temperature.
- It gives quantitative forecast of primary efficiency.
- It generates a complete primer analysis for a single primer or primer pair.
- It examines single primers or pairs of primers.
- It describes all of the formulas and references that are used in the primer analysis algorithm.

## 13.17 SimVector

SimVector can simulate cloning experiments and generate publication-quality maps from beginning to end. It can create circular and linear vector maps with a variety of colours, patterns, fonts and line forms. The enzyme names are shown in two font types, with the bacterium section in Italics, as is customary. It uses several font styles and colours in a single textual word anywhere on the globe, including function annotations.

## 13.18 Primer Premier

This software is described as the most comprehensive programme for designing as well as analysing PCR primers. Standard PCR primers, genotyping tests of SNP, multiplexing tests and secondary structure checks for the designed primers can be designed. Primers are selected before reporting the best ones in the series, in a classified order, for secondary, dimers, coat pins, homologies and physical properties. Load the gene of interest from NCBI, choose a search range and let Primer Premier choose the best primers for you.

## 13.19 Web Primer

It is a simple and easily controlled tool of primer designing for PCR or sequencing.

Steps to use this Web Primer:

For example: Taking actin-related gene 1 (ACT 1) (Fig. 13.8).

- Enter the DNA sequence that will be used to find primers (e.g. ACT1).
- Enter the start and end points of your target area.
- Enter the maximum product size (optional).
- Force endpoints of primers (optional).
- Enter Primer selection parameters like primer length, primer composition, etc.
- Click on pick primers (Fig. 13.9).

**FIGURE 13.8**

Picking primers in WebPrimer resource.

Primer pairs for : ACT1

| primer | start | len | product size | tm | gc% | any_th | end_th | hairpin | seq |
|---|---|---|---|---|---|---|---|---|---|
| primer-left-0 | 436 | 20 | | 58.43 | 50.00 | 0.00 | 0.00 | 0.00 | TCATGGTCGGTATGGGTCAA |
| primer-right-0 | 922 | 20 | 487 | 58.58 | 50.00 | 21.53 | 0.00 | 0.00 | TCAGCAGTGGTGGAGAAAGA |
| primer-left-1 | 432 | 21 | 487 | 58.00 | 51.38 | 0.00 | 0.00 | 0.00 | GGTATCATGGTCGGTATGGGT |
| primer-right-1 | 926 | 20 | 495 | 58.58 | 50.00 | 21.53 | 19.99 | 0.00 | TCTTTCAGCAGTGGTGGAGA |
| primer-left-2 | 462 | 21 | 495 | 59.10 | 47.62 | 15.74 | 0.00 | 0.00 | TCCTACGTTGGTGATGAAGCT |
| primer-right-2 | 929 | 20 | 468 | 57.74 | 50.00 | 21.53 | 6.60 | 0.00 | TTCTCTTTCAGCAGTGGTGG |
| primer-left-3 | 466 | 20 | 468 | 57.75 | 45.00 | 0.00 | 0.00 | 0.00 | ACGTTGGTGATGAAGCTCAA |
| primer-right-3 | 920 | 21 | 455 | 58.39 | 47.62 | 0.00 | 0.00 | 0.00 | AGCAGTGGTGGAGAAAGAGTA |
| primer-left-4 | 458 | 21 | 455 | 58.20 | 47.62 | 21.95 | 0.02 | 0.00 | AGACTCCTACGTTGGTGATGA |
| primer-right-4 | 938 | 22 | 481 | 58.52 | 40.91 | 0.00 | 0.00 | 0.00 | ACGGACAATTTCTCTTTCAGCA |

Showing 1 to 10 of 10 entries   10 ▾ records per page   ‹ 1 ›

**FIGURE 13.9**

Result page of WebPrimer.

## 13.20 Primer3

It is a free and simple online tool for creating primers and probes from a DNA sequence. It is the most widely used software due to the accessibility of a several parameters for designing primers with high specificity and accuracy.

## 13.21 The PCR suite

It is a UCSC-hosted online primer software that enables users to build primers that are unique to different templates styles, e.g. overlapping amplicons on templates, SNP primers (in a GenBank), exon primers and cDNA primers.

**NOTE: Read about the protocols for designing cloning primers in Chapter 14.**

## Further reading

Giegerich, R., Meyer, F., Schleiermacher, C., 1996. GeneFisher–software support for the detection of postulated genes. Proc. Int. Conf. Intell. Syst. Mol. Biol. 4, 68−77.

Haas, S.A., Hild, M., Wright, A.P.H., Hain, T., Talibi, D., Vingron, M., 2003. Genome-scale design of PCR primers and long oligomers for DNA microarrays. Nucleic Acids Res. 31 (19), 5576−5581.

Kalendar, R., Kospanova, D., Schulman, A.H., 2021. Transposon-based tagging in silico using FastPCR software. Methods Mol. Biol. 2250, 245−256.

Kalendar, R., Samuilova, O., Ivanov, K.I., 2017. FastPCR: an in silico tool for fast primer and probe design and advanced sequence analysis. Genomics 109, 312−319.

Kalendar, R., Lee, D., Schulman, A.H., 2014. FastPCR software for PCR, in silico PCR, and oligonucleotide assembly and analysis. Methods Mol. Biol. 1116, 271−302.

Koressaar, T., Remm, M., 2007. Enhancements and modifications of primer design program Primer3. Bioinformatics 23 (10), 1289−1291.

Petersohn, A., Brigulla, M., Haas, S., Hoheisel, J., Völker, U., Hecker, M., 2001. Global analysis of the general stress response of *Bacillus subtilis*. J. Bacteriol. 183 (19), 5617−5631.

Rose, T.M., Henikoff, J.G., Henikoff, S., 2003. CODEHOP (COnsensus-DEgenerate hybrid oligonucleotide primer) PCR primer design. Nucleic Acids Res. 31 (13), 3763−3766.

Untergasser, A., Cutcutache, I., Koressaar, T., Ye, J., Faircloth, B.C., Remm, M., Rozen, S.G., 2012. Primer3 - new capabilities and interfaces. Nucleic Acids Res. 40 (15), e115.

Wrobel, G., Kokocinski, F., Lichter, 2004. AutoPrime: selecting primers for expressed sequences. Genome Biol. 5, P11.

Xue-Franzen, Y., Haas, S.A., Brino, L., Gusnanto, A., Reimers, M., Talibi, D., Vingron, M., Ekwall, K., Wright, A.P.H., 2003. A DNA microarray for fission yeast: minimal changes after a temperature shift to 36 C. Yeast 21, 25−39. https://doi.org/10.1002/yea.1053.14745780.

# Primer designing for cloning

The gene of interest is generally amplified by the polymerase chain reaction from genomic or vector DNA prior to being cloned to a vector expression. The various steps that are involved in designing of primers for cloning are discussed as follows:

- Access NCBI and look for the sequence of the given gene in the search option for which the primer needs to be designed for cloning, e.g. we take here *Arabidopsis thaliana* WRKY transcription factor, its complete cds (Fig. 14.1).
- Open its flat file, copy the cds sequence in FASTA format.
- To check whether the frame of the targeted sequence is transcribable, use the ExPASy tool 'TRANSLATE' as shown in following figure (Fig. 14.2).

**(Note: For more details of ExPASy translate tool refer to Chapter 12: ExPASy Portal).**

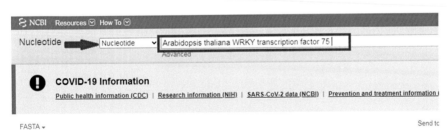

**FIGURE 14.1**

mRNA sequence of *Arabidopsis thaliana* WRKY

Bioinformatics for Everyone. https://doi.org/10.1016/B978-0-323-91128-3.00005-7

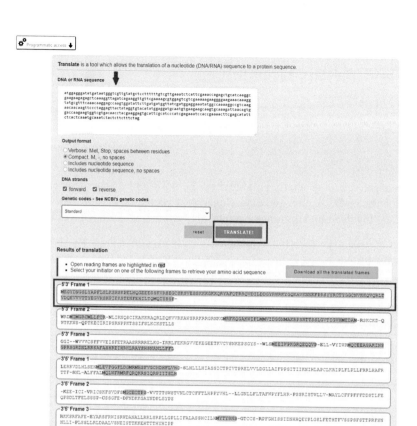

## FIGURE 14.2

Translation of sequence and ORFs

- If there is extra transcribed sequence before or after the genes that does not translate into protein, we have to remove those extra translatable sequences.
- After getting a fully translated frame, paste the targeted sequence in Ms-word, the first 18 nucleotides or bps will serve as forward primer. However, the last 18 nucleotides are copied and pasted in reverse complement and the generated sequence will serve as reverse primer.
- (Highlight the first 18 and last 18 nucleotides for ease)

➢ **ATGGAGGGATATGATAAT**GGGTCGTTGTATGCTCCTTTTTTGTCG
TTGAAATCTCATTCGAAACCAGAGCTGCATCAAGGCGAAGAAGA
GAGCTCAAAGGTTAGATCAGAAGGTTGTTCGAAAAGCGTGGAGT
CGTCGAAAAAGAAGGGGAAGAAACAAAGGTATGCGTTTCAAAC
AAGGAGCCAAGTGGATATTCTTGATGATGGTTATCGATGGAGGAA
ATATGGCCAAAAGGCCGTCAAGAACAACAAGTTCCCTAGGAGTT
ACTATAGGTGTACATATGGAGGATGCAATGTGAAGAAGCAAGTG
CAAAGATTAACAGTGGACCAAGAAGTGGTCGTGACAACCTACG
AAGGAGTGCATTCGCATCCCATCGAGAAATCCACCGAAAACTTCG
AGCATATTCTCACTCAAATGCAA**ATCTACTCTTCTTTCTAG**

➢ **Forward primer:** ATGGAGGGATATGATAAT

➢ **Reverse Primer:** ATCTACTCTTCTTTCTAG

➢ Reverse complement of last 18 nucleotides: CTAGAAAGAAGAGTA
GAT

- Reverse complement is used to convert a sequence of DNA into its reverse complement, or reverse-complement counterpart. By pasting the FASTA sequence in the text area given, you can easily get the reverse complement for your sequence by clicking on the 'submit' option (Fig. 14.3).

- Now the whole sequence is copied from the word and pasted in the given field on NEB cutter in the following way (Fig. 14.4).

- Click on submit to go ahead.

- It will display the restriction map of the sequence which enables to identify restriction sites within the cds sequence (Fig. 14.5).

- The restriction sites that are absent in the gene of interest are inserted in the forward and reverse primers. Click on '0 cutters' to select the enzymes that do not cut your target gene sequence. A long list is displayed as shown in the figure below (Fig. 14.6).

- Then select two restriction enzymes and perform their double digest using DoubleDigest Calculator (Fig. 14.7).

- DoubleDigest Calculator conveniently calculates the possible enzymatic reaction buffer, concentration of enzymes, conditions for incubation and additives that are required in our double digest reaction.

- A chart of Reaction Conditions for Restriction Enzymes are displayed.

Note: On the basis of high star activity or if restriction enzyme activity is less than 20%, buffer is not recommended.

- Here we selected BamHl (5′ G▾GATCC 3′ and 3′ CCTAG▲G 5′) and PstI (5′ CTGCA▾G 3′ and 3′ G▲ACGTC 5′).

- After selecting the suitable restriction enzymes, paste their 5′−3′ recognition sites ahead of the 18 bp sequence selected for both the forward and reverse primer in the following way.

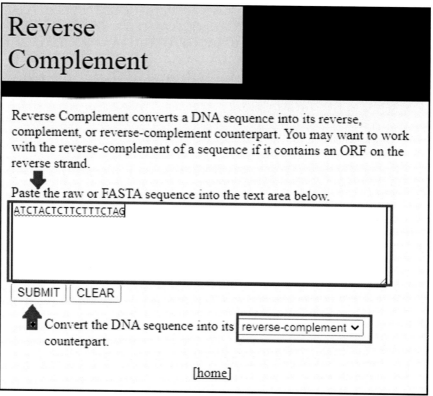

**FIGURE 14.3**

Reverse complement

This tool will take a DNA sequence and find the large, non-overlapping open reading frames using the E.coli genetic code and the sites for all Type II and commercially available sequence just once. By default, only enzymes available from NEB are used, but other sets may be chosen. Just enter your sequence and "submit". Further options will appear with **input file is 1 MByte, and the maximum sequence length is 300 KBases.** What's new in V2.0   Citing NEBcutter

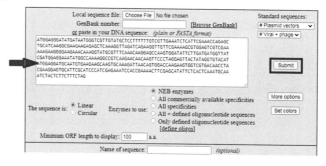

**FIGURE 14.4**

Sequence input in NEB

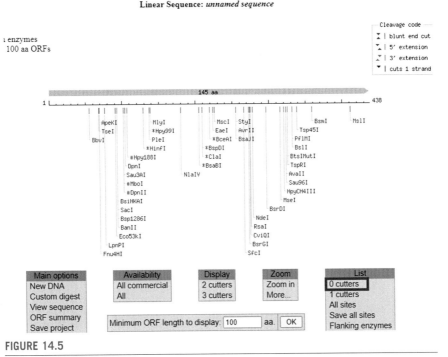

**FIGURE 14.5**

Linear sequence in NEB

> ➤ Forward primer: G˅GATC▴CATGGAGGGATATGATAAT
> ➤ Reverse primer: C▴TGCA˅GCTAGAAAGAAGAGTAGAT

- For our selected restriction enzymes, it's necessary to see their recognition and cut sites while cloning a gene.
- You may also put overhangs, so that enzymes fit on and will cut the vector efficiently in the following way.

  Forward primer: **ATAATA G˅GATC▴CATGGAGGGATATGATAAT**
  Reverse primer: **ATGATC C▴TGCA˅GCTAGAAAGAAGAGTAGAT**

- Use Oligocalc tool to check self-complementarity of the designed primers in order to avoid hairpin formation. Simply paste the sequences of both the primers designed in the field given and click on 'Self Complementarity' option (Fig. 14.8).
- After clicking on 'Self Complementarity' option, a new window is displayed showing the potential hairpin formation if any. Also the self-annealing sites are marked in red. Here we did not get any hairpin formation as shown in the following figure (Fig. 14.9).
- The desired target gene is incorporated within vector in such a way that the codons present in our primer are in frame with that of the vector to carry out expression.

# Enzymes that don't cut

## unnamed sequence

Number of cuts [= ▾] [0]  [OK]  [Save as text file]

| # | Enzyme | Specificity |
|---|--------|-------------|
| 1 | AatII | G‚ACGT˅C |
| 2 | Acc65I | G˅GTAC‚C |
| 3 | AccI | GT˅MK‚AC |
| 4 | AciI | C˅CG‚C |
| 5 | AclI | AA˅CG‚TT |
| 6 | AcuI | CTGAAG(N)$_{14}$‚NN˅ |
| 7 | AfeI | AGC˅GCT |
| 8 | AflII | C˅TTAA‚G |
| 9 | AflIII | A˅CRYG‚T |
| 10 | AgeI | A˅CCGG‚T |
| 11 | AhdI | GACNN‚N˅NNGTC |
| 12 | AleI | CACNN˅NNGTG |
| 13 | AlwI | GGATCNNNN˅N‚ |
| 14 | AlwNI | CAG‚NNN˅CTG |
| 15 | ApaI | G‚GGCC˅C |
| 16 | ApaLI | G˅TGCA‚C |
| 17 | ApoI | R˅AATT‚Y |
| 18 | AscI | GG˅CGCG‚CC |
| 19 | AseI | AT˅TA‚AT |
| 20 | AsiSI | GCG‚AT˅CGC |
| 21 | AvaI | C˅YCGR‚G |
| 22 | BaeGI | G‚KGCM˅C |
| 23 | BaeI | ‚(N)$_5$˅(N)$_{10}$ACNNNNGTAYC(N)$_7$‚(N)$_5$˅ |
| 24 | BamHI | G˅GATC‚C |
| 25 | BanI | G˅GYRC‚C |

**FIGURE 14.6**

Enzyme and their specificity

---

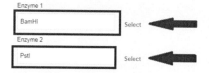

Select two restriction enzymes to get buffer recommendations for double digestion reactions:

Enzyme 1

[ BamHI ]  Select ⬅

Enzyme 2

[ PstI ]  Select ⬅

**FIGURE 14.7**

Double digestion of restriction enzymes

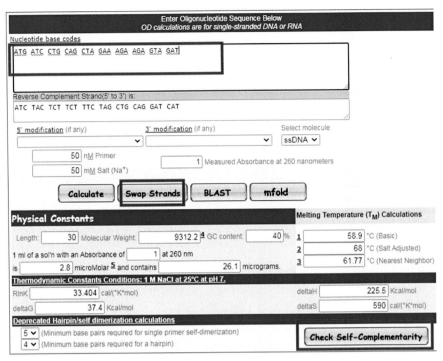

**FIGURE 14.8**

Swap strands in oligodt

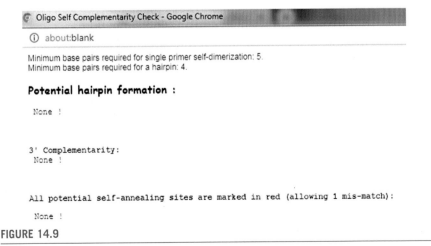

**FIGURE 14.9**

Hairpin formation

- A brief recap of primer designing for cloning is given below:
  - ➤ **ATGGAGGGATATGATAA**TGGGTCGTTGTATGCTCCTTTTTTGTCG
    TTGAAATCTCATTCGAAACCAGAGCTGCATCAAGGCGAAGAAGA
    GAGCTCAAAGGTTAGATCAGAAGGTTGTTCGAAAAGCGTGGAGT
    CGTCGAAAAAGAAGGGGAAGAAACAAAGGTATGCGTTTCAAAC
    AAGGAGCCAAGTGGATATTCTTGATGATGGTTATCGATGGAGGAA
    ATATGGCCAAAAGGCCGTCAAGAACAACAAGTTCCCTAGGAGTT
    ACTATAGGTGTACATATGGAGGATGCAATGTGAAGAAGCAAGTGC
    AAAGATTAACAGTGGACCAAGAAGTGGTCGTGACAACCTACGAA
    GGAGTGCATTCGCATCCCATCGAGAAATCCACCGAAAACTTCGAG
    CATATTCTCACTCAAATGCAA**ATCTACTCTTCTTTCTAG**
- **Forward primer** − ATGGAGGGATATGATAAT
  R.E-BamHI (5′ G▾GATCC 3′&3′ CCTAG▴G 5′)
  ATAATA G▾GATC▴CATGGAGGGATATGATAAT.

  Overhangs R.E site
- **Reverse primer** − ATCTACTCTTCTTTCTAG
  Its reverse complement − CTAGAAAGAAGAGTAGAT
  R.E-PstI (5′ CTGCA▾G 3′ & 3′ GACGT C 5′)
  ATGATC C▴TGCA▾GCTAGAAAGAAGAGTAGAT
  Note − R.E (restriction enzyme).

---

## Further reading

Arányi, T., Váradi, A., Simon, I., 2006. The BiSearch web server. BMC Bioinf. 7, 431.

Arvidsson, S., 2008. BMC Bioinf. 9, 465.

Bond, S.R., Naus, C.C., 2012. Nucl. Acids Res. 40 (Web Server issue), W209−W213.

Brandt, B.W., Bonder, M.J., Huse, S.M., Zaura, E., 2012. Nucl. Acids Res. 40, W82−W87.

Kibbe, W.A., 2007. OligoCalc: an online oligonucleotide properties calculator. Nucl. Acids Res. 35 (webserver issue). May 25.

Qu, W., 2012. Nucleic Acids Res. 40 (Web Server issue), W205−W208.

Stothard, P., 2000. The sequence manipulation suite: JavaScript programs for analyzing and formatting protein and DNA sequences. BioTechniques 28, 1102−1104.

Untergasser, A., Nijveen, H., Rao, X., Bisseling, T., Geurts, R., Leunissen, J.A., 2007. Primer3Plus, an enhanced web interface to Primer3. Nucleic Acids Res. (Web Server issue), W71−W74.

Vincze, T., Posfai, J., Roberts, R.J., 2003. NEBcutter: a program to cleave DNA with restriction enzymes. Nucleic Acids Res. 31, 3688−3691.

Yoon, H., Leitner, T., 2015. Bioinformatics 31, 1472−1474.

# Restriction analysis tools

15

## 15.1 Introduction

A restriction enzyme is a protein that recognises a short, unique sequence and only cuts the DNA in that particular site known as the target or restriction site. These proteins are available in microbes and are essential for the viral and other foreign DNA defence component. The names that have been given to restriction enzymes come from the organism in which they have been isolated like genus and strain. One of the most important and most widely used restriction enzymes is EcoRI. EcoRI refers to *Escherichia coli*'s first restriction enzyme, Strain RY13. There are more than 400 known restriction enzymes in microscopic organisms like bacteria that distinguish and cut more than 100 diverse DNA sequences. The progression of recombinant DNA technology prompted the finding of the restriction enzyme and to the clarification of their mechanism and activity particularity. Without a doubt, restriction enzymes are important proteins in numerous molecular science and genetic engineering procedures.

## 15.2 What is restriction mapping?

The restriction map is the portrayal of double-stranded DNA dependent on the situation of the restriction endonucleases cleavage sites. Digestion with uncommon restriction enzymes, which as a rule have 6-bp recognition sites, yields few enormous DNA parts. Most enzymes, then again, cut DNA all the more regularly and produce countless number of fragments (of not exactly a 100 to in excess of a 1000 bp long). By and large, restriction enzymes with 4-base recognition sites produce sections of 256 bases, while restriction enzymes with 6-base recognition sites produce fragments of 4000 bases.

## 15.3 Why is restriction mapping useful?

It has been utilised in a variety of fields. Restriction mapping in molecular biology is the first step in many recombinant DNA processes. DNA fragments cloning and subcloning into a range of vectors, mutagenesis-related studies and other procedures

BioInformatics for Everyone. https://doi.org/10.1016/B978-0-323-91128-3.00010-0

involving the definition of DNA are essential. On the other hand, although the sequence of the DNA is normally desirable, certain DNA manipulations can be carried out in practical terms without any prior knowledge of its sequence. Digestion by restriction enzymes are used in genetic fingerprinting and RFLP analysis. In medicine restriction mapping has a role to align possible organ donors in the DNA profiles; in biological studies for the investigation of wild animal and plant populations; in medical forensics for the analysing and examination of the paternity and crimes of DNA from the blood, hair, saliva and semen.

## 15.4 Webcutter 2.0

It is one of the important free detection online softwares for linear and circular DNA. The webcutter tool generates restriction maps of nucleotide sequences in a versatile manner, resulting in a nicely formatted output.

### 15.4.1 Step by step method

There are two ways to input your sequence. The DNA sequences can be copied and pasted, or entered into the box or the 'Browse … ' button allows you to import a sequence file from your device.

For example: Taking the DNA sequence of *Brassica oleraceae* isolate HDEM chloroplast, complete genome from the NCBI portal (Fig. 15.1).

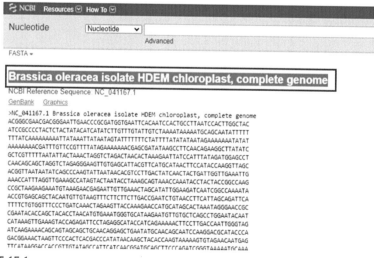

**FIGURE 15.1**

DNA sequence of *Brassica oleraceae* isolate HDEM chloroplast.

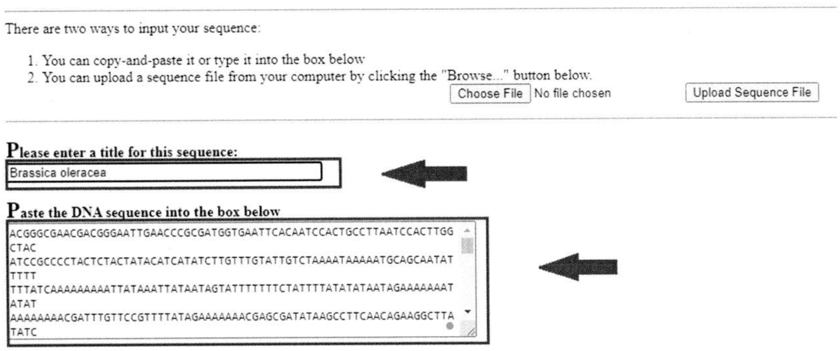

There are two ways to input your sequence:

1. You can copy-and-paste it or type it into the box below
2. You can upload a sequence file from your computer by clicking the "Browse..." button below.

[Choose File] No file chosen    [Upload Sequence File]

**Please enter a title for this sequence:**

Brassica oleracea ◄━━━━

**Paste the DNA sequence into the box below**

ACGGGCGAACGACGGGAATTGAACCCGCGATGGTGAATTCACAATCCACTGCCTTAATCCACTTGG
CTAC
ATCCGCCCCTACTCTACTATACATCATATCTTGTTTGTATTGTCTAAAATAAAAATGCAGCAATAT
TTTT
TTTATCAAAAAAAAATTATAAATTATAATAGTATTTTTTTCTATTTTATATATAATAGAAAAAAAT
ATAT
AAAAAAAACGATTTGTTCCGTTTTATAGAAAAAAACGAGCGATATAAGCCTTCAACAGAAGGCTTA
TATC

◄━━━━

**FIGURE 15.2**

Sequence in webcutter.

- Enter the title name for the sequence and then paste the DNA sequence into the box (Fig. 15.2).
- Select the type of analysis whether linear or circular (Fig. 15.3).
- You can choose enzymes of your choice for analysis or let the software choose all enzymes in the databases (Fig. 15.3).
- Click on 'Analyze sequence' (Fig. 15.3).
- The result page will give you restriction enzyme sites on your submitted sequences and it will also give table by enzyme name (Fig. 15.4A and Fig. 15.4B).

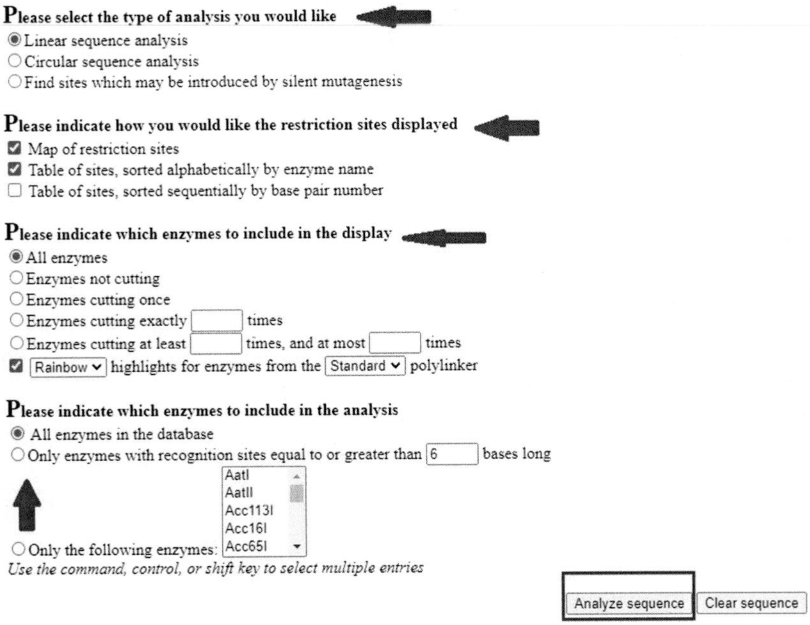

**Please select the type of analysis you would like** ◄━━━━
◉ Linear sequence analysis
○ Circular sequence analysis
○ Find sites which may be introduced by silent mutagenesis

**Please indicate how you would like the restriction sites displayed** ◄━━━━
☑ Map of restriction sites
☑ Table of sites, sorted alphabetically by enzyme name
☐ Table of sites, sorted sequentially by base pair number

**Please indicate which enzymes to include in the display** ◄━━━━
◉ All enzymes
○ Enzymes not cutting
○ Enzymes cutting once
○ Enzymes cutting exactly [    ] times
○ Enzymes cutting at least [    ] times, and at most [    ] times
☑ [Rainbow ▾] highlights for enzymes from the [Standard ▾] polylinker

**Please indicate which enzymes to include in the analysis**
◉ All enzymes in the database
○ Only enzymes with recognition sites equal to or greater than [6] bases long

|  |
|---|
| Aatl |
| Aatll |
| Acc113l |
| Acc16l |
| Acc65l |

○ Only the following enzymes: Acc65l
*Use the command, control, or shift key to select multiple entries*

[Analyze sequence]  [Clear sequence]

**FIGURE 15.3**

Choose enzymes.

**(A)** **Brassica oleracea**

1190 base pairs

**(B)**

| Enzyme name | No. of sites | Positions cuts | Recognition sequence |
|---|---|---|---|
| Acc113I | 1 | 516 | agt/act |
| AccB1I | 1 | 1147 | g/gyrcc |
| AccII | 1 | 27 | cg/cg |
| AciI | 4 | 28 76 564 770 | ccgc |
| AclWI | 1 | 1185 | ggatc |
| AcsI | 1 | 35 | r/aatty |
| AfaI | 2 | 516 855 | gt/ac |
| AflIII | 2 | 452 792 | a/crygt |
| AluI | 8 | 359 641 782 932 944 1019 1094 1127 | ag/ct |
| Alw21I | 1 | 824 | g∞gcw/c |
| AlwI | 1 | 1195 | ggatc |
| AlwNI | 1 | 944 | cagnnn/ctg |
| ApoI | 1 | 35 | r/aatty |
| AseI | 1 | 446 | at/taat |
| AsiSI | 1 | 984 | at/taat |
| Asp700I | 1 | 888 | gaann/nnttc |
| AspMI | 1 | 824 | g∞gcw/c |
| Asp59I | 1 | 1058 | g/gncc |
| AsuI | 1 | 1058 | g/gncc |
| AvaII | 1 | 1058 | g/gwcc |
| BanI | 1 | 1147 | g/gyrcc |
| Bbv12I | 1 | 824 | g∞gcw/c |
| BbvI | 6 | 131 360 642 933 1095 1131 | gcagc |
| BclI | 1 | 717 | t/gatca |
| BfaI | 7 | 303 309 360 366 599 725 867 | c/tag |
| BlpI | 1 | 823 | gc/tnagc |
| Bme18I | 1 | 1058 | g/gwcc |
| BmyI | 1 | 824 | gdgch/c |
| Bpu1102I | 1 | 823 | gc/tnagc |
| BsaJI | 2 | 410 964 | c/cnngg |
| Bsc4I | 3 | 410 550 1103 | ccnnnn/nnngg |
| Bse118I | 1 | 551 | r/ccggy |
| BseDI | 2 | 410 964 | c/cnngg |
| Bsh1236I | 1 | 27 | cg/cg |
| BshNI | 1 | 1147 | g/gyrcc |
| BsiMKAI | 1 | 824 | g∞gcw/c |
| BsiSI | 1 | 552 | c/cgg |
| BsiYI | 3 | 411 551 1104 | ccnnnn/nnngg |
| BslI | 3 | 411 551 1104 | ccnnnn/nnngg |
| BsoFI | 7 | 128 357 561 639 930 1092 1128 | gc/ngc |

**FIGURE 15.4**

A and B Result page.

## 15.5 WatCut

WatCut is a freely available online tool. It is used for mutation analysis, restriction analysis and single nucleotide polymorphism analysis.

**For restriction analysis (restriction mapping):**

- Search your DNA sequence for restriction enzyme cleavage sites by simply uploading a sequence file or pasting DNA sequence in the box.
- For example: Taking DNA sequence of *B. oleraceae* isolate HDEM chloroplast, complete genome from the NCBI portal (Fig. 15.1).
- Paste sequence in the empty box (Fig. 15.5).
- After pasting sequence, click on 'Submit new sequence'.
- The result page will give you results in graphical form, tabular form and restriction enzymes 'with sequences' (Fig. 15.6).

**For silent mutation analysis:**

Search for mutations in your primer that result in new restriction sites without modifying the encoded protein sequence.

- Paste your oligonucleotide sequence in the box.

For example: paste a random sequence like ATGGAGGGATATGATAAT in the box (Fig. 15.7).

- Click on 'submit sequence'.
- Select the correct reading frame and click on 'Analyze'.
- The result of silent mutation scan will show a site of mutations of the submitted oligonucleotide (Fig. 15.8).

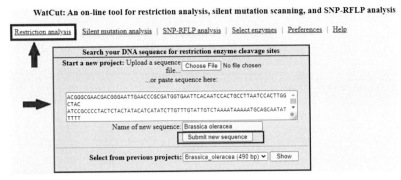

**FIGURE 15.5**

Sequence in watcut.

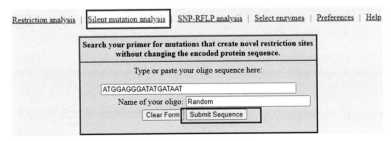

**FIGURE 15.6**

Result page.

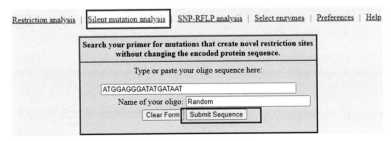

**FIGURE 15.7**

Sequence input.

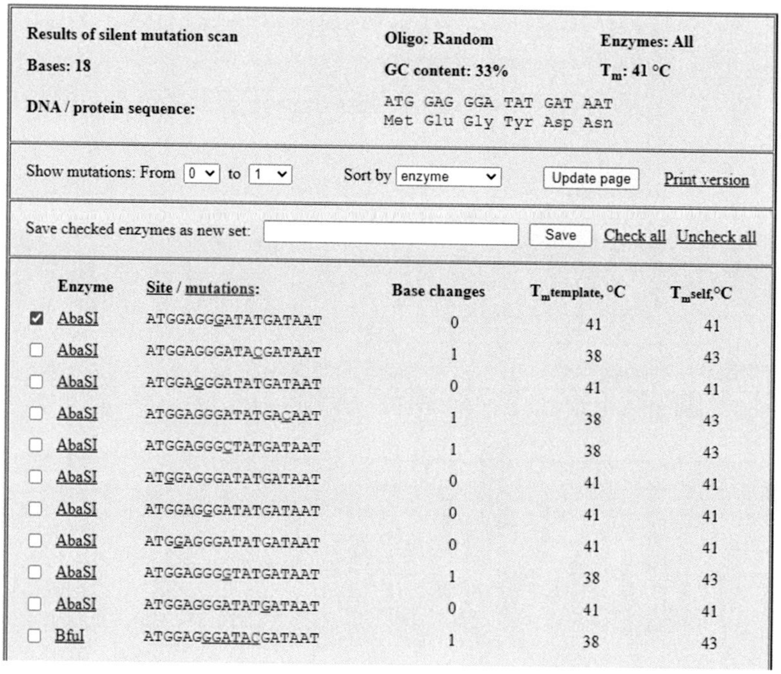

| | Enzyme | Site / mutations: | Base changes | $T_m$template, °C | $T_m$self,°C |
|---|---|---|---|---|---|
| | **Results of silent mutation scan** | | **Oligo: Random** | **Enzymes: All** | |
| | **Bases: 18** | | **GC content: 33%** | **$T_m$: 41 °C** | |
| | **DNA / protein sequence:** | | ATG GAG GGA TAT GAT AAT<br>Met Glu Gly Tyr Asp Asn | | |

Show mutations: From [0 ▾] to [1 ▾]    Sort by [enzyme ▾]    [Update page]    Print version

Save checked enzymes as new set: [                    ]    [Save]    Check all  Uncheck all

| | Enzyme | Site / mutations: | Base changes | $T_m$template, °C | $T_m$self,°C |
|---|---|---|---|---|---|
| ☑ | AbaSI | ATGGAGGGATATGATAAT | 0 | 41 | 41 |
| ☐ | AbaSI | ATGGAGGGATACGATAAT | 1 | 38 | 43 |
| ☐ | AbaSI | ATGGAGGGATATGATAAT | 0 | 41 | 41 |
| ☐ | AbaSI | ATGGAGGGATATGACAAT | 1 | 38 | 43 |
| ☐ | AbaSI | ATGGAGGGCTATGATAAT | 1 | 38 | 43 |
| ☐ | AbaSI | ATGGAGGGATATGATAAT | 0 | 41 | 41 |
| ☐ | AbaSI | ATGGAGGGATATGATAAT | 0 | 41 | 41 |
| ☐ | AbaSI | ATGGAGGGATATGATAAT | 0 | 41 | 41 |
| ☐ | AbaSI | ATGGAGGGGTATGATAAT | 1 | 38 | 43 |
| ☐ | AbaSI | ATGGAGGGATATGATAAT | 0 | 41 | 41 |
| ☐ | BfuI | ATGGAGGGATACGATAAT | 1 | 38 | 43 |

**FIGURE 15.8**

Silent mutation results.

## 15.6 Restriction enzyme picker

REPK identifies sets of four available restriction enzymes that, when combined, uniquely distinguish designated sequence groups from a FASTA format sequence file supplied for use in T-RFLP. This software will help you select particular enzymes which can distinguish the various groups in your database if you are using a database with recognised sequences.

## 15.7 Restriction Analyzer

It is a freely available software that has several uses like the following:

- It is used to carry out in silico restriction analysis.
- It is used to find the absent and unique sites more rapidly.
- It displays the results in tabular and graphical form.
- It is also used to analyse restriction fragments.
- It simulates a gel electrophoresis.

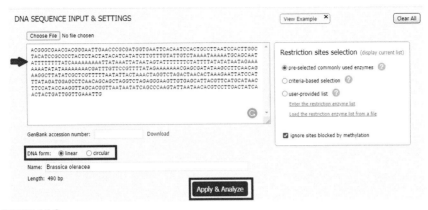

**FIGURE 15.9**

Sequence input in Restriction Analyzer.

## 15.7.1 Step by step method

- Choose a file from your computer to upload or simply paste DNA sequence of interest.

  For example: Taking DNA sequence of *B. oleraceae* isolate HDEM chloroplast, complete genome from the NCBI portal as shown in (Fig. 15.1).

- Paste sequence in the open box (Fig. 15.9).
- Choose the form of DNA whether circular or linear.
- Click on 'Apply and Analyze'.
- The result page will display restriction sites overview, restriction fragments and annotated sequences (Fig. 15.10).

## 15.8 Restriction Comparator

Restriction Comparator is an online app designed that is used in bioinformatics for a different purposes. Some of which are as follows:

- It is used to carry out parallel restriction analysis
- It compares two sequences at the same time
- It gives distinctive sites for restrictions
- It is also used to visualise restriction patterns

## 15.9 Restriction enzyme digest of DNA

It is one of the simplest tool that is freely available online for restriction analysis.

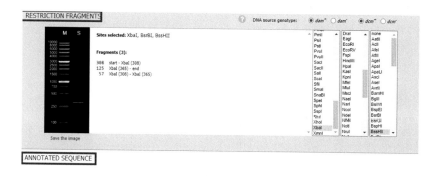

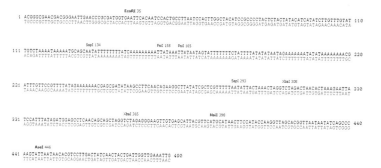

**FIGURE 15.10**

Restriction site overview.

## 15.10 RestrictionMapper

It is one of the freely available online tool for mapping of restriction endonuclease sites on a DNA sequence.

### 15.10.1 Step by step methods

- Open restrictionmapper using link www.restrictionmapper.org.

  For example: Taking DNA sequence of *B. oleraceae* isolate HDEM chloroplast, complete genome from the NCBI portal as shown in (Fig. 15.1).

- Name your sequence and paste in the open box (Fig. 15.11).
- Choose the form of DNA whether circular or linear.
- Click on 'Map Sites'.
- The result page will show map sites (Fig. 15.12).

  WebDSV — is a simple molecular biology software for creating, editing and analysing DNA sequences, as well as marking and visualising sequence features and

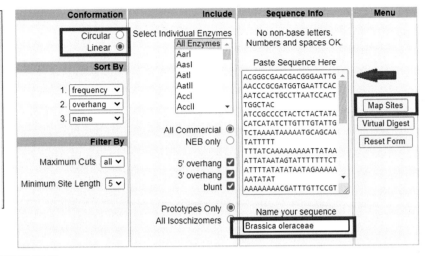

**FIGURE 15.11**

Sequence input in RestrictionMapper.

generating plasmid maps. One can analyse sites with WebDSV, perform silicon molecular cloning and create PCR primers.

In silico restriction digest of complete genomes — It enables computerised digestion of more than 300 genomes of prokaryotes as well as SPFG electrophoretic fragment separation.

## 15.11 **Sequence extractor**

This software is used to produce a restriction map and polymerase chain reaction primer. Protein translations as well as intron/exon boundaries are depicted. It is more often used to build DNA constructs in silico. The main features of sequence extractor are as follows:

- It supports template sequences in GenBank, EMBL, FASTA and raw formats.
- It shows the forward as well as reverse translations listed in a GenBank or EMBL entry.
- It does not compute new translations but uses protein sequences listed in GenBank or EMBL entrance.
- Restriction sites may be shown, as well as a summary of restriction site locations.
- Imperfect primer sites can be found.

Note: To learn about the most basic protocol for performing Restriction Analysis Using NEBcutter, see Chapter 16.

**Name:** Brassica oleraceae

**Conformation:** linear

**Overhang:** five_prime, three_prime, blunt

**Minimum Site Length:** 5 bases

**Maximum Number of Cuts:** all

**Included:** all commercial, prototypes only

**Noncutters:** AarI, AatII, AbsI, AccI, AclI, AcyI, AflII, AgeI, AjuI, AlfI, AloI, AlwNI, ApaI, BglII, BplI, Bpu10I, BsaAI, BsaBI, BsaXI, BseMII, BsePI, BseRI, BseSI, BseYI, BsgI, Bsn DrdI, Eam1105I, Eco31I, Eco47III, Eco57I, Eco57MI, EcoNI, EcoRII, EcoRV, Esp3I, FalI, NaeI, NarI, NcoI, NdeI, NheI, NmeAIII, NotI, NruI, NspI, OliI, PacI, PasI, PflMI, PfoI, PleI ScaI, PI-SceI, SduI, SexAI, SfaNI, SfiI, SgfI, SgrAI, SgrDI, SmaI, SmlI, SnaBI, SpeI, SphI,

| Name | Sequence | Site Length | Overhang | Frequency | Cut Positions |
|------|----------|-------------|----------|-----------|---------------|
| BtrI | CACGTC | 6 | blunt | 1 | 455 |
| AflIII | ACRYGT | 6 | five_prime | 1 | 452 |
| ApoI | RAATTY | 6 | five_prime | 1 | 35 |
| BtgZI | GCGATG | 6 | five_prime | 1 | 42 |
| EcoP15I | CAGCAG | 6 | five_prime | 1 | 384 |
| EcoRI | GAATTC | 6 | five_prime | 1 | 35 |
| FauI | CCCGC | 5 | five_prime | 1 | 32 |
| FokI | GGATG | 5 | five_prime | 1 | 56 |
| StyI | CCWWGG | 6 | five_prime | 1 | 410 |
| VspI | ATTAAT | 6 | five_prime | 1 | 446 |
| BtsI | GCAGTG | 6 | three_prime | 1 | 46 |

**FIGURE 15.12**

Result page- map sites.

## Further reading

Collins, R.E., Rocap, G., 2007. REPK: an analytical web server to select restriction endonu-cleases for terminal restriction fragment length polymorphism analysis. Nucleic Acids Res. 35 (Database issue), W58–W62.

Heinrichs, A., 2007. Making the cut: discovery of restriction enzymes. Nat. Milest. 8, S7.

Meselson, M., Yuan, R., 1968. DNA restriction enzyme from *E. coli*. Nature 217, 1110–1114.

Raghava, G.P.S., 2001. A web server for computing size of DNA/Protein fragment using graphical method. Biotech Softw. Internet Rep. 2, 198–200.

Smith, H.O., Wilcox, K.W., 1970. A restriction enzyme from Hemophilus influenzae. I. Purification and general properties. J. Mol. Biol. 51, 379–391.

Vincze, T., Posfai, J., Roberts, R.J., 2003. NEBcutter: a program to cleave DNA with restriction enzymes. Nucleic Acids Res. 31, 3688–3691.

Maarek, Y.S., Jacovi, M., Shtalhaim, M., Ur, S., Zernik, D., Ben-Shaul, I.Z., 1997. WebCutter: a system for dynamic and tailorable site mapping. Comput. Netw. ISDN Syst. 29 (8–13), 1269–1279.

# Restriction analysis using NEBcutter

16

## 16.1 Step-by-step tutorial

The various steps to perform restriction mapping using the freely available online software NEBcutter2 programme are given below:

There are a number of ways to insert your sequence of interest in the submission box which are as follows:

1. You can choose your file from the computer by clicking on the 'Choose file' option.
2. You can simply enter GenBank number or even can browse for an accession number using GenBank.
3. You can simply copy your sequence and paste it in the box.

For example: Taking the DNA sequence of *Brassica oleraceae* isolate HDEM chloroplast, complete genome from the NCBI portal (Fig. 16.1).

- Enter the title name for the sequence (Optional) and then paste the DNA sequence into the box (Fig. 16.2).
- Select the type of analysis whether linear or circular (Fig. 16.2).
- You can choose enzymes proved by the NEB tool or simple choose enzymes with all commercially available specificities.
- Click on 'More options' to popup a new tab with additional options which can be selected like met modifications, the type I enzyme uses, changing genetic codes and searching a selected region of the inserted DNA sequence.
- Click on 'submit' option.

When you press the 'Submit' button, the search results are shown for enzymes which are once cut (Fig. 16.3).

- The colour on top of the page describes various cleavage codes and enzyme names.
- One can also select two or three cutter enzymes that is shown in the bottom box, new redrawn sequence will be shown.
- You may make a red mark by clicking on the horizontal string representing the DNA sequence once or twice. Location or area of interest can be zoomed in and out to get more detail out of it.

Bioinformatics for Everyone. https://doi.org/10.1016/B978-0-323-91128-3.00020-3

**159**

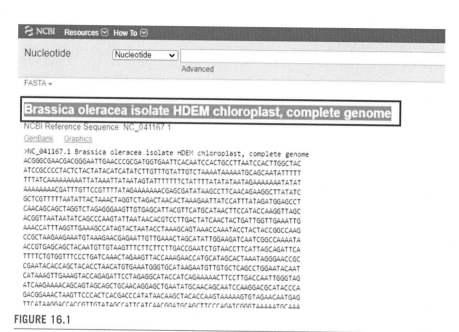

**FIGURE 16.1**

DNA sequence of *Brassica oleraceae* isolate HDEM chloroplast.

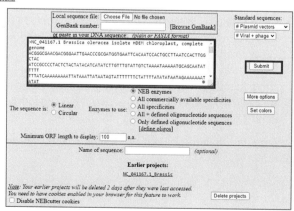

**FIGURE 16.2**

Linear or Circular analysis selection.

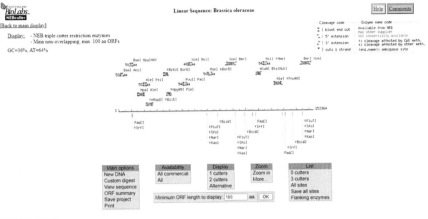

**FIGURE 16.3**

Submission of analyses.

- There is also a 'Main options' shown at the left bottom where the 'Custom digest' option is used to draw maps with enzyme of interest.
- The 'View sequence' option is used to view the submitted sequence.
- 'ORF summary' results in gene table, their coordinates and lengths of poly-peptide at GenBank.

  For instance, Fig. 16.4 displays those enzymes which were not able to cut DNA.

- One can point or click on the features that are displayed in the results tab. It will show additional information like site of recognition and position where restriction enzyme cuts.

# Enzymes that don't cut

## Brassica oleraceae

Number of cuts = ∨ 0      OK      Save as text file

| # | Enzyme | Specificity |
|---|--------|-------------|
| 1 | AscI | GG˅CGCG˄CC |
| 2 | AsiSI | GCG˄AT˅CGC |
| 3 | FseI | GG˄CCGG˅CC |
| 4 | NotI | GC˅GGCC˄GC |
| 5 | SbfI | CC˄TGCA˅GG |
| 6 | SfiI | GGCCN˄NNN˅NGGCC |

**FIGURE 16.4**

Enzymes that don't cut.

- To know the complete information of enzyme, click on the displayed name of enzyme.
- Open ORF Sequence by clicking on 'ORF' option (Fig. 16.5) which shows the coding regions as well as deduced protein sequences.

There are additional options like flanking restriction enzyme sites. The feature 'Locate multiple cutters that excise this ORF' shows flanking sites for restriction enzymes (Fig. 16.6).

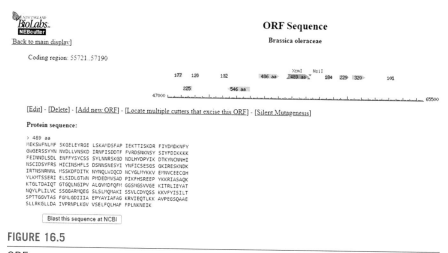

**FIGURE 16.5**

ORF sequence.

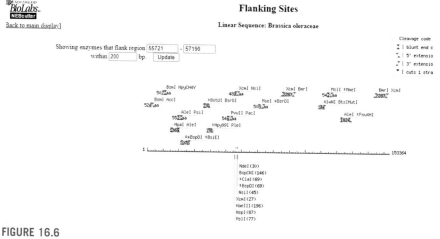

**FIGURE 16.6**

Flanking sites.

# Further reading

Collins, R.E., Rocap, G., 2007. REPK: an analytical web server to select restriction endonucleases for terminal restriction fragment length polymorphism analysis. Nucleic Acids Res. 35 (Database issue), W58—W62.

Heinrichs, A., 2007. Making the cut: discovery of restriction enzymes. Nat. Milest. 8.

Meselson, M., Yuan, R., 1968. DNA restriction enzyme from *E. coli*. Nature 217, 1110—1114.

Roberts, R.J., Halford, S.E., 1993. Type II restriction enzymes. In: Linn, S.M., Lloyd, R.S., Roberts, R.J. (Eds.), Nucleases. Cold Spring Harbor Laboratory Press, pp. 35—88.

Roberts, R.J., Vincze, T., Posfai, J., Macelis, D., 2003. REBASE—restriction enzymes and methyltransferases. Nucleic Acids Res. 31, 418—420.

Saiki, R.K., Gelfand, D.H., Stoffel, S., Scharf, S.J., Higuchi, R., Horn, G.T., Mullis, K.B., Erlich, H.A., 1988. Primer-directed enzymatic amplification of DNA with a thermostable DNA polymerase. Science 239, 487—491.

Smith, H.O., Wilcox, K.W., 1970. A restriction enzyme from Hemophilus influenzae. I. Purification and general properties. J. Mol. Biol. 51, 379—391.

Vincze, T., Posfai, J., Roberts, R.J., 2003. NEBcutter: a program to cleave DNA with restriction enzymes. Nucleic Acids Res. 31, 3688—3691.

# KEGG database

17

KEGG is most widely used and the most important resource database that combines genetic, chemical and systemic functional information. In the fully sequenced genome, in particular, gene catalogues are connected to the cell's, organism's and high-level system's systemic functions which comprise three kinds of molecular webs: KEGG pathway maps, BRITE functional hierarchies and KEGG modules. The KEGG Orthology (KO) framework connects genomes to molecular networks. Diseases and medication are also included in the molecular networks of KEGG.

The KEGG database was established in 1995. At the beginning of KEGG's establishment, it consisted database of four types only viz., Pathway, Genes, Compound and Enzyme. KEGG pathway mapping was performed through ENZYME only because the database contained only of metabolic pathway maps. KEGG was greatly extended later: PATHWAY augmented by BRITE and MODULE; GENES extended to GENOME; GLYCAN and REACTION supplemented to COMPOUND, and KEGG Pathway Mapping substituted for ENZYME. In addition, KEGG has been used more extensively for the study not only of genomics but also transcriptomics, proteomics and glycomics.

## 17.1 Objectives

- Automate and standardise the annotation of existing information about biological systems.
- Maintain genome-sequenced gene catalogues.
- Using LIGAND, maintain catalogues of chemical reactions occurring in living cells.
- Develop novel informatics technologies to aid in the prediction of biological systems and the design of additional experiments.

### 17.1.1 Structure of the KEGG database

The KEGG sub-information library provides online representation of biological structures that are made up of molecular components of different genes, proteins

Bioinformatics for Beginners, https://doi.org/10.1016/B978-0-323-91128-3.00001-X

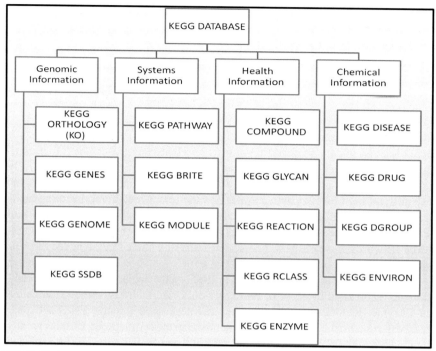

**FIGURE 17.1**

An overview of KEGG databases.

and chemical substances. The interactions, reactions and relationships between these components form a regulatory network diagram (system information), which also includes health information related to drugs and diseases.

Several of the KEGG databases are discussed briefly in the sections below (Fig. 17.1).

## 17.2 KEGG DRUG

The KEGG DRUG is an integrated, unit focussed on the chemical structure and/or chemical portion of an active ingredient and is an extensive drug knowledge resource for approved drugs in Japan, the United States and Europe. Each KEGG DRUG entry has D numbers and original annotations are associated with KEGG, which include therapeutic goals, metabolism of medicines and other information from the network molecular interaction.

## 17.3  KEGG BRITE

This database is an assortment of BRITE functional hierarchy files also known as htext or hierarchical text for hierarchic classifications of different aspects of biological structures. KEGG BRITE contains several kind of partnerships, in comparison to KEGG PATHWAY, restricted to biological interactions and reactions. This database hierarchy includes two classes for genes, proteins and for other substances.

## 17.4  KEGG GENOME

KEGG GENOME is a series of KEGG species, which include organisms that have full genome sequences and are classified by a three- or four-letter organism code, as well as selected viruses with disease relevance. MGENOME, a series of metagenome sequences from environmental samples, complements KEGG GENOME (ecosystems).

## 17.5  KEGG GENES

KEGG GENES is a list of complete genomes of cellular organisms and viruses derived from publicly available resources, primarily NCBI RefSeq and GenBank, and annotated by KEGG using the KO classification system. The collection is augmented by a KEGG-developed collection of functionally characterised proteins extracted from published literature.

## 17.6  KEGG PATHWAY

It is a sequence of hand-drawn pathway diagrams that reflect our current understanding of molecular interaction, reaction and relationship networks.

## 17.7  KEGG DISEASE

KEGG DISEASE is a list of disease entries that focusses exclusively on perturbants, while the molecular networks underlying the majority of diseases remain unknown. Each entry is designated by an H code and includes a list of recognised genetic factors (disease genes), environmental factors, pathogens and therapeutic drugs.

Several of the analysis tools included in the KEGG database include the following:

- **KEGG Mapper:** Software for mapping KEGG PATHWAY/BRITE/MODULE
- **BlastKOALA:** Annotation of KOs and KEGG mapping using BLAST

- **GHOSTX:** Used for annotations and mapping
- **KOALA:** KO annotation and KEGG mapping using HMM profiles
- **BLAST/FASTA:** Checks for sequence similarity
- **SIMCOMP:** Looks for chemical structures that are similar

## 17.8 KEGG PATHWAY database

KEGG pathways comprise several KEGG pathways drawn by researchers manually based on the literature of current research, which depict metabolic processes, processes for environmental knowledge, cellular processes, biological systems, human diseases and drug production. The most important and widely used in all databases is KEGG Pathway.

- Map number: Refers to a reference pathway, which is a simplified, informative metabolic diagram of general reference significance based on current information. A point can also represent a gene, the enzyme encoded by this gene, or the reaction in which this enzyme participates.
- Org number: Species-specific pathway; the aim of this is to replace the K-numbered genes with the corresponding genes in each species.
- ko number: Orthologous genes; dots in the KO pathway indicate orthologous genes.
- rn number: A point in a chemical reaction path represents only the reaction, reactant and form of reaction in which the point is involved.

### 17.8.1 Applications

- Through comparing graphs, we can automatically detect conserved gene clusters across multiple genomes.
- Utilised to identify clusters of enzymes that share a common feature.
- Data browsing and retrieval
- Stimulation and modeling

## 17.9 Protocol 1: using KEGG database

1. Open KEGG's website using www.kegg.jp/. The homepage provides database's entry points and research methods used most frequently.
2. The KEGG2 web service key entry point on the homepage provides a complete database list and computational resources by clicking the KEGG2 content table (Fig. 17.2).
3. Click on KEGG PATHWAY to return to the homepage. In the KEGG2 tab, you can also click on a KEGG PATHWAY connection.

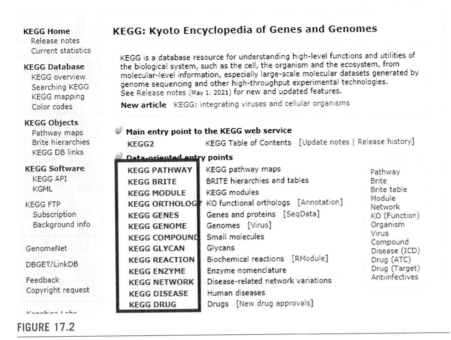

**FIGURE 17.2**

Data-oriented entry points.

4. The KEGG PATHWAY database page is now opened. This page lists all KEGG pathway maps in Categories 0–7 along with links. They are divided into four kinds here.

Category 0–1 = Metabolic pathway maps

Category 2–5 = Regulatory pathway maps

Category 6 = Disease pathway maps

Category 7 = Drug structure maps (Fig. 17.3)

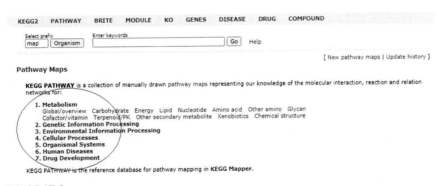

**FIGURE 17.3**

Pathway maps.

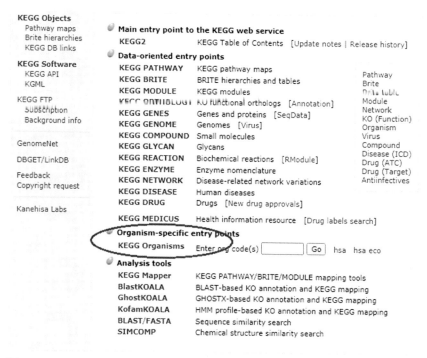

**FIGURE 17.4**

Organism-specific entry points.

5. Go back to the homepage and click on 'KEGG organisms' (Fig. 17.4).
6. A page KEGG Organisms: Complete Genomes is displayed with a unique letter code for various organisms, such as 'rno', for *Rattus norvegicus*, identifies each genome (rat).
7. The links on the left side have helpful details and documents on the KEGG homepage. Tap on 'Current statistics', for instance, to keep the check of KEGG database entries (Fig. 17.5).
8. Click on 'KEGG' to search for KEGG-related databases.
   For example, we search for heat shock protein hsf 70 here (Fig. 17.6).
9. The following page is displayed with a number of results (Fig. 17.7).
10. Click on one of the entry and a page is displayed with a lot of information. Here the Entry field includes an accession number.
    a. The SSDB and Motif fields display search resources for the KEGG SSDB database.
    b. The Position field here indicates position of gene on genome.
    c. The AA seq and NT seq fields are particularly used for retrieving the sequence data for further study (Fig. 17.8).

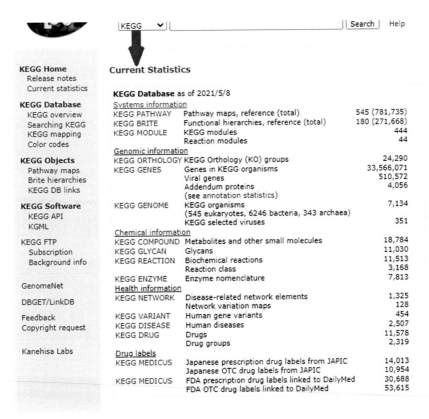

**FIGURE 17.5**

Curren statistics of KEGG Database.

Current Statistics

**FIGURE 17.6**

hst 70 search.

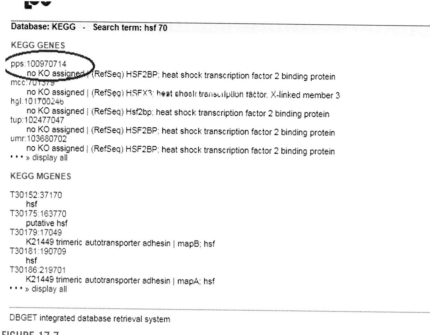

FIGURE 17.7

FIGURE 17.7

KEGG GENES.

## 17.10 Protocol 2: using KEGG pathway database

1. Go to the KEGG main page and then click on the KEGG PATHWAY (Fig. 17.9).
2. In order to review a daily metabolic chart, click Pentose pathway under carbohydrate metabolism (map00030) (Fig. 17.10).
3. The objects on the map are depicted by a number of signs, which in different types of maps can have a slightly different interpretation.
   a. Rectangles — proteins
   b. Smaller circles — organic compounds, glycans and other molecules
   c. Ovals — links to other pathway maps
   To understand different notations press on the 'Help' option.
4. Alternatively you can look for a gene in search field given on the KEGG PATHWAY database page, e.g. we search for WRKY here and click on go (Fig. 17.11).
5. A page is displayed which reveals the pathway of searched gene along with its thumbnail image as well as description (Fig. 17.12).
6. On clicking the thumbnail image the zoomed in view of the pathway is visualised. Our searched gene appears in red colour to show its position in the pathway (Fig. 17.13).

| Entry | 100970714　　　　CDS　　　　T02283 |
|---|---|
| Gene name | HSF2BP |
| Definition | (RefSeq) heat shock transcription factor 2 binding protein |
| Organism | pps　Pan paniscus (bonobo) |
| SSDB | Ortholog　Paralog　GFIT |
| Motif | Pfam: DUF383 MutS_III Exonuc_VII_L Mustang<br>Motif |
| Other DBs | NCBI-GeneID: 100970714<br>NCBI-ProteinID: XP_003823901<br>UniProt: A0A2R9B233 |
| LinkDB | All DBs |
| Position | 21 |
| AA seq | 334 aa　AA seq　DB search<br>MGEAGAAEEACRHMGTKEEFVKVRKKDLERLTTEVMQIRDFLPRILNGEVLESFQKLKIV<br>EKNLEKKEQELEQLKMDCEHFKARLETVQADDIREKKEKLALRQQLNEAKQQLLQQAEYC<br>TEMGAAACTLLWGVSSSEEVVKAILGGDKALKFFSITGQTMESFVKSLDGDVQELDSDES<br>QFVFALAGIVTNVAAIACGREFLVNSSRVLLDTILQLLGDLKPGQCTKLKVLMLMSLYNV<br>SINLKGLKYISESPGFIPLLWWLLSDPDAEVCLHALRLVQSVVLEPEVFSKSASGFRSSL<br>PLQRILAMSKSRNPRLQTAAQELLEDLRTLEHRV |
| NT seq | 1005 nt　NT seq<br>atgggcgaagcgggcgccgctgaggaggcctgccggcacatgggaactaaagaggaattt<br>gttaaagtcagaaagaaggatctggaacggctgacaactgaagtgatgcaaatacgggac<br>ttcttacccagaatactaaatggggaggtgctggagagcttccagaaattaaagattgta<br>gaaaaaacctggaaagaaagagcaagaattagagcagctgaaaatggattgtgagcac<br>tttaaagcccgcctggaaaccgtgcaggccgacgacataagagagaagaaggagaaactg<br>gctcttcgacagcagttgaatgaagcgaagcgacaactcctgcagcaggcagagtattgt<br>acagaaatgggagcagcagcgtgtaccctcttgtggggtgtctccagcagtgaggaagtc<br>gtcaaggccattttgggaggagataaagctttgaagttttcagcatcactggtcaaaca<br>atggagagttttgtgaagtcgttagatggtgatgtccaggagctggattcggatgaaagt<br>cagtttgttttcgctctggctggaattgtcacgaatgttgctgctatagcatgtggtcgt<br>gaattcttggttaattcaagccgggtgctcttggacaccatattgcaacttctgggagac<br>ttgaagccaggacagtgtaccaaactcaaagtgctaatgctgatgtccctatacaatgta<br>agcatcaatttgaaaggcttgaaatacatcagcgagagtccaggattcatccctttgctg<br>tggtggcttttgagtgatccagatgcagaggtgtgccttcacgcactgaggcttgtgcag<br>tctgtggttctggaacctgaagtcttctccaagtcggcctctgggttccggagctccctg<br>cccctgcaacgcatcctggcaatgtccaagagccgcaacccccgcctgcaaaccgcagcc<br>caggagctcctggaagacctccgcactctggagcatcgtgtgtag |

DBGET integrated database retrieval system

## FIGURE 17.8

Entry of a gene.

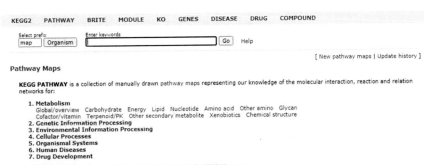

## FIGURE 17.9

Pathway search.

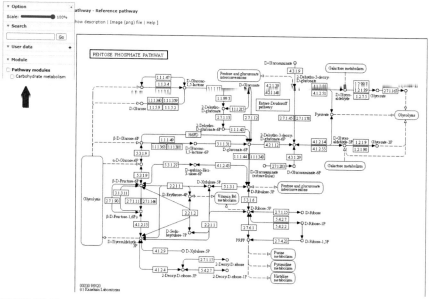

**FIGURE 17.10**

Pathway modules.

**FIGURE 17.11**

WRKY search in KEGG2.

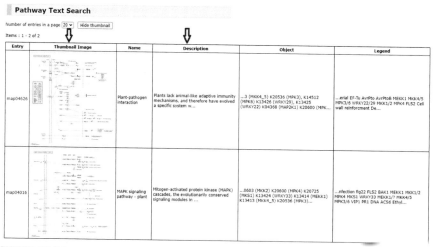

FIGURE 17.12

Pathway text search.

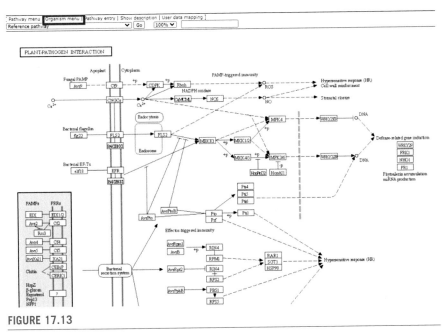

**FIGURE 17.13**

Organism menu.

**7.** The pull-down menu of organisms can be used to colourise the parts.

   **a.** For example: '*Oryza sativa japonica*' can be selected from grass family to show a green coloured pathway with the rice genes involved (Fig. 17.14).

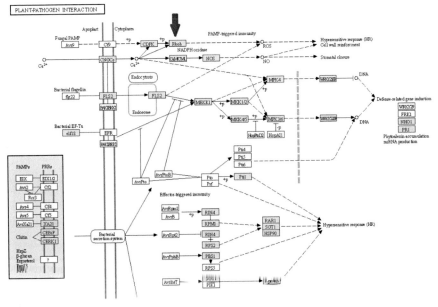

**FIGURE 17.14**

Plant-Pathogen interaction.

## Further reading

Kanehisa, M., Goto, S., Sato, Y., Furumichi, M., Tanabe, M., 2012. KEGG for integration and interpretation of large-scale molecular data sets. Nucleic Acids Res. 40, D109–D114.

Kanehisa, M., Goto, S., 2000. KEGG: kyoto encyclopedia of genes and genomes. Nucleic Acids Res. 28, 27–30.

Tanabe, M., Kanehisa, M., 2012. Using the KEGG database resource. In: Current Protocols in Bioinformatics.

# Database for annotation, visualisation and integrated discovery

## 18.1 Introduction

Biological analysis of a broad list of genes derived from experiments such as microarray genes is a great challenge. The establishment of database for annotation, visualisation and integrated discovery (DAVID) in 2003 and other high-process functional annotation tools addressed the challenge. DAVID is capable of extracting biological features and sense from vast gene lists.

The bioinformatics resource DAVID is an integrated biological know-how base (http://david.niaid.nih.gov) tool designed for systematic bio-signification from a massive gene–protein lists. DAVID is capable of processing any sort of gene list regardless of the genomic platform or software package used. It offers an integrated knowledge base from the most frequently used bioinformatic tools. The tools in the Bioinformatic Resources DAVID serve the objective that a broad gene list resulting from genomic research can be functionally interpreted. The newly added DAVID Bioinformatics Resources contents, features and tool suites would address many things that other methods did not address extensively:

1. Expanding DAVID Knowledge Base on biologic data significantly, integrating over 20 identifiers of gene or protein and provide 40 well-known categories or more of useable annotations from hundreds of databases available for public.
2. Addressing the enhanced interactions among many genes through the development of novel algorithms.
3. DAVID Pathway Viewer can be used to visualise genes.
4. Also, providing users with the capability to design and use personalised gene backgrounds while performing traditional gene-term enrichment analysis.

## 18.2 Tools

DAVID Bioinformatics Resources are newly updated with DAVID Knowledge Base.The five web-based tool suites provided by DAVID are provided in the sections below.

## 18.3 Functional annotation tool

This tool helps users to do mapping of functional annotation, enrichment analysis-related functional annotation and functional clustering based on gene-to-annotation relationships.

## 18.4 Gene functional classification tool

This tool is used to produce gene-to-gene similarity matrix of the genes based on functional annotation that is shared from multiple functions. This new algorithm for clustering divides closely related genes into functional groups.

## 18.5 Gene ID conversion tool

This tool helps its users can convert gene IDs to other identifier forms by using it with DAVID Knowledge base robust gene ID mapping portal. Users can also identify and assess the unclear or contaminating accessions included in a user list.

## 18.6 Gene name viewer

This method is used to identify the corresponding gene names for each unique gene ID. In addition, it also provides links to the DAVID Gene Report, where each gene is profiled in detail.

## 18.7 NIAID pathogen genome browser

NIAID Pathogen Browser can be used to screen species with biologically important keywords of interests for the most relevant genes. It may help scientists understand the genes associated with a pathogen of interest (Table 18.1).

**Table 18.1** Some important websites.

| | |
|---|---|
| DAVID Home Page | http://david.niaid.nih.gov |
| DAVID Knowledgebase Download | http://david.abcc.ncifcrf.gov/knowledgbase |
| DAVID Functional Annotation Tool Suite | http://david.abcc.ncifcrf.gov/summary.jsp |
| DAVID Gene Functional Classification Tool Suite | http://david.abcc.ncifcrf.gov/gene2gene.jsp |
| DAVID Gene ID Conversion Tool | http://david.abcc.ncifcrf.gov/conversion.jsp |
| DAVID Gene Name Batch Viewer | http://david.abcc.ncifcrf.gov/list.jsp |
| DAVID NIAID Pathogen Browser Tool | http://david.abcc.ncifcrf.gov/GB.jsp |

## 18.8 Terminology

### 18.8.1 Annotation category

A group of sources of annotation gathering related biological queries.

### 18.8.2 Annotation source

A separate category database.

### 18.8.3 DAVID gene ID

Internal ID created in DAVID framework on 'DAVID Gene concept'.

### 18.8.4 DAVID ID%

After the user's input gene IDs have been converted to the corresponding DAVID gene ID, the percentage of DAVID genes are listed in the list of specific annotations.

### 18.8.5 DAVID knowledgebase

It is represented DAVID Oracle databases that collect a wide variety of publicly available bioinformatics annotation information.

### 18.8.6 EASE score

An alternate name for Fisher Exact DAVID statistics, referring to a single-tail Fisher Exact probability value used for study of gene enrichment.

### 18.8.7 Term

A detailed annotation source.

## 18.9 DAVID file formats

DAVID may upload tab-delimited data/files. The first file column should contain the gene ID for a single gene list and an optional value for the second column (e.g. fold change, *P*-value, etc.). Remove the headings of the column and save the file (as Tab delimited text file). Choose File > Save As > and then choose Text (*.txt) to convert the excel file in this format. For saving your annotated gene list as an Ms excel file from your browser simply select File > Save As > and then type the.xlsx file name and save on your hard drive. This file can then be opened in Ms Excel.

## 18.10 Functions

DAVID bioinformatics tools can help users in a number of ways:

- converting gene IDs as well as diagnosing and solving gene ID-related problems
- finding gene names from a list
- functionally related gene groups can be discovered
- identifying enriched annotation terms
- gene and disease associations can be linked easily
- functional domains as well as motifs can be found
- proteins that show property of interaction can be listed
- searching for functionally similar genes in genome

## 18.11 Protocol

The steps for submitting a user's gene ID to DAVID are as follows:

- To upload a gene list, visit http://david.abcc.ncifcrf.gov.
- Submit a list of genes or use the built-in demo lists.
- You can simply paste interested gene IDs in the open box (A) or upload file from your computer in box (B).
- Choose the correct form of gene identifier.
- Choose the list type whether gene list or background.
- Click on the 'Submit List' option (Fig. 18.1).
- The resources menu page provides access to DAVID analytic modules. By clicking on a specific tool's connection, you will be taken to the corresponding analytic module for analysing list of current genes, which is highlighted in the gene list manager (Fig. 18.2).
- Choose one of DAVID Tools, for example, on the tools menu page, Click on 'Functional Annotation Chart' to access the tool suite's 'Summary Page'. Select functional annotation categories of interest by accepting the default seven or by extending the tree beside each key category to select or deselect functional annotation categories of interest. Then, at the bottom of the page, click the 'Functional Annotation Map' button to access a chart report (Fig. 18.3).
- A window is displayed. Investigate the 'Functional Annotation' findings. For a particular annotation word, to view additional related terms, click on 'RT' (related terms). To view a list of all related genes, click on the 'blue bar'. Additionally, to view genes on a pathway's picture, click on the pathway's name as shown in figure below (Fig. 18.4).
- Click on 'Functional Annotation Clustering' to access 'Summary Page'. Select annotation categories, then press on 'Functional Annotation Clustering' icon at the bottom of the page.

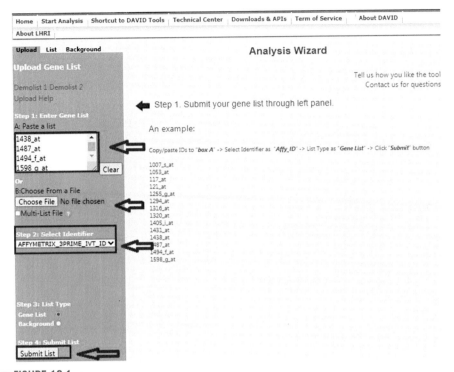

**FIGURE 18.1**

Uploading gene list.

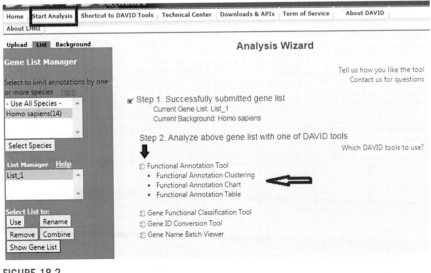

**FIGURE 18.2**

Gene list manager.

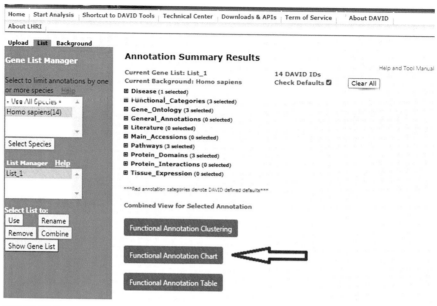

**FIGURE 18.3**

Annotation summary result.

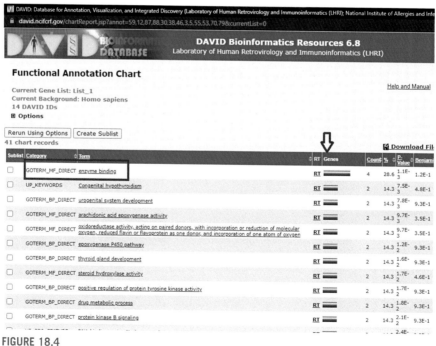

**FIGURE 18.4**

Functional annotation list

- Investigate the implications of the 'Functional Annotation Clustering' procedure. By clicking on the term's name, a more detailed explanation will appear. To view all associated genes for a particular word, click on the 'blue bar'. Click on the red 'G' to display a list of all genes associated with the cluster's names as shown in figure below (Fig. 18.5).
- Click on 'Functional Annotation Table' to access the tool suite's 'Summary Page'. Select annotation categories, then press the 'Functional Annotation Table' button at the bottom of the page. To view a comprehensive overview of a gene of interest, click on the annotation keywords (Fig. 18.6).
- Return to start page by pressing the header 'Start Analysis'.
- To classify input gene list into gene classes, click on another tool, for example, 'Gene Functional Classification Tool'. You can click on the red 'T' (term reports) to see a list of the gene group's related biology. Additionally, by clicking on the 'green icon', you can access the two-dimensional view.
- Then click the 'Gene Name Batch Viewer' icon. This will list all the gene names. You can click on a gene's name to access additional details. Additionally, by selecting 'RG' (associated genes), you can conduct a quest for additional functionally related genes (Fig. 18.7).

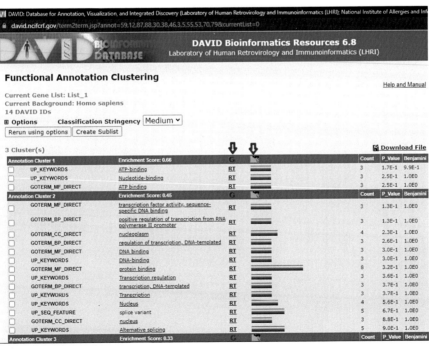

**FIGURE 18.5**

Functional annotation clustering

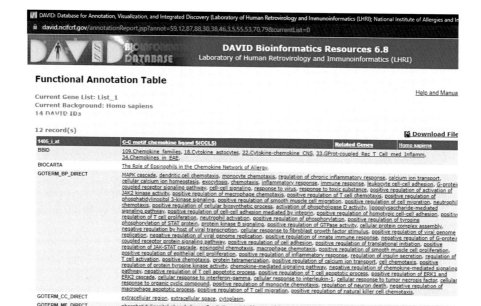

**FIGURE 18.6**

Functional annotation table.

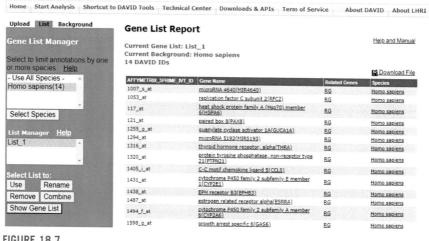

**FIGURE 18.7**

Gene list report.

# Further reading

Dennis Jr., G., Sherman, B.T., Hosack, D.A., Yang, J., Gao, W., Lane, H.C., Lempicki, R.A., 2003. DAVID: database for annotation, visualization, and integrated discovery. Genome Biol. 4, P3.

Hosack, D.A., Dennis Jr., G., Sherman, B.T., Lane, H.C., Lempicki, R.A., 2003. Identifying biological themes within lists of genes with EASE. Genome Biol. 4, R70.

Huang, D.W., Sherman, B.T., Tan, Q., Kir, J., Liu, D., Bryant, D., Guo, Y., Stephens, R., Baseler, M.W., Lane, H.C., Lempicki, R.A., 2007. DAVID bioinformatics resources: expanded annotation database and novel algorithms to better extract biology from large gene lists. Nucleic Acids Res. 35, W169–W175.

Huang, D.W., Sherman, B.T., Lempicki, R.A., 2008. Systematic and integrative analysis of large gene lists using DAVID bioinformatics resources. Nat. Protoc. 4 (1), 44–57.

# Genome analysis browsers 19

## 19.1 Introduction

Genome browsers are indispensable for displaying and decoding the plethora of data types that can be associated with genomic positions. These involve genetic variation, transcription and numerous forms of regulatory data such as methylation and transcription factor binding, as well as disease associations. The wider genome browsers act as data archives for significant public databases, allowing for the visualisation and analysis of a variety of data forms. Additionally, you can upload your own data to any of the publicly available genome browsers. This tool has an extensive role in computational molecular biology, and evolutionary research. The genome browser provides users with a graphical interface for browsing, searching, retrieving and analysing genomic sequence and annotation details.

A genome browser is a computer programme that visually shows genomic data. It takes usually very large files, such as whole genome FASTA files, and organises them so that we as users can make sense of the data contained inside. Genome browsers are typically designed to combine various types of data stored in various types of data files. For instance, annotation files containing information about the position of genes in the genome can be loaded into a genome browser to allow for visual inspection of the genes' locations. This is critical since we can more intuitively interpret results when we view data in a genomic context rather than in isolation (i.e. a single gene sequence). By enabling the viewing of one type of data in the context of another, genome browsers may reveal critical information about gene regulation in normal development and disease.

## 19.2 Web-based genome browsers

These type of browsers significantly advance biology research because of their adaptability and high-quality data. Web-based genome browsers' primary functions and features are data visualisation, retrieval, analysis and customisation. There are two popular groups of web-based genome browsers: those that support multiple species and those that support only one species. Numerous genome browsers combine sequences and annotations for hundreds of organisms, facilitating cross-species comparisons. The other one species-specific genome browsers, their only aim is to focus primarily on a single model organism containing annotations. Ensembl and The University of California, Santa Cruz (UCSC), are the two commonly used general genome browsers.

## 19.3 The university of California, Santa Cruz, genome browser

UCSC main tools are as follows:

- **Genome Browser** — it is a graphical representation of genes, their arrangement and associated annotation tracks.
- **BLAT** — a technique for alignment for DNA sequences to a reference genomic.
- **Custom Tracks** — it displays your submitted data alongside that of the browser.
- **Table Browser** — manipulation of large amounts of data and downloads, as well as intersections and joins among data sets.
- **Session** — the process which helps share ones data with others.
- **PCR** — obtaining deoxyribose nucleotide that has been bracketed by a primer pairs.
- **COVID-19 Research** — explore coronavirus data sets using the SARS-CoV-2 genome browser.
- **Data Integrator** — it combines data from several sources inside the Genome Browser database.
- *In-silico* **PCR** — it helps to align polymerase chain reaction-related primer pairs to the genome.
- **Track Hubs** — import and display external data tracks for tracking hubs.
- **REST API** — returns JSON-formatted data (Fig. 19.1).

In addition to serving as a gateway to the NCBI portal, the UCSC Genome Browser also offers access to genome assemblies collected from other sequencing centres as well as from the NCBI portal. The primary features are as follows:

- Examine the characteristics of specific chromosomal regions
- Conduct research on individual genes as well as gene collections
- Locate sequences and markers
- Retrieve annotation data for particular regions or the entire genome
- Visualise your own data in conjunction with other annotations
- Make a comparison between a region of one genome and the genomes of other organisms

**The GB is often used for the following purposes:**

- It is used in the process of searching for genes and disease-associated genes that have been previously identified.
- It displays orthologous genes in the genomes of other species.

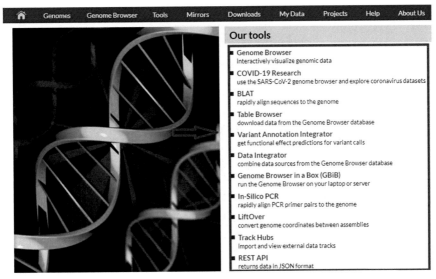

**FIGURE 19.1**

UCSC Genome Browser.

- It identifies enzymes for regeneration and sequence-tagged site.
- It conducts a search for single nucleotide polymorphisms.
- It visualises data from microarrays.
- It Identifies mRNAs and expressed sequence tags from other species.
- It develops illustrations for research-based journals.

## 19.4 Protocol

1. Open your web browser and navigate to http://genome.ucsc.edu.
2. In the top left corner, click either 'Genomes' or 'Genome Browser' (Fig. 19.2).
3. Here you can enter the species' name and the assembly ID. You may enter various types of information in the field's labelled 'position or search term'. These include gene names, specific regions, keywords and IDs.
4. To illustrate, we will check for the ell2 gene in the Human assembly from March 2006 and the following page will show with several matches. Choose the appropriate entry (Fig. 19.3).
5. If you want to see annotated assembly visually, click on submit button. It will present the assembly in its default location with the default annotation tracks.
6. The result page for the GB annotation track can be partitioned into a few sections. The browser page fills in as the information show and is encircled by various control regions, including route controls above and underneath, a

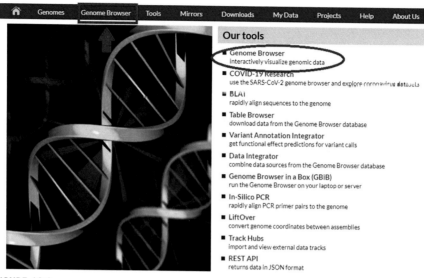

**FIGURE 19.2**

Clicking on Genome Browser.

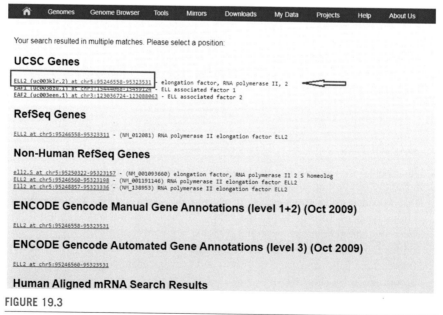

**FIGURE 19.3**

UCSC genes.

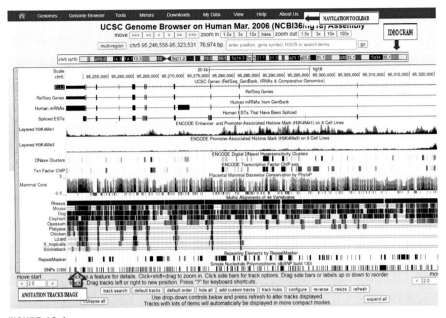

**FIGURE 19.4**

UCSC Genome Browser on Human Mar 2006.

chromosome ideogram on the *Homo sapiens* and some different congregations that demonstrates the window's position on the chromosome, and track controls coordinated by class at the lower part of the page (Fig. 19.4).

7. The browser picture is open for configuration and can be easily used for publication or presentation purposes. The Base Position track is located at the very top of the picture and displays a sequence of numbers. The annotation tracks are stacked below the Base Position track in the picture.

8. The site navigation toolbar is situated at the highest point of the page. Beneath that are two columns of catches for getting to the explained genome show. Following that, for human congregations and some different genomes, a chromosome ideogram is shown — the red imprint demonstrates correctly what region of the chromosome is extended in the tracks picture. Beneath that, the genome comment tracks picture shows the explained genome in a horizontal orientation, with the chromosome's short arm on the left.

9. In certain assemblies, a chromosome shading key is utilised. At long last, the track controls are coordinated by classification at the lower part of the list. Individual annotation tracks may be added or removed from the monitor using these controls shown in following figure (Fig. 19.5).

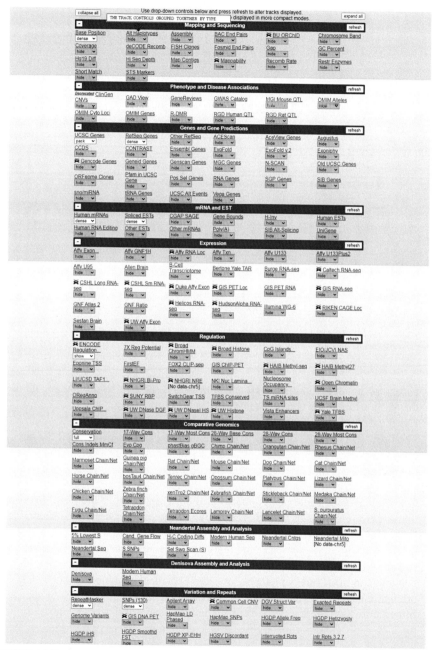

**FIGURE 19.5**

Track controls.

## 19.5 ENSEMBL genome browser

The genome browser developed by the Ensembl project has a rich featured user interface. The data of sequences were obtained from EMBL and other public databases. Ensembl hosts a variety of genomic databases and tools for comparative genomics, variation analysis, gene regulation and epigenetics. It searches over 80 genomes, ranging from alpacas to zebrafish. Additionally, Ensembl offers methods for determining the phenotypic effects of genetic variations and comparing your data to previously published genomic variation.

## 19.6 **Protocol**

1. Go to http://www.ensembl.org/index.html to access Ensembl (Fig. 19.6).
2. Select any desired species and assembly, here we go with *Homo sapiens*, and search for EAF2 gene. To see the search results, choose 'By Species' and then click on 'Homo sapiens' and then 'EAF2 gene'.
3. Click on the desired search result and a page will display as follows (Fig. 19.7):
4. Click on 'Region in Detail' to access additional tracks and navigation options (such as zooming). Three picture boxes are shown in this View. The 'Chromosome 3' depicts chromosome 3 with a red box enclosing the area in which we are currently located (Fig. 19.8).
5. The next image zooms in on chromosome 3 includes 'Contigs', Ensembl/Havana genes, non-coding RNA (ncRNA) genes and ncRNA pseudogenes. In this box, we see our EAF2 gene which includes an IQCCB1 gene upstream of it. This is the place where we can tap into each gene to acquire additional information about every gene.
6. The bottom image illustrates how we can conceal and reveal all of Ensembl's tracks. To add or delete tracks, navigate to the left-side navigation and click the 'Configure this tab' link. You click on the 'Select' box next to a desired track

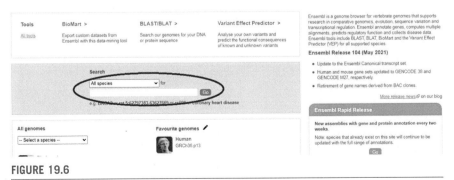

**FIGURE 19.6**

Ensembl homepage.

**FIGURE 19.7**

EAF2 gene.

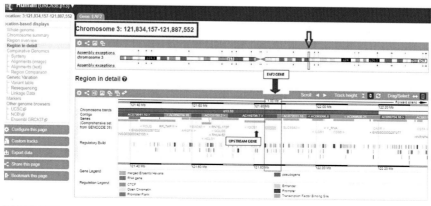

**FIGURE 19.8**

Chromosome detail.

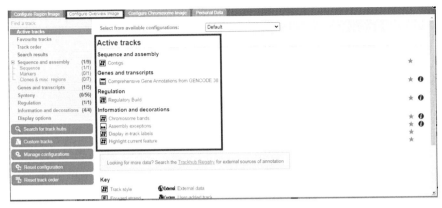

**FIGURE 19.9**

Ensembl's tracks.

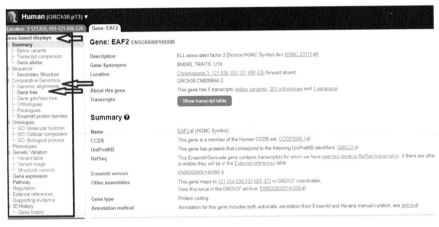

**FIGURE 19.10**

Gene based displays.

and then choose a group of tracks on the left to see if they will be shown. Finally, in the popup window's top right corner, click on the 'Save and Close' button (Fig. 19.9).

7. In the left menu, click on 'Gene-based displays' to access features that are often critical for comprehending the gene structure and regulation of a desired gene, such as comparative genomics, ontologies, genetic variation, etc (Fig. 19.10).

8. By clicking on the 'Genomic alignments' icon, you will be able to view the alignment of desired genes genomic with different organisms.

   Additionally, under comparative genomics, we can obtain a gene tree for our query. For instance, if we conduct a search for the EAF2 gene tree, the following results are returned (Fig. 19.11).

9. Under the gene expression you can also look for the pathways associated (Fig. 19.12).

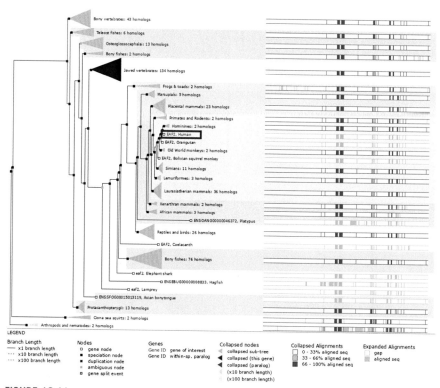

**FIGURE 19.11**

Gene tree.

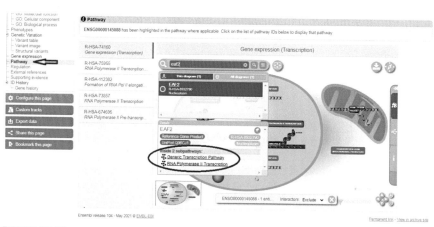

**FIGURE 19.12**

Associated pathways.

## 19.7 Standalone annotation browsers and editors

These browsers allow advanced operations like modify and save annotations that are not available in the majority of web-based browsers.

## 19.8 Apollo

Apollo is a Java programme that can import and export a variety of data formats, including GMOD's Chado database schema, XML, GenBank and GFF3. One of the biggest benefits of its existence is that it makes it possible for users to apply their own annotations using a graphical user interface and then save their changes to a remote database or local file. However, the usefulness of Apollo as a genome browser is limited by the maximum number of sequence features that can be shown at one time, which prevents it from working well for views of DNA that exceed a megabase in length.

## 19.9 The IGB

The Integrated Genome Browser (IGB) is another stand-alone browser based on Java. The big advantage of IGB is that it works well in tandem with DAS (Direct Access Storage) servers. IGB will be intelligent about where it gets the data, by looking to the DAS1 and DAS2 DAS servers and retrieving only the amount of data required. As expected, since creation occurred at Affymetrix, Affymetrix whole genome analysis data works well with the data used in this project. IGB seamlessly scrolls and zooms over lengthy sequences of numerous features, even after the data have been loaded.

## 19.10 Artemis

Artemis is another Java-based browser developed at the Sanger Institute in 2003. The genome visualisation system designed by Artemis has a three-panel user interface that visualises the genome at varying resolutions. The ability to view and edit sequence and annotation data is made possible by Artemis. It is capable of working with some of the most widely used sequence and function file formats, including EMBL, GENBANK, FASTA, GFF3 and BLAST alignment files. At Artemis Research, we focus on curating gene models, which is made easier because we have nested the six-frame translation and stop codons in the gene model. The visual offset of spliced exons into the reading frame is another useful characteristic of eukaryotic genomes.

## Further reading

Fujita, P.A., Rhead, B., Zweig, A.S., 2010. The UCSC genome browser database. Nucleic Acids Res. 39, D876—D882.

Karolchik, D., Baertsch, R., Diekhans, M., 2003. The UCSC genome browser database. Nucleic Acids Res. 31, 51—54.

Skinner, M.E., Uzilov, A.V., Stein, L.D., 2009. Browse: a next generation genome browser. Genome Res. 19, 1630—1638.

Torarinsson, E., 2010. Methods in molecular biology. Genome Brow. 703, 53—65.

Wang, J., Kong, L., Gao, G., Luo, J., 2013. A brief introduction to web-based genome browsers. Briefings Bioinf. 14 (2), 131—143.

Zweig, A.S., Karolchik, D., Kuhn, R.M., Haussler, D., Kent, W.J., 2008. UCSC genome browser tutorial. Genomics 92, 75—84.

# Next-generation alignment tools

20

## 20.1 Introduction

The following five new-generation sequencing (NGS) technologies are the most widely utilised today: Illumina's sequencing by synthesis, Roche's 454 pyrosequencing, SOLiD sequencing-by-ligation, IonTorrent semiconductor sequencing and Oxford Nanopore Technology. The type of reads produced and the types of sequencing errors that are introduced influence the various techniques that may be employed. As of this moment, Illumina and SOLiD are the only technologies that are capable of synthesising all three types of sequencing reads. On platforms like Illumina, SOLID or IonTorrent, the number of base pairs each scan can be defined. To get a 75-bp Read length with SOLiD, 300-bp Read length with Illumina or a 400-bp sequencing run, a desirable sequencing run type should be selected. For the most part, the average read lengths are 700 base pairs, 10 kilobases and 15 kilobases, while the maximum read lengths range from 1 kilobase, 10 kilobases and 15 kilobases for the 454, Nanopore and PacBio platforms. The error rate ranges from 0% in Illumina to 30% in Oxford Nanopore Technology.

Traditional sequence alignment tools like BLAST, on the other hand, are incompatible with NGS. Millions of mostly short sequences must be aligned in order to extract useful information from NGS data. The vast amounts of data produced by modern sequencing machines are much too slow for BLAST and comparable methods to process. The advent of these devices sparked the development of a new generation of read aligners that are much faster.

The majority of the mapping algorithms/tools listed require users to understand how the algorithm works in order to execute the required commands. NGS mapping and alignment can be done in a variety of ways, with many of them oriented toward consistency refinement. In most cases, detailed user guides are provided for each tool (Figs. 20.1 and 20.2).

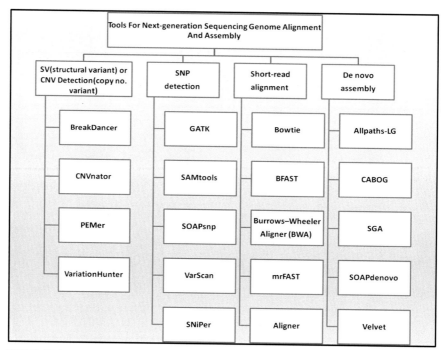

**FIGURE 20.1**

Tools for next-generation sequencing genome alignment and assembly.

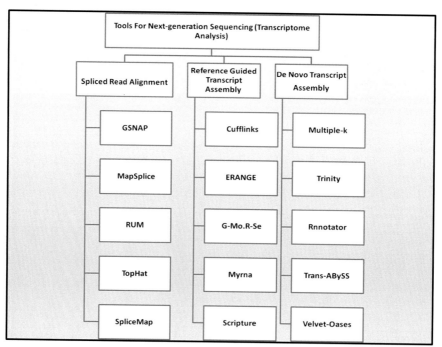

**FIGURE 20.2**

Tools for next-generaation sequencing (Transcriptome analysis).

## 20.2 Novoalign

The Novoalign system indexes the human genome. The Hash table is constructed similar to GSNAP by splitting reads into oligomers (overlapping). Using the Needleman–Wunsch algorithm, the mapping phase decides the global optimum alignment. 'Novoindex' and 'Novoalign' are two steps in the NovoAlign process. The first stage involves indexing the genome, and the second stage aligns the reads to the indexed genome. This software does not allow the maximum amount of precise matches or mismatches. For accurately mapping NGS readings to a reference database, one must utilise Novoalign and NovoalignCS.

## 20.3 mrFAST/mrsFAST

The tools mrFAST and mrsFAST are used to index the human genome. To index the genome's k-mers, they create a collision-free hash table. Both mrFAST and mrsFAST were created using the similar method; however, mrsFAST only supports mismatches to run faster, while as mrFAST supports both gaps and mismatches. In other words, mrsFAST can be used for any experiments that do not have gaps, but mrFAST should only be used for experiments that do not have gaps. Using the other tools, such as mrFAST and mrsFAST, requires having the mapping positions available for reading; in contrast, the accessible mapping locations are needed in a variety of applications, including finding structural variations.

## 20.4 FANGS

The FANGS indexing system is for genome searching. The Roche 454 sequencer yields lengthy reads, and hence the reading workflow is optimised for processing these long reads.

## 20.5 RMAP

RMAP is a read indexing tool. RMAP, like MAQ, pre-processes the reads to create a hash table, which it then compares to the reference genome to extract mapping positions. Genome indexing is the subject of the majority of newly established software.

## 20.6 BWT

The Burrows–Wheeler Transform, i.e. BWT is a memory-efficient data indexing technique that traverses a data block with a small memory footprint. Ferragina and Manzini extended BWT to a newer data structure in order to enable exact matching which was named FM index. The algorithm improves lookup efficiency in cases where a single read can match several positions in the genome by converting the genome to an FM index. The increased productivity, however, comes at the cost of a slightly longer index construction time than hash tables.

## 20.7 Bowtie

Bowtie is a short-read memory-efficient aligner. It achieves more than 35-bp per hour alignment of short reads to the human genome. The bowtie index uses Burrows–Wheeler indexes to keep the genome's memory footprint modest. The development and integration stages for Bowtie are bowtie-build and bowtie. In the first stage, indexing of the reference genome occurs (i.e. the build stage), and in the second stage, generating of a list of alignments occurs (i.e. the generate stage). The two versions of Bowtie are called Bowtie and Bowtie 2. Bowtie 2 is built to handle reads with length over 50 bps and also includes options not available with Bowtie.

## 20.8 BWA

BWA is yet another approach based on BWT. In BWA, the Ferragina and Manzini algorithm, also known as Bowtie, is used to locate exact matches using the concordance created by Bowtie. These three instructions are called 'bwa index', 'bwa aln' and 'bwa samse'. First, the reference genome is indexed. Second, the suffix array is searched for all of the hits to every read in the data set. Finally, coordinates from the suffix array are converted to the reference genome and SAM alignments are produced.

## 20.9 SOAP2

SOAP2 differs from other BWT-based applications. To fasten the process of exact matching, it indexes the reference genome using BWT and hash table techniques. In order to find inexact matches, it uses a 'split-read method', in which the read is separated into fragments based on the number of mismatches. '2bwt-builder' and 'soap' are two successive commands that are used to execute SOAP2. The Burrows–Wheeler index is created by the first instruction, and alignments are done by the second. The maximum permitted number of mismatches is two.

## 20.10 BFAST

BFAST is a powerful and efficient method for performing billions of short sequence alignments quickly and accurately. In two stages, BFAST accomplishes alignment. First BFAST recognises candidate alignment sites (CALs) for each reading using several reference genome indexes. Secondly the readings on each CAL are matched to the best match using gapped local alignment.

## 20.11 Next-generation sequencing alignment tools — websites

| Algorithm/Tools | Website |
|---|---|
| AB SOLiD map reads | http://solidsoftwaretools.com/gf/project/mapreads/frs/ |
| Allpaths-LG | http://www.broadinstitute.org/software/allpaths-lg/blog/?page_id=12 |
| AGILE | http://users.eecs.northwestern.edu/smi539/agile_x86_64_0.3.0 |
| BreakDancer | http://sourceforge.net/projects/breakdancer |
| BFAST | http://sourceforge.net/projects/bfast/files/bfast/0.6.4/bfast-0.6.4d.tar.gz/download |
| BOAT | http://boat.cbi.pku.edu.cn/ |
| Bowtie | https://sourceforge.net/projects/bowtie-bio/files/bowtie/0.12.7 |
| BWA | http://sourceforge.net/projects/bio-bwa/files/ |
| BS Seeker | http://sourceforge.net/projects/bsseeker/files/BSSeeker04-232010/examples.tgz/download |
| BWT-SW | http://i.cs.hku.hk/ckwong3/bwtsw/bwtsw-20070916.tar.gz |
| CNVnator | http://sv.gersteinlab.org/cnvnator/ |
| CABOG | http://wgs-assembler.sf.net |
| CloudBurst | http://sourceforge.net/projects/cloudburst-bio/files/cloudburst/ |
| ERANGE | http://woldlab.caltech.edu/erange/ERANGE3.2.tgz |
| Exonerate | http://www.ebi.ac.uk/guy/exonerate/exonerate-2.2.0.tar.gz |
| FusionHunter | http://bioen-compbio.bioen.illinois.edu/FusionHunter/ |
| FusionMap | http://www.omicsoft.com/fusionmap/ |
| G-Mo.R-Se | http://www.genoscope.cns.fr/externe/gmors |
| GASSST | http://www.irisa.fr/symbiose/projects/gassst/Gassst_v1.23.tar.gz |
| GMAP | http://www.gene.com/share/gmap/src/gmap-2007-09-28.tar.gz |
| GNUMAP | http://dna.cs.byu.edu/gnumap/download.cgi |
| GSNAP | http://research-pub.gene.com/gmap/src/gmap-gsnap-2011-03-28.tar.gz |
| HMMSplicer | http://derisilab.ucsf.edu/index.php?software=105 |
| Myrna | http://bowtie-bio.sourceforge.net/myrna |
| MapSplice | http://www.netlab.uky.edu/p/bioinfo/MapSpliceDownload |
| Maq | http://sourceforge.net/projects/maq/files/maq/0.7.1/ |
| MOM | http://mom.csbc.vcu.edu/node/14 |
| Mosaik | http://code.google.com/p/mosaik-aligner/downloads/list |
| mr(s)FAST | http://sourceforge.net/projects/mrfast/files/mrfast/mrfast-2.0.0.2/ |
| MUMmer | http://sourceforge.net/projects/mummer/files/mummer/3.22/MUMmer3.22.tar.gz/download |

*Continued*

| Algorithm/Tools | Website |
| --- | --- |
| MuMRescueLite | http://genome.gsc.riken.jp/osc/english/software/src/MuMRescueLite_090522.tar.gz |
| NovoAlign | http://www.novocraft.com/download.html |
| NSMAP | https://sites.google.com/site/nsmapforrnaseq/home/nsmap |
| PALMapper | http://ftp.tuebingen.mpg.de/fml/raetsch-lab/software/palmapper/palmapper-0.4-rc4.tar.gz |
| PASS | http://pass.cribi.unipd.it/cgi-bin/pass.pl?action=Download |
| PASSion | https://trac.nbic.nl/passion/wiki/Download |
| PERM | http://code.google.com/p/perm/downloads/detail?name=PerMSource0.2.9.9.zip&can=2&q= |
| ProbeMatch | http://pages.cs.wisc.edu/jignesh/probematch/ |
| QPALMA | ftp://ftp.tuebingen.mpg.de/pub/fml/raetsch-lab/software/qpalma/qpalma-0.9.2-rc1.tar.gz |
| RazerS | http://www.seqan.de/downloads/projects.html |
| RMAP | http://www.cmb.usc.edu/people/andrewds/rmap/rmap_v2.05.tbz2 |
| SOAPsnp | http://soap.genomics.org.cn/soapsnp.html |
| SNiPer | http://www.tgen.org/research/index. cfm?pageid=623 |
| Segemehl | http://www.bioinf.uni-leipzig.de/Software/segemehl/segemehl_0_0_9_3.tar.gz |
| SeqMap | http://biogibbs.stanford.edu/jiangh/seqmap/download/seqmap-1.0.13-src.zip |
| SHRiMP | http://compbio.cs.toronto.edu/shrimp/releases/ |
| SliderII | http://www.bcgsc.ca/downloads/slider/SliderII.tar.gz |
| SOAPaligner/soap2 | http://soap.genomics.org.cn/down/SOAPaligner-v2.20-Linux-x86_64.tar.bz2 |
| SOCS | http://socs.biology.gatech.edu/Download.html |
| SpliceMap | http://www.stanford.edu/group/wonglab/SpliceMap/download.html |
| SplitSeek | http://solidsoftwaretools.com/gf/project/splitseek/frs/ |
| SSAHA2 | http://www.sanger.ac.uk/resources/software/ssaha2.html |
| Stampy | http://www.well.ox.ac.uk/stampy-registration |
| SWIFT Suit | http://bibiserv.techfak.uni-bielefeld.de/download/tools/swift.html |
| Trinity | http://trinityrnaseq.sourceforge.net |
| Tophat | http://tophat.cbcb.umd.edu/downloads/tophat-1.3.3.Linux_x86_64.tar.gz |
| Velvet | http://www.ebi.ac.uk/~zerbino/velvet |
| Vmatch | http://www.zbh.uni-hamburg.de/vmatch/Vmatchlic.pdf |
| VarScan | http://varscan.sourceforge.net |
| Zoom | http://www.bioinformaticssolutions.com/products/zoom/download.php |

# Further reading

Abouelhoda, M.I., Kurtz, S., Ohlebusch, E., 2004. Replacing suffix trees with enhanced suffix arrays. J. Discrete Algorithm. 2 (1), 53−86.

Broder, A.Z., Glassman, S.C., Manasse, M.S., Zweig, G., 1997. Syntactic clustering of the web. Comput. Netw. ISDN Syst. 29 (8−13), 1157−1166.

Burrows, M., Wheeler, D., 1994. A Block Sorting Lossless Data Compression Algorithm. Technical Report 124. Digital Equipment Corporation, Systems Research Center, 130 Lytton Avenue Palo Alto, CA 94301.

Butler, J., MacCallum, I., Kleber, M., Shlyakhter, I., Belmonte, M., Lander, E., Nusbaum, C., Jaffe, D., 2008. ALLPATHS: De novo assembly of whole-genome shotgun microreads. Genome Res. 8, 810−820.

Campagna, D., Albiero, A., Bilardi, A., Caniato, E., Forcato, C., Manavski, S., Vitulo, N., Valle, G., 2009. PASS: a program to align short sequences. Bioinformatics 25 (7), 967−968.

Chen, Y., Souaiaia, T., Chen, T., 2009. PerM: efficient mapping of short sequencing reads with periodic full sensitive spaced seeds. Bioinformatics 25 (19), 2514−2521.

Clement, N.L., Snell, Q., Clement, M.J., Hollenhorst, P.C., Purwar, J., Graves, B.J., Cairns, B.R., Johnson, W.E., 2010. The GNUMAP algorithm: unbiased probabilistic mapping of oligonucleotides from next-generation sequencing. Bioinformatics 26 (1), 38−45.

Eaves, H.L., Gao, Y., 2009. MOM: maximum oligonucleotide mapping. Bioinformatics 25 (7), 969−970.

Gibbs, A.J., McIntyre, G.A., 1970. The diagram, a method for comparing sequences. Its use with amino acid and nucleotide sequences. Eur. J. Biochem. 16 (1), 1−11.

Gotoh, O., 1982. An improved algorithm for matching biological sequences. J. Mol. Biol. 162 (3), 705−708.

Hoffmann, S., Otto, C., Kurtz, S., Sharma, C.M., Khaitovich, P., Vogel, J., Stadler, P.F., Hackermüller, J., 2009. Fast mapping of short sequences with mismatches, insertions and deletions using index structures. PLoS Comput. Biol. 5 (9), e1000 502.

Homer, N., Merriman, B., Nelson, S.F., 2009. BFAST: an alignment tool for large scale genome resequencing. PLoS One 4 (11), e7767.

Jiang, H., Wong, W., 2008. SeqMap: mapping massive amount of oligonucleotides to the genome. Bioinformatics 24, 2395−2396.

Kurtz, S., Phillippy, A., Delcher, A., Smoot, M., Shumway, M., Antonescu, C., Salzberg, S., 2004. Versatile and open software for comparing large genomes. Genome Biol. 5 (2), R12.

Li, H., Ruan, J., Durbin, R., 2008. Mapping short DNA sequencing reads and calling variants using mapping quality scores. Genome Res. 18, 1851−1858.

Lin, H., Zhang, Z., Zhang, M.Q., Ma, B., Li, M., 2008. Zoom! Zillions of oligos mapped. Bioinformatics 24 (21), 2431−2437.

Li, R., Li, Y., Kristiansen, K., Wang, J., 2008. SOAP: short oligonucleotide alignment program. Bioinformatics 24, 713−714.

Li, H., Homer, N., 2010. A survey of sequence alignment algorithms for next-generation sequencing. Briefings Bioinf. 11 (5).

Metzker, M.L., 2010. Sequencing technologies [mdash] the next generation. Genome Res. 11, 31−46.

Needleman, S.B., Wunsch, C.D., 1970. A general method applicable to the search for similarities in the amino acid sequence of two proteins. J. Mol. Biol. 48 (3), 443−453.

Ruffalo, M., LaFramboise, T., Koyut-rk, M., 2011. Comparative analysis of algorithms for next-generation sequencing read alignment. Bioinformatics 27 (20), 2790–2796.

Rumble, S.M., Lacroute, P., Dalca, A.V., Fiume, M., Sidow, A., Brudno, M., 2009. SHRiMP: accurate mapping of short color-space reads. PLoS Comput. Biol. 5 (5), e1000 386.

Schatz, M.C., 2009. CloudBurst: highly sensitive read mapping with MapReduce. Bioinformatics 25 (11), 1363–1369.

SHRiMP - Short Read Mapping Package. http://compbio.cs.toronto.edu/shrimp/(accessed 4 February 2016).

Smith, T.F., Waterman, M.S., 1981. Identification of common molecular subsequences. J. Mol. Biol. 147, 195–197.

Smith, A., Xuan, Z., MQ, Z., 2008. Using quality scores and longer reads improves accuracy of solexa read mapping. BMC Bioinf. 9, 128.

Weese, D., Holtgrewe, M., Reinert, K., 2012. RazerS 3: faster, fully sensitive read mapping. Bioinformatics 28 (20), 2592–2599.

Weiner, P., 1973. Linear pattern matching algorithms. In: Proceedings of the 14th Annual Symposium on Switching and Automata Theory (Swat 1973). IEEE Computer Society, Washington, DC, pp. 1–11.

Yang, X., Charlebois, P., Gnerre, S., Coole, M., Lennon, N., Levin, J., Qu, J., Ryan, E., Zody, M., Henn, M., 2012. De novo assembly of highly diverse viral populations. BMC Genom. 13 (1), 475.

Zhang, G., Fedyunin, I., Kirchner, S., Xiao, C., Valleriani, A., Ignatova, Z., 2012. FANSe: an accurate algorithm for quantitative mapping of large scale sequencing reads. Nucleic Acids Res. 40 (11), e83.

# Molecular marker storage databases and data visualisation

# 21

## 21.1 Introduction

The identification and analysis of genetic diversity is critical in plant breeding, and its importance is growing as genome sequencing technology advance. Characterising genetic variation and aiding in genomic breeding requires accurate genetic markers. Developing specialised bioinformatics systems and complicated databases is necessary for the processing and storing of an increased amount of molecular marker data. In general, species-specific molecular marker databases comprise several genetic, genomic and phenotypic features. Many molecular marker databases offer information on a wide range of different types of markers for a wide range of different species, while others focus solely on a single type of marker).

Molecular markers have numerous applications in plant breeding, and their ability to detect the presence of a gene (or genes) encoding a desirable trait has led to the development of marker-assisted selection (MAS). The advancement of these technologies enables the breeding process to be accelerated. A desirable quality, for example, may only be noticed in mature plants, but MAS allows researchers to screen for the feature much earlier in the plant's life cycle. Additionally, molecular markers enable simultaneous selection for a variety of different plant features. Additionally, they are used to identify specific plants carrying a particular resistance gene without exposing the plant to the pest or pathogen in question.

## 21.2 Marker storage databases

Marker databases range in size from large, centralised repositories that store data for multiple species to small, specialised databases used for very specific reasons. The larger libraries frequently lack detailed analytic capabilities, whereas the smaller systems may integrate more species-specific data. The dbSNP is rapidly becoming the de facto standard repository for SNP data, and there are a plethora of additional species-specific marker databases.

Bioinformatics for Everyone. https://doi.org/10.1016/B978-0-323-91128-3.00004-5

## 21.3 dbSNP

The dbSNP is a public domain (refer to a discrete region of a protein that is thought to fold independently of the rest of the protein and to have its own function) archive for a large collection of common genetic polymorphisms. dbSNP mostly contains SNP data for humans and other vertebrates, and it also has some data for plants. The dbSNP database was created to facilitate submissions and research on a wide variety of biological issues like

- Physical mapping
- Analyses of function
- The field of pharmacogenomics
- Evolutionary research

## 21.4 Using dbSNP

- Go to dbSNP via https://www.ncbi.nlm.nih.gov/snp/. In the given field search for your desired query (Fig. 21.1).
- Here we search for CFTR gene in *Homo sapiens* (Fig. 21.2).
- Click on the desired search result and a detailed Reference SNP (rs). Report is displayed as shown in the following figure (Fig. 21.3).
- The Variant Details tab provides information on Genomic Placement, Gene and Amino Acid alterations, while the HGVS tab has HGVS designations.

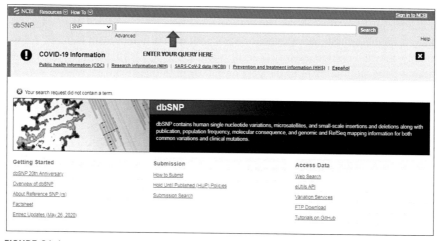

**FIGURE 21.1**

dbSNP homepage.

**FIGURE 21.2**

CFTR search.

## 21.5 HapMap

The HapMap Consortium compiles and catalogues data on genetic variations in humans (The International HapMap Consortium, 2003). There are two basic techniques for data access: GBrowse, each of which is customised to a certain sort of user. Over 3.1 million human SNPs have been genotyped in a geographically diversified sample of 270 individuals as part of the HapMap project. The International HapMap Project's objective is to create a haplotype map of the human genome, dubbed the HapMap that will reflect the most prevalent patterns of human DNA sequence variation. The HapMap is projected to be a critical resource for researchers looking for genes associated with health, disease and drug and environmental response.

## 21.6 IBISS

The Commonwealth Scientific and Industrial Research Organization of Australia developed the Interactive Bovine in silico SNP Database (IBISS) (CSIRO). It is a collection of 523,448 Bovine SNPs that were found using a proprietary analytical workflow using 324,031 ESTs. The database can be searched using keywords, accession numbers or by doing a BLAST search against an entry sequence. Additionally, users can search for markers using a linked genome browser.

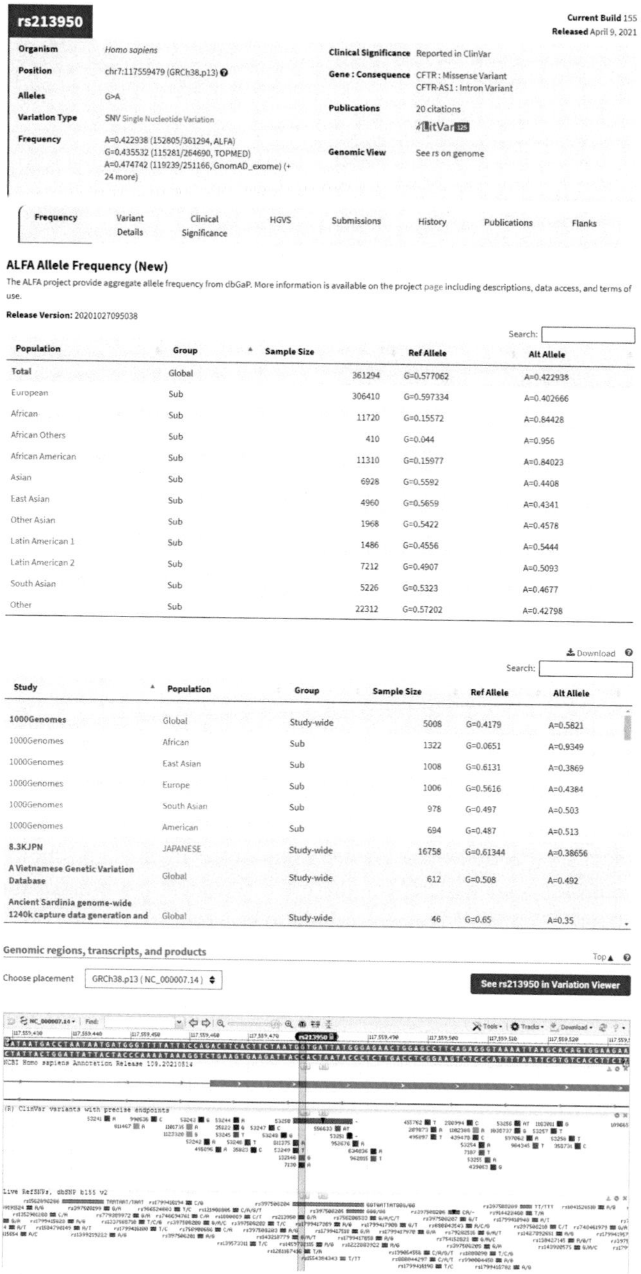

**FIGURE 21.3**

dbSNP results.

## 21.7 **Gramene**

The Gramene database (http://www.gramene.org/) contains a variety of different types of markers derived from the rice, maize, grape and *Arabidopsis* genomes. This website has a search engine, which enables visitors to look up specific markers. Details about each marker are shown in text format, including database cross-references and map coordinates associated with CMap chromosomes. One of the primary objective of Gramene's mission is to connect and integrate genomes via standardised functional annotation and comparative analysis. Gramene gives the following information:

- Reference genomes that have been completely constructed.
- Ontology-based annotation and comparative analysis.
- Additional community data, including genetic variation, expression, and methylation.
- The Plant Reactome pathway portal is a one-stop shop for analysing metabolic and regulatory pathways in plants.
- Compile previously published data on comparison maps, markers and QTL.

## 21.8 **Using GRAMENE**

- To access Gramene go to your browser and type http://www.gramene.org/. The homepage of Gramene is displayed. In the given field, search for species, pathways, etc (Fig. 21.4).

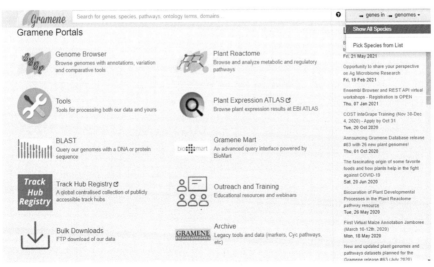

FIGURE 21.4

Gramene home page.

- Users can choose their species of interest to display a gene or a genomic region, and launch Genome Browser window, e.g. here we are looking for BADH rice gene in the *Oryza sativa indica* group.
- The genomic location of your desired gene is displayed as shown in the following figure (Fig. 21.5).

By clicking on 'homology option' a phylogram is displayed which shows the relationships between this gene and others similar to it (Fig. 21.6).

A graphical presentation of the different related processes, enzymes, metabolites and cofactors is shown as part of a pathway, illustrated in a step-by-step manner. Additional resources including UniProt, PIR, ChEBI, PubChem, PubMed and GO are available for searching for gene loci and proteins (Fig. 21.7).

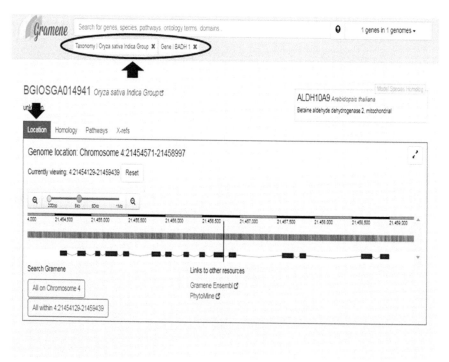

**FIGURE 21.5**

Genomic location of searched gene.

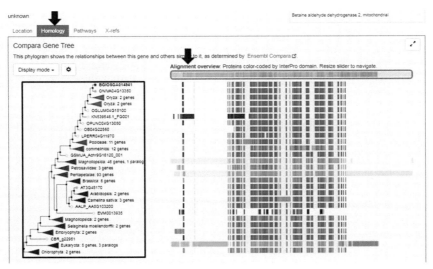

**FIGURE 21.6**

Phylogram.

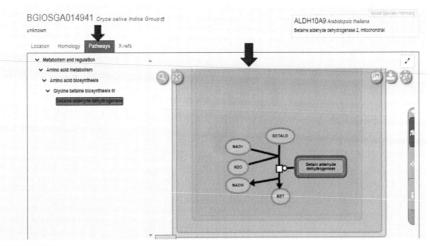

**FIGURE 21.7**

Pathways.

## 21.9 Techniques for data visualisation

Currently available methods for visualising molecular markers fall into two basic categories.

## 21.10 Graphical map viewer

The NCBI map viewer: The molecular genetic markers, genome assemblies and other annotations are visualised using sets of graphically aligned maps in the NCBI Map Viewer (http://www.ncbi.nih.gov/mapview). Also, it gives users the ability to see numerous levels of annotation for a given chromosomal segment at the same time.

CMap: It is a genomic and physical map visualisation and comparison tool. It is especially successful when it is used to compare maps between species that are closely related. The CMap software was first developed for the Gramene project, and it has since been used to compare genetic maps for many animal breeds, including cattle, pigs and honeybees. The CMap database was created to allow for a range of mapping applications to be implemented with ease.

MAPMAKER: MAPMAKER carries out multipoint linkage analyses, i.e. the assessment for dominant, recessive and codominant markers of all recombination fractions and uses a simple two-point approach to load connection groups, with the use of a transitive process on the maximum two-point probabilistic distances and LOD scores.

## Reference

The International HapMap Consortium, 2003. The International HapMap Project. Nature 426, 789−796. https://doi.org/10.1038/nature02168.

## Further reading

Duran, C., Edwards, D., Batley, J., 2009. Molecular marker discovery and genetic map visualisation. In: Edwards, D., Stajich, J., Hansen, D. (Eds.), Bioinformatics. Springer, New York, NY. https://doi.org/10.1007/978-0-387-92738-1_8.

Lai, K., Lorenc, M.T., 2015. Chapter 4 molecular marker databases. In: Methods in Molecular Biology. Springer Science and Business Media LLC.

# Introduction to computer-aided drug design

## 22

**Drug design** is the inventive process of finding new medications based on the knowledge of a biological target. Computer-aided drug design (CADD) includes finding, developing and analysing medicines and related biological active compounds by computer methodologies. The use of CADD methodologies speeds up the early stages of chemical development while guiding and speeding up drug discovery. Virtual screening, virtual library design, lead optimisation, de novo design and other computational approaches are all covered in CADD. It is a reasonable and methodical technique that concentrates scientists' attention on the most promising chemicals, eliminating the effort needed to test their potency in synthetic and biological laboratories.

## 22.1 CADD includes

- Drug research and development processes are being expedited with the use of computing power.
- Identifying and optimising novel medications with the use of chemical and biological knowledge on targets and ligands.
- An *in silico* approach to filter design using ADMET, which results in the screening of most promising candidates.

  The advantages of CADD include

- It is used for conducting a limited number of experiments, smaller libraries of compounds are picked from a larger chemical database.
- Lead compounds' optimisation causes changes in drug metabolism and pharmacokinetics properties as absorption, distribution, metabolism, excretion and the potential for toxicity.
- Since it decreases the chance of drug resistance, it will produce lead compounds, which target the cause of the problem.
- The production of high-quality data sets and libraries, which can be optimised for high molecular diversity or similarity, are two common results of CADD.
- Cost-effective.
- Reasonable substitute for traditional drug discovery.
- Time and labor efficient.

Bioinformatics for Everyone. https://doi.org/10.1016/B978-0-323-91128-3.00002-1

## 22.2 Databases

### 22.2.1 PubChem

The data in this database are available to the public through the National Institutes of Health, an encyclopedia of tiny molecules. While these complex compounds exist within RNA, it also includes information on larger molecules such as nucleotides, carbohydrates, lipids, peptides and chemically modified macromolecules.

**Example:** Retrieve detailed information about Oseltamivir using PubChem

- Open PubChem official website (https://pubchem.ncbi.nlm.nih.gov/) and search for Oseltamivir (Fig. 22.1).
- Click on 'Oseltamivir' and the following hits are obtained.
- Open the entry of Compound that best matches the search (Fig. 22.2).

The entry contains the detailed information about Oseltamivir. You get a wealth of information including Structure, Names and Identifiers, as well as Chemical and Physical characteristics (Fig. 22.3).

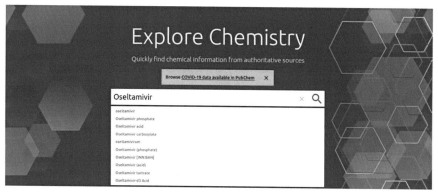

**FIGURE 22.1**

Pubchem official website.

**FIGURE 22.2**

Pubchem compound search.

COMPOUND SUMMARY

# Oseltamivir

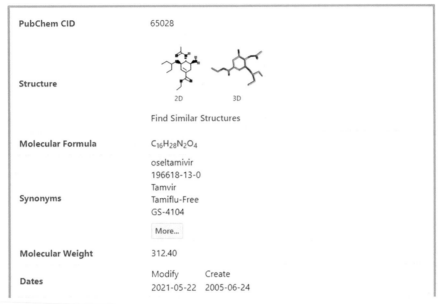

| PubChem CID | 65028 |
|---|---|
| Structure | 2D    3D<br>Find Similar Structures |
| Molecular Formula | $C_{16}H_{28}N_2O_4$ |
| Synonyms | oseltamivir<br>196618-13-0<br>Tamvir<br>Tamiflu-Free<br>GS-4104<br>More... |
| Molecular Weight | 312.40 |
| Dates | Modify        Create<br>2021-05-22   2005-06-24 |

**FIGURE 22.3**

Compound summary.

**Exercise:**

Search and study the information about drug chloramphenicol using PubChem

- Detailed information about Compounds, Substances and Bioassays can be searched using PubChem (Fig. 22.4).

**FIGURE 22.4**

Drug search using Pubchem.

## 22.3 DrugBank

DrugBank is a unique, complete, free-access, online resource in bioinformatics and chemicals that combines extensive drug information and extensive drug goal information. DrugBank has made it possible to view a comprehensive picture of possible drug targets by combining extensive drug (i.e. chemical, pharmacological and pharmaceutical) data with comprehensive drug target (i.e. sequence, structure and route) information. Information about drug and its target can be retrieved by providing any search term such as drug name, target name, Pathway or Indications of a disease.

**Example:** Retrieve detailed information about Oseltamivir using DrugBank.

Open DrugBank official website (https://www.drugbank.ca/) and enter the Drug name. (Select the tab which is to be entered as a search term, here Drug name is to be searched. Hence, 'Drugs' tab is selected.) (Fig. 22.5).

The entry of Drug Oseltamivir opens and detailed information of the drug can be studied. Number of targets, Enzymes, Transporters and Biointeractors are mentioned at the top of the entry and the entry contains detailed information about drugs and its targets (Fig. 22.6).

**Exercise:**

1. Report the name of the target molecules and their respective molecular weight for the drug Oseltamivir.
2. Report the UniProt ID of the Enzyme(s) involved in metabolism of drug Oseltamivir.
3. Report gene name and Functions of the Transporter protein(s) for the drug Oseltamivir.
4. Report names of various Bio interactions shown by Oseltamivir and provide the names of interacting Drugs and interacting groups.

**FIGURE 22.5**

Drugbank homepage.

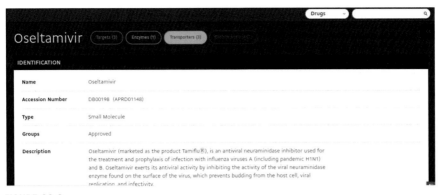

**FIGURE 22.6**

Detailed information of drug.

**Example:** Search for Drug and Target information in the DrugBank providing Structure.

Click on search tab at the top right corner, dropdown will appear. Then, click on 'Chemical Structure'. Following window will appear. Draw the structure in the window provided. Click on search (Fig. 22.7).

Results are obtained (Fig. 22.8).

In the same way, DrugBank can also be searched using molecular weight of the drug/target as the search term (Fig. 22.9).

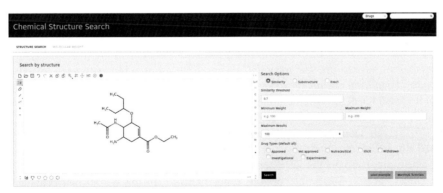

**FIGURE 22.7**

Chemical structure search.

Results 1 — 2 of approximately 2 results

‹ Previous  Next ›

| | | Oseltamivir | $C_{16}H_{28}N_2O_4$ |
|---|---|---|---|
| DB00198 | | 196618-13-0 | |
| Score: 1 0 | | approved | Mono mass: 312.204907394 |
| nemenn | | Oseltamivir acid | $C_{14}H_{24}N_2O_4$ |
| Score: 0 956 | | 16722?-45-8 | Mono mass: 284.173607266 |
| | | experimental | |

**FIGURE 22.8**

Result page.

STRUCTURE SEARCH    **MOLECULAR WEIGHT**

**Search by Molecular Weight**

Minimum weight              Maximum weight

e.g. 100                    e.g. 200

Drug Types (default all):

☐ Approved   ☐ Vet approved   ☐ Nutraceutical   ☐ Illicit   ☐ Withdrawn   ☐ Investigational   ☐ Experimental

**Search**                                                        CLEAR

**FIGURE 22.9**

Molecular weight search.

## 22.4 ZINC DB

ZINC is a library of commercially accessible compounds for virtual screening that is free to the community. Over 230 million purchasable chemicals are in 3D ready-to-ship ready-to-use forms, making ZINC an amazing resource for customers. In addition to 750 million chemicals you can buy, there are over 750 million more that you can find analogues for under a minute with ZINC. In ZINC DB, we can search using one substance or multiple substances at once Search using one substance.

In 'search using one' option, name of Substance, structure of substance, SMILES, InChI, etc., can be given as input.

**Example:** Retrieve the ZINC entry for Aspirin.

Under 'Search using one' option, Enter 'Aspirin' in the search box provided (Fig. 22.10).

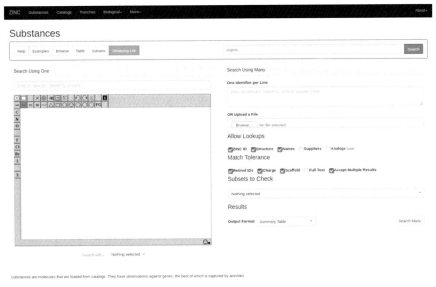

**FIGURE 22.10**

ZINC DB homepage.

Click on search, a window with matching entries to Aspirin will appear (Fig. 22.11).

Click on Aspirin. ZINC entry for Aspirin will appear (Fig. 22.12).

Search using many substances.

Multiple ZINC IDs/SMILES/InChI could be provided in the 'Search using Many' option and output could be obtained in the form of sdf file/SMILES.

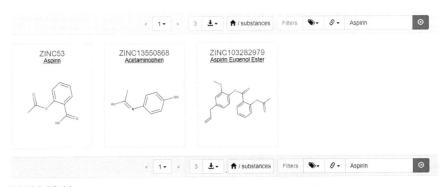

**FIGURE 22.11**

Aspirin matching entries.

**FIGURE 22.12**

ZINC entry for aspirin.

## 22.5 PDB

RCSB-PDB is one of the important resource powered by the Protein Data Bank archive. It offers information on the 3D forms of proteins, nuclear acids and complex components, helping students to have the whole understanding, from protein synthesis to health and disease, on all aspects of biomedicine and agriculture.

PDB can be searched by providing

1. **Text-based query:**
   PDB ID, Protein name, etc., can be entered in the search box.
2. **Sequence based query:**
   Protein sequence can be provided in the sequence search option.

   **Search by using PDB ID as query:**
   **Example:** Retrieve and download the pdb file for PDB ID: 3K39.

Open the official website of RCSB-PDB (https://www.rcsb.org/) and in the search box enter the PDB ID: 3K39 (Fig. 22.13).

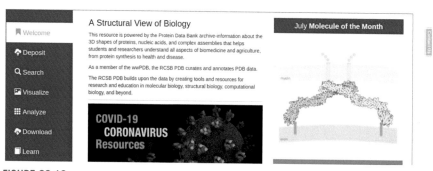

**FIGURE 22.13**

Protein Data Bank (PDB).

Click on the entry 3K39 (Fig. 22.14).

The PDB entry is displayed (Fig. 22.15):

Downloading PDB file:

Click on the 'Downloads files' tab. Drop down will appear. Select PDB format.

A pop-up window will appear. Select option of Save File and click on OK. The pdb file will be saved in the Downloads folder (Fig. 22.16).

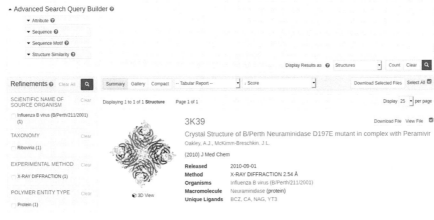

**FIGURE 22.14**

3K39 structure.

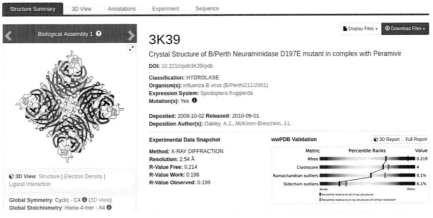

**FIGURE 22.15**

PDB for 3K39.

**FIGURE 22.16**

Saving PDB file of 3K39.

**Exercise:**

1. Report Method and Resolution of the given entry and confirm if the protein structure has a resolution in accepted range or not.
2. Report if the given protein is mutated or not? If mutation is present, report the location of mutation and visualise it in the sequence (Fig. 22.17).
3. Report total number of chains present in the given entry.
4. Report if the given entry contains ligand(s). If present, make a list of ligands present.
5. Report the UniProt accession ID for the given entry.

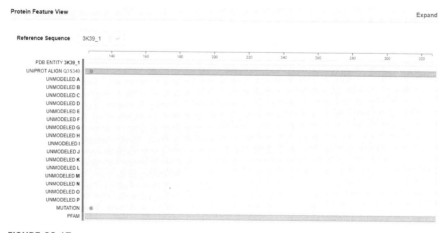

**FIGURE 22.17**

Protein feature view.

Search by using protein sequence as query:

Click on the Search tab. Then select the sequence search option (Fig. 22.18).

Click on 'Advanced Search-Sequence search' (Fig. 22.19).

Enter the protein sequence (without the header). Then click on the search option represented by magnifying glass symbol (Fig. 22.20).

Relevant protein structure entries are displayed in the results (Fig. 22.21)

**FIGURE 22.18**

Search tab.

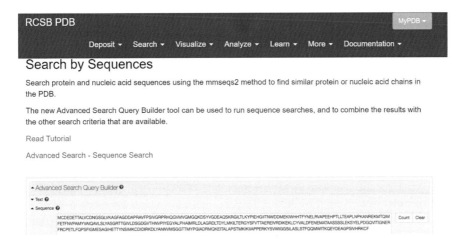

**FIGURE 22.19**

Advanced search-sequence search.

**FIGURE 22.20**

Advanced search query builder.

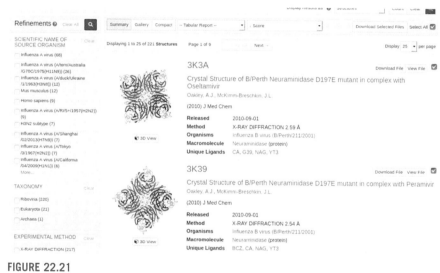

**FIGURE 22.21**

Protein structure entries.

## 22.6 ModBase

ModBase is a database of comparative protein structure models. Target protein structure is obtained from PDB. But, if the target protein is not found in PDB, then search for the template Protein/Homologous Protein PDB ID in ModBase.

**Example:** Retrieve the model for Target protein for which Template is PDB ID 1G9K

- Select 'Property' as Template or Homolog PDB code and enter PDB ID 1G9K and keep the 'Organism' as ALL (default) and then click on search (Fig. 22.22).

Homology models are obtained (Fig. 22.23).

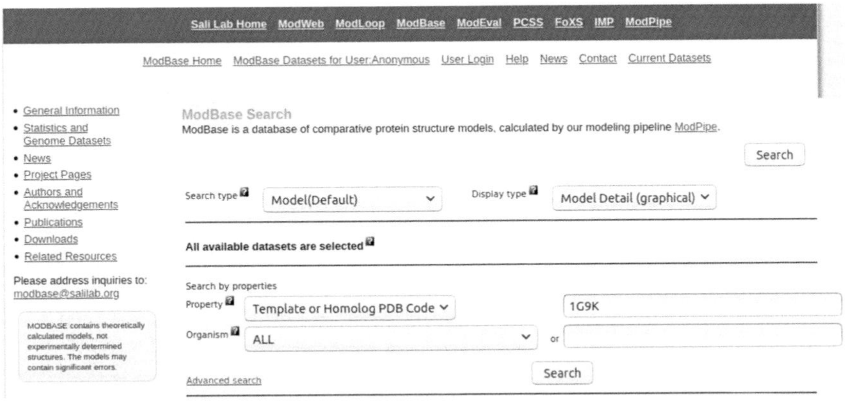

**FIGURE 22.22**

ModBase search.

**FIGURE 22.23**

Model overview.

## 22.7 File formats

### 22.7.1 MDL molfile

An MDL molecular file format is a file format that describes molecules' atoms, bonds, connectivity and coordinates. The molfile is made up of some header information, the Connection Table, which contains atom information, bond connections and kinds, and sections for more sophisticated information.

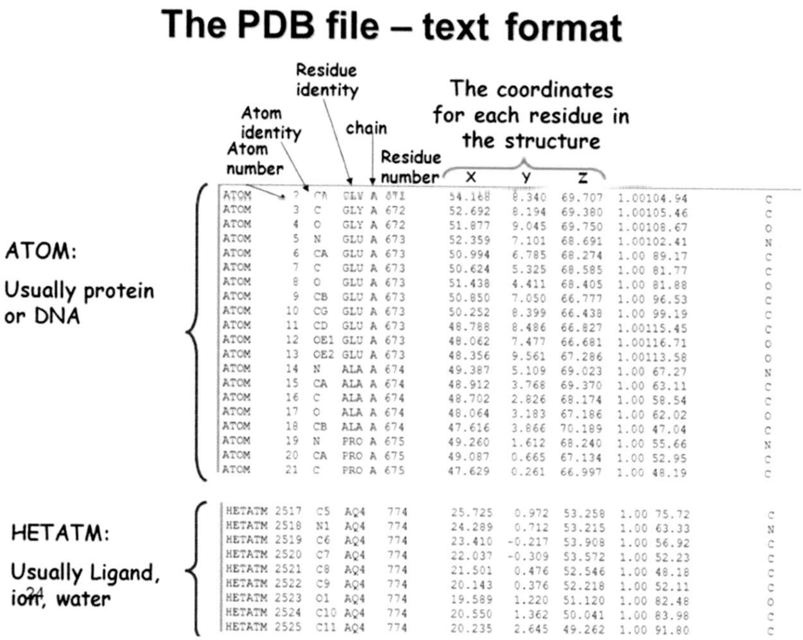

# The PDB file – text format

**FIGURE 22.24**

Protein Data Bank-Text format.

## 22.7.2 sdf

SDF is one of the series of MDL-designed chemical-data file formats intended for structural information in particular. 'SDF' means structure-data file, and SDF files wrap in molfile format (MDL molfile). The lines consisting of four dollar signs ($$$$) are the limit of several compounds. The ability to include connected data is one aspect of the SDF format. Multiple molecules can be present in sdf file, separated by '$$$$'.

## 22.7.3 PDB

The Protein Data Bank (pdb) is a textual file format that describes the three-dimensional structures of molecules stored in the Protein Data Bank (Fig. 22.24).

## Further reading

Andreoli, F., Del Rio, A., 2015. Computer-aided molecular design of compounds targeting histone modifying enzymes. Comput. Struct. Biotechnol. J. 13, 358–365.

Copeland, R.A., Olhava, E.J., Scott, M.P., 2010. Targeting epigenetic enzymes for drug discovery. Curr. Opin. Chem. Biol. 14, 505–510.

Del Rio, A., Varchi, G., 2016. Molecular design of compounds targeting histone methyltransferases. Epi-Informatics 257−272.

Drewes, G., 2012. Future strategies in epigenetic drug discovery. Drug Discov. Today Ther. Strat. 9, e121−e127.

Hamm, C.A., Costa, F.F., 2011. The impact of epigenomics on future drug design and new therapies. Drug Discov. Today 16, 626−635.

Roy, K., 2019. Multi-target drug design using chem-bioinformatic approaches. In: Methods in Pharmacology and Toxicology.

Tomar, V., Mazumder, M., Chandra, R., Yang, J., Sakharkar, M.K., 2018. Small molecule drug design. In: Reference Module in Life Sciences.

# BioEdit in bioinformatics

BioEdit is a free and open-source sequence analysis programme that makes use of plugins to interact with other apps to provide a deeper analysis. It can import an almost-unlimited range of sequence formats (including SCL, SEQ, TXT and FAS) and it makes use of the powerful programme ReadSeq. If you cannot remember a sequence, you have the option to open it as text in BioEdit. This means they can be pasted straight from the clipboard, or copied from another application or the NCBI website. There are many of free apps (ClustalX, formatdb, localBlast) available to download online (i.e. NCBI). Adding new applications is a tedious and time-consuming process. The alternative perspective is that the main advantage may be a GUI for the format and BLAST command-line application.

## 23.1 Features

- These four modes of manual alignment are selected and slid, have a dynamic grab and drag, allow for the insertion and deletion of gaps using a mouse click and use text editing-like editing.
- The colour alignment and editing with distinct colour tables of nucleic acid and amino acid and complete backdrop colour control.
- Alignment shading built on dynamic information.
- Generate and display ABI chromatograms with a polished appearance.
- Lock grouped sequence alignment for synchronised hand alignment modifications.
- It is possible to annotate a series with graphical features and other dynamic views such as feature annotation tooltips.
- Lock sequence to prevent unintentional modifications.

## 23.2 Protocol: sequence alignment using BioEdit

### 23.2.1 Step by step tutorials

To begin with, you need to retrieve your personal sequences, which can be your full genome sequence or certain genes. NCBI will provide you with this information.

Bioinformatics for Everyone. https://doi.org/10.1016/B978-0-323-91128-3.00023-7

**For Example**: Let us head over to the NCBI site and pick up four sequences of the *Brassica* gene.

- Save these sequences in Notepad on your desktop in FASTA format (Fig. 23.1).
- You can import these sequences.
  Insert New Alignment File >. There are various ways to do this, but the quickest way is to choose 'Import Sequences' > 'Sequence Alignment File' > 'Choose text file that saves FASTA sequences or just copy and paste sequences'.
- Open Bioedit > click on File > Click on new alignment (Fig. 23.2).
- Click on sequence > New sequence (Fig. 23.3).
- Type name of the sequence and select sequence type whether DNA, RNA, protein, etc.
- Select font size and paste your sequence.
- Click on Apply and Close.

Sequences for bioedit - Notepad

File Edit Format View Help

>Brassica oleracea var. viridis
CGGGTAATTTTTGTGGTTTTAAACCCAAGTGGGGCCCCAACCCTTCTGGCGGGGGGCACGTTCGCCTGGG
TGTCACAAATCGTCGTCCCCCATCCTCTCGAGGATATCGGACGGAAGCTGGTCTCCCGTGTGTTACCGC
ACGCGGTTGGCCAAAATCCTAGCTAAGGATGCCAGGAGCGTCTTGACATGCGGTGGTGAATTCAATTCTC
GTCAAATCGTCTGTCGTTTCGGTCCGAAAGCTCTTGGTGATCTACAATGTCCTCAACGCGAGCACTATCG
CAAATGCGCCAGTTTAAGCAAATAAATAGTACCC

>Brassica napus isolate Na1_(
TCGTAACCTGGAAACAGAACGACCCGAGAACGTTGAAACATCACTCTCGGTGGGCCGGTTTCTTAGCTGA
TTTCGTGCCTACCGATTCCGTGGTTATGCGTTCGTCACCGGCCCAGTTTCGGTTGGATCATACGCATAGC
TTCCGGATATCACCAAACCCCGGCACGAAAAGTGTCAAGGAACATTCAACTAAACGGCCTGCTTTCGCCA
ACCCGGAGACGGTGTTTGTTCGGAAGCAGTGCTGCAATGTAAAGTCTAAAACGACTCTCGGCAACGGATA
TCTCGGCTCTCGCATCGATGAAGAACGTAGCGAAATG

>Brassica villosa isolate T160
TGCGGAAGGATCATTGTCGTAACCTGGAAACAGAACGACCTGAGAACGTTGAAACATCACTCTCGGTGGG
CTGGTTTCTTAGCTGATTCTTGCCTACCAATTCCGTGGTTATGCGTTTGTCCCCGGCTAAGTTTCGGTTA
GATTATACGCATAGCTTCCGGATATACCAAACCCCGGCACGAAAAGTGTCAAGGAACATTCAACTAAACG
GCCTGCTTTCGCCAACCCGGAGACGGTGTTTGTTCGGAAGCAGTGCTGCAATGTAAAGTCTAAAACGACT
CTCGGCAACGGATATCTCGGCTCTCGCATCGATGAAGAACGTAGCGAAAT

>Brassica oleracea clone Bol-44
ACCTGGTTGATCCTGCCAGTAGTCATATGCTTGTCTCAAAGATTAAGCCATGCATGTGTAAGTATGAACG
AATTCAGACTGTGAAACTGCGAATGGCTCATTAAATCAGTTATAGTTTGTTTGATGGTAACTACTACTCG
GATAACCGTAGTAATTCTAGAGCTAATACGTGCAACAAACCCCGACTTCTGGAAGGGATGCATTTATTAG
ATAAAAGGTCGACGCGGGCTCTGCCCGTTGCTCTGATGATTCATGATAACTCGACGGATCGCATGGCCTT
AGTGCTGGCGACGCATCATTCAAATTTCTGCCCTATCAACTT

FIGURE 23.1

Sequences in notepad.

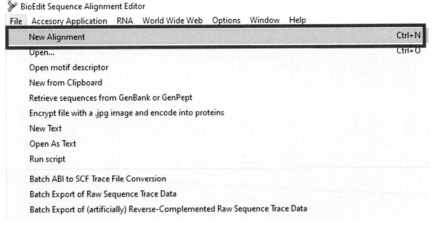

**FIGURE 23.2**

New Alignment in BioEdit.

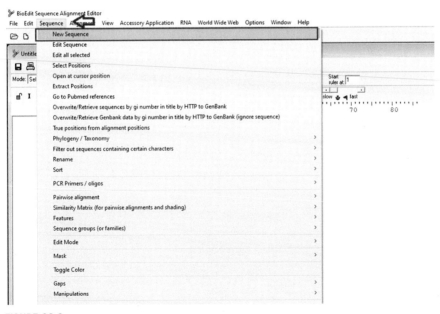

**FIGURE 23.3**

New Sequence in BioEdit.

All steps are shown in Fig. 23.4.

- You can launch ClustalW from the Accessory menu once all the sequences have been selected (Fig. 23.5).
- Select all sequence > Accessory Application > ClustalW Multiple alignment > Run ClustalW > OK > Alignment (Fig. 23.6).
- You can also view these alignments graphically. Click on File > Graphic view (Fig. 23.7).

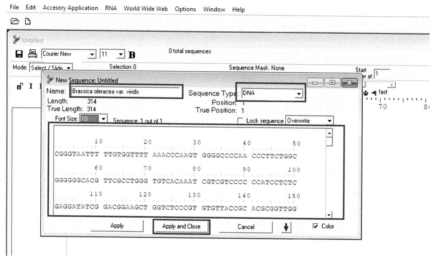

**FIGURE 23.4**

Sequence entry in BioEdit for analysis.

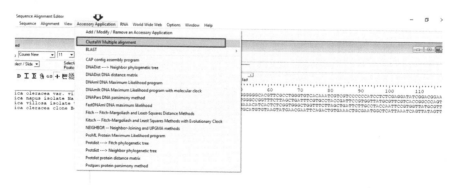

**FIGURE 23.5**

Launch ClustalW in BioEdit.

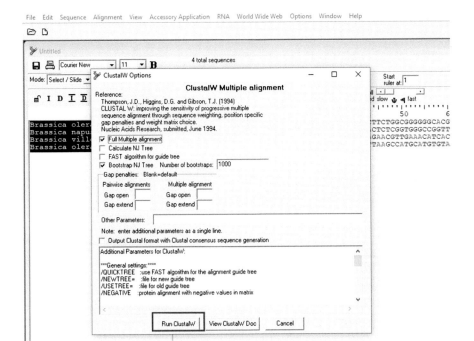

**FIGURE 23.6**

ClustalW alignment.

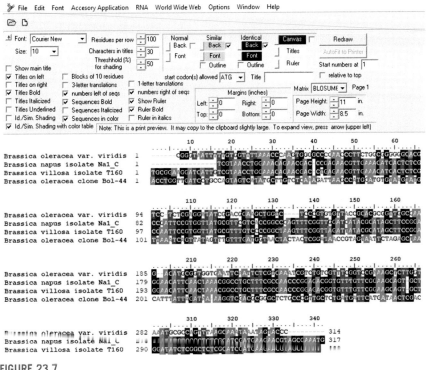

**FIGURE 23.7**

Graphical View of Sequences.

**FIGURE 23.8**

Generating a reverse complement sequence.

## 23.3 Protocol: putting forward and reverse sequences together using BioEdit

1. Select the Reverse **fasta** form file name from the left hand side (e.g. BR_3.g1) and press **Shift + Ctrl + R** to generate a reverse complement strand. Now the forward and reverse sequences are running in the same direction and have (mostly) the same nucleotides (Fig. 23.8).
2. Double click on the file name to the left of the sequence to open a new editing window.
3. Highlight and copy the entire sequence (**Ctrl + C**).
4. Go to the Forward sequence fasta window. Select '**new sequence**' under the 'Sequence' feature in the top tool bar.
   a. Paste your Reverse sequence in the new window (**Ctrl + V**).
   b. Rename this new sequence 'R' in the 'Name' field.
   c. Select 'DNA' for 'Sequence Type' to get the appropriate nucleotide colours.
   d. Select 'Apply and Close'. Now both sequences should show up in your Forward window.

## Further reading

BioEdit, http://www.mbio.ncsu.edu/BioEdit/.
ClustalW, http://www.imtech.res.in/pub/mirror_sites/ebi/dos/clustalW.
Henry Stewart publications 1467−5463, 2004. Briefings Bioinf. 5 (1), 82−87.
Thompson, J.D., Higgins, D.G., Gibson, T.J., 1994. ClustalW: improving the sensitivity of progressive multiple sequence alignment through sequence weighting, position specific gap penalties and weight matrix choice. Nucleic Acids Res. 22, 4673−4680.

# Index

'*Note*: Page numbers followed by "f" indicate figures and "t" indicate tables.'

Printed in the United States
by Baker & Taylor Publisher Services